Praise for
The Best Spiritual Writing series

"Zaleski's compilation of spiritual writi[ng] exceptional place. . . . It is a curious lit[tle] the diverse forms, voices, topics, gradually coalesce into something bigger and more elegant, something spiritual and extraordinary."
—*Publishers Weekly* (starred review)

"There is enough here to feed the hungry heart for years to come."
—Phyllis Tickle, author of *The Great Emergence*

"Illuminating . . . This anthology, as always, is a rich feast."
—*National Catholic Reporter*

"Zaleski has repeated his annual miracle, uniting another year's worth of various and thought-provoking pieces. Essential for individuals who have read earlier volumes, and an excellent place to start for those who have not." —*Library Journal* (starred review)

"[A] luminous collection." —*Chicago Tribune*

"Like a very fine friend returned from a year's voyaging, laden with delights and treasures to share, Philip Zaleski brings us, here again, another trove of well-wrought, luminous, soul-bracing gifts."
—Thomas Lynch, author of *The Undertaking* and *Apparition & Late Fictions*

"[A] reliably bracing volume." —*Booklist* (starred review)

"Those who embrace variety will find plenty to sink their teeth into."
—*The Christian Science Monitor*

The Best
Spiritual Writing

2012

Edited by

PHILIP ZALESKI

Introduction by

PHILIP YANCEY

PENGUIN BOOKS

PENGUIN BOOKS

Published by the Penguin Group

Penguin Group (USA) Inc.,

375 Hudson Street, New York, New York 10014, U.S.A.

Penguin Group (Canada), 90 Eglinton Avenue East, Suite 700, Toronto,
Ontario, Canada M4P 2Y3 (a division of Pearson Penguin Canada Inc.)

Penguin Books Ltd, 80 Strand, London WC2R 0RL, England

Penguin Ireland, 25 St Stephen's Green, Dublin 2,
Ireland (a division of Penguin Books Ltd)

Penguin Group (Australia), 250 Camberwell Road, Camberwell,
Victoria 3124, Australia (a division of Pearson Australia Group Pty Ltd)

Penguin Books India Pvt Ltd, 11 Community Centre,
Panchsheel Park, New Delhi—110 017, India

Penguin Group (NZ), 67 Apollo Drive, Rosedale, Auckland 0632,
New Zealand (a division of Pearson New Zealand Ltd)

Penguin Books (South Africa) (Pty) Ltd, 24 Sturdee Avenue,
Rosebank, Johannesburg 2196, South Africa

Penguin Books Ltd, Registered Offices:
80 Strand, London WC2R 0RL, England

First published in Penguin Books 2011

3 5 7 9 10 8 6 4 2

Selection and preface copyright © Philip Zaleski, 2011
Introduction copyright © Philip Yancey, 2011
All rights reserved

Pages 269–271 constitute an extension of this copyright page.

ISBN: 9780143119906

Printed in the United States of America
Set in Adobe Garamond Pro • Designed by Elke Sigal

Contents

Foreword

Newman and Hemingway—is it possible to think of two authors more unalike?—thought best and wrote best while standing erect, the former with pen and ink at a lectern, the latter hammering away at a Royal typewriter crammed into a bookcase. Nietszche developed his most daring ideas while striding through the German mountains; it was there that he composed much of *Thus Spake Zarathustra*. Archimedes and Nabokov dallied with the muses while soaking in the tub, while Proust wrote in bed, flat on his back, idly brushing away the madeleine crumbs. A writer (any artist) can create in almost any position: sitting, standing, lying, walking, even floating—whether in water or, as in the case of the cellist Charlotte Moorman, in air.

But there is another posture to consider, and it is this that I wish to explore. The great theologian Hans Urs von Balthasar hit upon it about half a century ago, when he talked about the necessity for *la théologie à genoux*, which we might translate as *theology on one's knees*, or *kneeling theology*. Balthasar did not mean this literally; he meant that theology must be informed by prayer, with all that complements that most necessary, ordinary, and mysterious of actions; above all, that theology must possess an active sense of the transcendent, a felt certainty that I exist in relation to something—

or someone—purer, greater, nobler than myself, something that stands, in Plato's famous formulation, as absolute beauty, truth, and goodness.

What I would like to propose is an adaptation of Balthasar's words; that the spiritual writer—the spiritual artist—needs to practice *l'art à genoux*, or *kneeling art*.

This is not a new idea, although I have framed it in a new metaphor. *L'art à genoux* surrounds us. Every time I visit the local Catholic parish, here in the rolling hills of western Massachusetts, my eyes turn toward a small wooden sculpture to the right of the altar. The carving depicts Virgin and Child, in the form of Our Lady of Walsingham, commemorating an appearance of Mary to a Saxon noble woman in Norfolk, England, in 1061. The site of this apparition is now a major international pilgrimage destination, featuring both Catholic and Anglican shrines; the statue in our little church replicates in miniature the image found in the Catholic "Slipper Chapel." It displays all the customary Walsingham iconography: Mary, gowned in blue, crowned in glory, on a high-backed throne, gesturing toward her young son, who sits astride her left knee. He holds a book in his left hand, while his right is raised in blessing. A sprig of lilies rests by the Virgin's right shoulder.

I don't know who carved this sculpture or how old it is. What interests me is the air of calm dignity it possesses, the atmosphere of contemplative grace it bestows. It doesn't strive for originality or gaudiness or brilliance of any sort. It simply is: sweet and serene in its silent regard. Yet it also calls. It calls us to ponder its beauty, its grace, its purity of invention and aspect, its intimations of the transcendent, its otherworldly goodness. Can a statue be good? Yes, I believe so: this statue is good. To me, it epitomizes *l'art à genoux*.

It may be that spiritual art, at the peak of aspiration and execution, contains in it something not of the artist's making, something not of this world. When the artist creates at a supernal level, he or she may be participating in what Louis Massignon, adapting the terminology of the Islamic mystic al-Hallaj, termed the "virgin point" of contact between God and the human being, where mystical exchange takes place. Newman, in his magnificent Oxford University sermons, offers an account of this elevated, enchanted, ecstatic view of the artistic vocation as it operates in the realm of music:

> Is it possible that that inexhaustible evolution and disposition of notes, so rich yet so simple, so intricate yet so regulated, so various yet so majestic, should be a mere sound which is gone and perishes? Can it be that those mysterious stirrings of heart, and keen emotions, and strange yearnings after we know not what, and awful impressions from we know not whence, should be wrought in us by what is unsubstantial, and comes and goes, and begins and ends in itself? It is not so; it cannot be. No, they have escaped from some higher sphere; they are the outpourings of eternal harmony, in the medium of created sound; they are echoes from our home; they are the voice of angels, or the *Magnificat* of saints, or the living laws of Divine governance, or the Divine attributes, something are they beside themselves, which we cannot compass, which we cannot utter.

For Newman, music pours into the composer from "a higher sphere"; the composer who is attuned to *l'art à genoux* transmits what he hears from above, rather than inventing in his workshop below (and this is why Newman might say that Beethoven, his favorite composer, could discern celestial harmonies even while nearly stone-deaf).

In order to understand better this kneeling art—and the demands it places upon the artist—let's look at the life and work of the painter-saint Fra Giovanni of Fiesole (c. 1400–1450), better known as Blessed Fra Angelico. Much of the earliest information about Fra Angelico comes from Giorgio Vasari's *Lives of the Artists*, a sixteenth-century compendium of biographies of medieval and Renaissance painters, engravers, sculptors, and the like. Vasari makes his admiration for Fra Angelico clear at the outset, declaring him to be "both an accomplished painter and illuminator, and also a worthy priest; and for the one reason as much as the other he should be honored by posterity." Vasari understates the case. Fra Angelico was more than "accomplished," more than "worthy"; he was a consummate spiritual artist and a saint, whose frescoes for the Friary of San Marco in Florence, where he lived as a Dominican friar for many years, rank among the greatest achievements of the Renaissance. Of these works, Vasari says with perfect accuracy that "in their bearing and expression, the saints painted by Fra Angelico come nearer to the truth than the figures done by any other artist."

The key word here is *truth*. Fra Angelico sought truth and then sought to transmit it to others. Art for him was not a vehicle for subjective gratification, for personal statement or emotional expression (although his paintings are deeply felt and capture, as Vasari indicates, the personality of the saints). For Fra Angelico, art was a means of spiritual investigation and religious devotion, a path, through beauty and goodness, toward truth.

How did Fra Angelico conduct this artistic search? Here Vasari is tight-lipped but does offer a few crucial details. The most significant, of course, is that Fra Angelico was a friar, pledged to a life of austerity, prayer, and contemplation. Vasari took the trouble to interview an ancient friar who, in his youth, had known some intimate friends of the painter; from him Vasari learned that Fra Angelico had been "a modest and peaceable man of great holiness," who led a "simple and devout life." These are, admittedly, pious generalities, although they gain credence from Vasari's source; more compelling are the following concrete details about Fra Angelico's life: that he was chaste, quiet, and slow to anger, that he turned down opportunities for high rank in his order, preferring the practice of obedience to that of giving orders; that he once said that "anyone practicing the art of painting needed a quiet and untroubled life," that he never retouched his work, believing that his first impressions came from God, a view corollary to Newman's musical views, and, most tellingly, that "he would never take up his brushes without a prayer."

For Fra Angelico, then, art was a spiritual way. In this understanding, he anticipated both the greatest poet and the greatest composer that the West has yet produced. Dante, in his celebrated letter to Can Grande, states that the purpose of his *Commedia* is "to remove those living in this life from the state of misery and to lead them to the state of bliss." His incomparable art may dazzle, shock, delight, or astound our senses, feelings, imagination, and intellect—but its aim is to save souls. And Bach, who regularly penned *J.J.* (*Jesu, Juva*, "Jesus, Help") at the start of his sacred compositions and *S.D.G.* (*Soli Deo Gloria*, "To only God the Glory") at the finish, famously declared that "the aim and final end of all music should be none other than the glory of God and the refreshment of the soul." We know in broad outline the spiritual practices that anchored the art of these two men. Dante was an ardent Catholic, who, under the heavenly influence of Beatrice Portinari, repented his youthful excesses and led a sober, devout, and studious life. Bach was an ardent Lutheran, a church organist, harpsichordist, and musical director in Leipzig for nearly thirty years, where he steeped himself in the liturgical and devotional practices of his faith, faithfully annotated his family Bible, and poured his creative energies into cantatas and passions whose musical architecture often models fundamental Christian themes such as the Trinity, the Crucifixion, and the Resurrection.

I hasten to add, in light of the above examples, that *kneeling art* is not an exclusively Christian or European prerogative. In fact, the image of Our Lady of Walsingham in my local parish reminds me, in its iconography and in its enveloping peacefulness, of statues I have seen from ancient Egypt that depict Isis balancing upon her knees the baby Horus. Similar achievements can be found in almost every traditional culture—Jewish, Muslim, Hindu, Buddhist—as well as in our own modern scientific one. Consider, for example, Islamic calligraphy, a quintessential art in a civilization based upon a revealed book, one that proclaims that God "teaches by the pen" (Qur'an 96:4). "There is no letter which does not worship God," runs an early Sufi saying. Islamic calligraphers undertake a long and strict apprenticeship, which entails studying the Qur'an, reciting numerous liturgical and supererogatory prayers, and, often, performing extra daily ablutions before beginning work, in keeping with another saying that goes, "Purity of writing is purity of soul." These aspiring calligraphers learn, too, the art of concentration. Scholar of Islam Annemarie Schimmel tells a legend about one calligrapher in Tabriz who was so single-minded that, while focused intently upon inscribing a perfect *waw* (an Arabic letter), he completely missed a great earthquake that shook the city while he worked.

Invariably, this rigorous training takes place under the guidance of a master, himself a participant in a lineage of calligraphers going back centuries and often affiliated with a Sufi order. Sometimes these masters make extraordinary demands upon their pupils, as in this outré account from a Naqshbandi Sufi text:

> Cut a fresh pen for *thuluth* and *naskh* [types of Arabic script], wrap them in paper, take two fingers deep dust out from Shaykh Hamdullah's tomb, recite the blessing over the Prophet and the glorification; then bury them in a Friday night [at the master's tomb]. After one week take them out, and whenever you begin to practice, write the first line with them, then the rest with other pens (from Annemarie

Schimmel, *Calligraphy and Islamic Culture* (NY: NYU Press, 1984).

Other practices tied to this sacred craft convey a rich cargo of religious meaning. Thus Schimmel reports that in Istanbul, calligraphers have been taught to make their ink from the lampblack coating the lamps in the Süleymaniye mosque, for then "not only was the raw material for their ink of good quality, but it also carried the *Baraka* of the mosque."

Once you start to look for it, this sort of spiritual instruction for the budding or mature artist crops up everywhere. Black Elk has detailed the ablutions, penances, prayers, and so on that precede the Oglala Sioux *wiwanyag wachipi* (Sun Dance). These preparations are absolutely indispensable, for, as he says, "this dance will be an offering of our bodies and souls to *Wakan-Tanka* ["Great Mystery" or "God"] and will be very *wakan*" ["holy"]; this attention to every traditional detail reveals, incidentally, the folly of New Age adaptations of Native American practices, which, cutting corners in order to seek out the "heart" of the ritual, actually eviscerate it. Similar preparatory practices can be found in the Confucian cultures of East Asia, where the art of poetry, one of the highest attainments of wisdom, requires a firm education in all the Confucian virtues, including dignity, humbleness, honesty, moderation, love of goodness, self-examination, attention to ritual, and continual remembrance of heaven (*t'ien*). The tea ceremony, in both its Chinese and Japanese forms, contains comparable injunctions and requires a lengthy apprenticeship in order to learn, to near perfection, a complex choreography of gestures, postures, and actions. Each of these sacred rituals functions as a supreme artistic expression of a traditional worldview; those who prepare for these rituals become, after years of training, the bearers of that culture's religio-artistic wisdom.

In a more modern idiom, the sermons and devotions of Gerard

Manley Hopkins, as well as his magnificent nature notebooks, reveal a great deal about how a post-Enlightenment religious man might cultivate his art. The same goes for the writings of Van Gogh, Gauguin, and Kandinsky. Much can be gleaned from Blake's annotations, Coleridge's notebooks, or Tolkien's correspondence. It is very difficult to distill to its essence the collective wisdom of millennia on the spiritual disciplines of artists, but we may venture this much: that the spiritual artist (and thus the spiritual writer) does well to place himself or herself before God, at the beginning and end of work, and ponder the following set of questions, a variation on the celebrated title of Gauguin's most celebrated canvas:

Who am I? Why do I work? What will I give to the world?

In these three small questions, it seems to me, may be found the seeds of *l'art à genoux.*

Many thanks to the essayists and poets who contributed material to this year's volume, and to Philip Yancey for his splendid introduction. My thanks also to Carolyn Carlson and all the folks at Viking Penguin, to Kim Witherspoon and David Forrer of Inkwell Management, and, as always, to my beloved Carol, John, and Andy.

PHILIP ZALESKI

Introduction

IF I HAD TO CHOOSE THE MOST IMPORTANT CHALLENGE FOR THOSE who write about spiritual matters, it would be finding the proper balance between art and propaganda. The nonfiction writer has to express the spiritual message in a structure and style that satisfies the demands of artistic integrity, while the fiction writer struggles to enfold a nonintrusive message within a believable narrative.

The selections in this book—essays, poems, reflections, meditations—come from writers who are exploring a spiritual dimension, yet all of the contributors know that many readers wonder whether such a spiritual dimension even exists. We are probing the invisible, after all. How can those of us who believe describe our experiences in a way that communicates to the skeptical or uncommitted?

Religious art has gained a reputation for erring on the side of propaganda. As a result, in the modern West novels and especially films with an explicit Christian theme provoke mild condescension if not actual ridicule in some circles. Much of this secular resistance is hypocritical, for Christians are not the only propagandists at work. I could name many baldly propagandistic works from the fields of science and politics: the New Atheists do not strive for objectivity; Michael Moore unashamedly makes documentaries with a targeted message; and the most successful movie of all time, *Avatar*, is hardly subtle. Clearly, some kinds of propaganda find wider acceptance than others.

One novelist known for his religious views stated the tension clearly:

> If someone were to tell me that it lay in my power to write a novel explaining every social question from a particular viewpoint that I believed to be the correct one, I still wouldn't spend two hours on it. But if I were told that what I am writing will be read in twenty years' time by the children of today, and that those children will laugh, weep, and learn to love life as they read, why then I would devote the whole of my life and energy to it.

The author of those words, Leo Tolstoy, nevertheless vacillated between art and propaganda. Twenty years, even a hundred years after his death people are still laughing, weeping, and learning to love life as they read his books, while others are also reflecting on, arguing with, and reacting to his ideas on social, moral, and, yes, religious questions. Although in this quote Tolstoy claims to come down firmly on the side of art, veins of propaganda run through his novels and short stories, inspiring some readers and alienating others. And in nonfiction works like *What Is Art?* the great novelist tilts unmistakably toward propaganda.

The word *propaganda* carries the scent of unfair manipulation or distortion of means to a particular end; rather, I use the original sense of the word as coined by a pope who formed the Sacred Congregation *de Propaganda Fide* in the seventeenth century in order to spread the faith. As a Christian writer, I admit that I do strive for propaganda in this sense. When I write, I want readers to consider a viewpoint I hold to be true, and I assume the same applies for those who write from the perspective of other religions or no religion at all.

Religious institutions such as the church, once a dominant force in encouraging artistic expression, now lag far behind—in no small part, I believe, because of an imbalance between art and propaganda. Like a bipolar magnet, the writer of faith feels the tug of opposing forces: a desire to communicate what gives life meaning counteracted by an artistic inclination toward self-expression and form that any "message" might interrupt. The result: a constant, dichotomous pull toward both propaganda and art. The best—and, ironically, most convincing—spiritual writing achieves a delicate balance between the two.

Some writers of faith yield too easily to the pull toward propaganda and away from art. They would react to Tolstoy's statement with disbelief: to choose a novel that entertains and fosters a love for life over a treatise that solves every social (better yet, religious) question of mankind! How can a person waste time with mere aesthetics—beautiful music, eye-pleasing art, lively literature—when injustice rules the nations and the decadent world hurtles toward destruction? Is this not fiddling while Rome burns? Publishers regularly send me novels that tend toward propaganda (fictionalized Bible stories and fantasies about the Second Coming) and away from the artful.

Somewhere in this magnetic field between art and propaganda the spiritual writer must work. One force tempts us to lower artistic standards and proclaim a message we truly believe while another tempts us to tone down or alter the message for the sake of aesthetics. Having lived in the midst of this tension for several decades, I have come to recognize it as mostly healthy. Apparent success often lies with the extremes: for example, a writer may well succeed in the religious subculture by erring on the side of propaganda, but ever so slowly the fissure between the religious and secular worlds will yawn wider and we will find ourselves writing and selling books to ourselves alone. On the other hand, the writer of faith cannot simply absorb the sensibilities of the larger world, which often has little tolerance for faith expression.

C. S. Lewis explored the polarity in the address "Learning in Wartime," delivered to Oxford students who were trying to concentrate on academics while their friends fought in the trenches of Europe and staved off the German aerial assault on London. How, asked Lewis, can creatures who are advancing every moment either to heaven or hell spend time on such comparative trivialities as literature, art, mathematics, or biology, let alone Lewis's own field of medieval literature?

The most obvious answer for a writer of faith is that God himself invested great energy in the natural world. As the Hebrew Bible records, God inspired followers, "people of the Book," to employ a variety of literary forms that endure as masterpieces. As for biology and physics, everything we know about them derives from painstakingly tracing clues from God's original act of creation. We live in a divinely created but imperfect (the theologians say "fallen") world. Beauty abounds, and we are right to seek it and seek to reproduce it. Yet tragedy and despair also abound, and we must fully address the human condition even as we point toward rumors of transcendence. That is why I embrace both art and propaganda, resisting pressure to conform to one or the other.

As I have lived with the tension between art and propaganda throughout my writing career, I have learned a few guidelines that allow for a synthesis of the two. Whenever I break one of these guidelines, I sense that I have tilted too far toward one side or the other. In either case my message gets lost, whether through pedantic communication or through a muddle of empty verbiage. Because I believe contemporary writers of faith mainly err on the side of propaganda, not art, my guidelines speak primarily to that error.

1. An artful propagandist takes into account the ability of the audience to perceive.

For the writer of faith who wants to communicate to a secular audience, I cannot stress this caution too strongly. In effect we must consider two different sets of vocabulary. Words that have a certain meaning to me as a Christian may have an entirely different, sometimes even antithetical, meaning to my secular listener. Consider a few examples. *Pity* once derived from *piety*: by responding to the poor and the needy, a person reflects God and is therefore pietous, or full of pity. Similarly, as any reader of the King James Version knows, *charity* is an example of God's grace, a synonym for love, as in the famous passage from I Corinthians 13 frequently read at weddings. Over the centuries the meanings of both words soured, and any theological overtones faded away. "I don't want pity!" or "Don't give me charity!" a needy person protests today.

Similarly, many words we now use to express personal faith may miscommunicate rather than communicate. The phrase *Our Father* or *Son of God* or even a single word such as *God* or *Allah* or *karma* may summon up wildly inappropriate images unless the writer goes on to explain what he or she means. *Love*, a vital theological word, has lost much of its meaning—for a current understanding of the word, surf the radio and listen to popular music stations. The word *redemption* most often relates to recycling centers, and few cultural analogies can adequately express that concept. I continue to use the word *evangelical* (meaning "good news"), though many of my friends have abandoned it because a secular audience hears it as a synonym for the "bad news" of *fundamentalism* or the *Religious Right*.

As words change in meaning, a writer of faith must adapt accordingly, selecting words and metaphors that fit the culture. A concept will only make sense if the audience has the ability to perceive it. If I see a three-year-old girl putting herself in danger, I must warn her in terms she can understand. If she decides to stick her finger first into her mouth and then into an electrical outlet, I will not respond by searching out my *Home Handyman Encyclopedia* and launching into a monologue on amps, volts, and electrical resistance. Rather, I will more likely grab her hand and say something like, "There's fire in there! You'll be burned!" Although the outlet box contains no literal fire, I will choose an expression that communicates to the comprehension level of a three-year-old.

Andrew Young learned an essential lesson of survival during the civil rights struggle. "Don't judge the adversary by how you think," he says. "Learn to think like the adversary." Later, as the U.S. ambassador to the United Nations, he tried to apply that lesson during the days of the Iran hostage crisis when news accounts were using such adjectives as "insane, crazed, demonic" to describe Iranian leaders. Those labels, said Young, do nothing to facilitate communication. To understand Iran, we must first consider their viewpoint. To the militants who overthrew him, the Shah of Iran was as brutal and vicious as Adolf Hitler; therefore they reacted to the United States, which offered refuge to the Shah, as we would respond to a country that sheltered Hitler.

In a parallel way, when writers of faith attempt to communicate to unbelievers and skeptics, we must first think through their assumptions and imagine how they will receive the message we are conveying. That process will affect the words we choose, the form, and, most important, the content we can get across. If we err on the side of too much content, the net effect is the same as if we had included no content, at least for those not precommitted to our beliefs. Quoting a verse from the Bible or Qu'ran has little meaning to one who does not accept them as divine revelation. Contributors to this volume from other professional fields, such as science or literary criticism, honor this principle intuitively; religious professionals and enthusiastic converts have to work at it.

Alexander Solzhenitsyn learned an important lesson after his release from the concentration camps when his writing finally began to find acceptance in Soviet literary journals. In *The Oak and the Calf* he recalls, "Later, when I popped up from the underground and began lightening my works for the outside world, lightening them of all that my fellow countrymen could hardly be expected to accept at once, I discovered to my surprise that a piece only gained, that its effect was heightened, as the harsher tones were softened."

Solzhenitsyn walked a tightrope between art and propaganda. Too much lightening and softening threatened to dilute the message. *There's really no need to capitalize God—that's archaic*, the Soviet censors coaxed him. *If you want us to publish your fine novel about Ivan Denisovich, merely cross out this one problematic line.* Solzhenitsyn resisted those two requests; he capitalized God and left in the controversial passage, "I crossed myself, and said to God: 'Thou art there in heaven after all, O creator. Thy patience is long, but thy blows are heavy.'" Acceding to such pressure would efface his whole message, he decided.

Whenever a believer addresses a secular audience, he or she must maintain a balance between presenting a heartfelt message and adapting it to the readers' level of comprehension. People of faith encounter the spiritual world everywhere; God seems fully evident to us. In contrast, the secular mind questions how anyone can find God in the maze of cults, religions, and media mountebanks, all clamoring for attention against the background of a godforsaken planet. Unless we truly understand that viewpoint, and speak in terms the secular mind can understand, our words will have the exotic though useless ring of a foreign language.

2. Artful propaganda works like a deduction rather than a rationalization.

Psychologists describe a process of rationalization in the human mind that they label *cognitive dissonance*. Under normal conditions the human mind, resistant to a state of tension and disharmony, works to patch things up with a self-affirming process of rational-ization.

My article is rejected. Instantly I start consoling myself with the knowledge that hundreds of manuscripts were rejected that day. The editor could have started off the day with a bad breakfast or an argument with his kids. Perhaps no one even read my manuscript. Or if they read it, somehow they missed my point. Any number of factors arise to account for the rejection, my mind's way of calming the dissonance caused by this jarring bit of bad news.

I define the process of rationalization very simply: it occurs when a person already knows the end result and reasons backward. The conclusion is a given; I merely need to find a way to support that con-clusion.

I encountered an example of rationalization some years ago while researching an article on a particular Christian mission, the Wycliffe Bible Translators. Since rumors of Wycliffe's CIA involve-ment were proliferating at the time, I felt it essential to investigate them and so I telephoned outspoken critics of Wycliffe. One, a pro-fessor in a New York university, insisted that Wycliffe was definitely subsidized by the CIA. I asked for proof. "It's quite obvious," he re-plied. "They claim to raise their thirty-million-dollar annual budget from fundamentalist churches. You and I both know there's not thirty million dollars available from that source. Obviously, they're getting it from somewhere else." Had that professor done a little re-search, he would have discovered that at the time, each of the five top television evangelists was collecting more than fifty million dollars annually in donations from religious sympathizers. Certainly the pool of resources in the United States was large enough to account for Wycliffe's contributions, but this professor started from a fore-gone conclusion and reasoned backward.

Solzhenitsyn heard a startling rationalization when the Soviet editor Lebedev said to him, "If Tolstoy were alive now and wrote as he did then [meaning against the government] he wouldn't be Tolstoy." Lebedev's opinion about his government was so firmly set that he could not allow a plausible threat to it and so he rationalized that Tolstoy would be a different person and thinker under a new regime.

Much of religious literature has an echo of rationalization. I get the sense that the author starts with a fixed conclusion and sets out to supply logical support for that conclusion. What I read about depression, suicide, abortion, divorce, addiction, and homosexuality often seems written by people who begin with a foregone conclusion and who have neither been through nor fully understood the anguished steps that are the familiar path to a person struggling with those issues. No wonder the "how-to" articles and books do not ring true.

A conclusion has impact only if the reader has been primed for it by moving along preliminary steps. To quote the philosopher William James, "In the metaphysical and religious sphere, articulate reasons are cogent for us only when our inarticulate feelings of reality have already been impressed in favor of the same conclusion." The end must be the consummation of what went before, not the starting place.

C. S. Lewis and J. R. R. Tolkien, who wrote fiction that reflected a Christian worldview, dismissed well-meaning Christian readers who sought to identify all the latent symbolism in the *Chronicles of Narnia* and *Lord of the Rings* series. Even though some parallels were obvious, both authors denied that had been their intent. Characters may indeed point to spiritual truth, yet they do so most effectively by shadowing forth a deeper, underlying truth. One cannot argue backward and view Aslan and Gandalf as mere symbolic representations—that would shatter their individuality and literary impact.

The modern Catholic writer Walker Percy once said about his craft, "Fiction doesn't tell you what you don't know. It tells you what you know but don't know that you know." Good spiritual writing does something just as subtle, making the point inside the reader before the reader consciously acknowledges it.

3. Artful propaganda must be "sincere."

I put the word *sincere* in quotes because I refer to its original meaning only. Like many words, sincere has been so twisted by modern commercialism that it ends up meaning its opposite.

Consider a timid salesman who doesn't mix well at social gatherings and doesn't show assertiveness on sales calls. His manager sends him to a Dale Carnegie course in order to improve his self-confidence. "You must be *sincere* to be successful in sales," he is coached, and then begins to practice various techniques. *Start with the handshake—it must be firm, confident, steady. Here, try it a few times. Now that you have that down, let's work on eye contact. See, when you shake my hand, you should be staring me right in the eye. Don't look away or even waver. Stare straight at me—that's a mark of sincerity. Your customer must feel you really care.* For a fee of several hundred dollars our insecure salesman learns techniques of sincerity. His next customers are impressed by his conscientiousness, his confidence in his product, and his concern for them, all because he has learned a new body language.

An acquired technique to communicate something not already present is precisely the opposite of the true meaning of *sincere*. Propaganda becomes bad propaganda because of the cosmetic cover-ups that writers apply to their work. If we portray reality in a truly sincere way, then the details of the work will reinforce its central message. If not, readers will spot the flaws and judge our work accordingly.

Solzhenitsyn's memoir also tells of the brief period under communism when the Soviet government acknowledged his genius and thought (fatally, as it turned out) he might be a writer they could manipulate. Write moral and uplifting literature, they admonished him; be sure to exclude all "pessimism, denigration, surreptitious sniping." Tone down criticism, they told him. Edit your realistic portrayals of communism's faults so as to soften the overall effect. I laughed aloud when I first read his account of that scene, because the advice Solzhenitsysn got from communist censors bears striking resemblance to what I sometimes hear from evangelical publishers. Every power, whether spiritual or secular, desires moral, uplifting literature—as long as they get to define what constitutes moral and uplifting.

Writers of faith are tempted to omit details of struggle and realism that do not fit neatly into the propaganda message. Or we include scenes that have no realism simply to reinforce our point. So convinced are we of the reality of the spiritual world that we do injustice to the natural world, a much messier place. Even the untrained observer can spot the flaws, and it only takes a slight defect here or there to ruin a work of art.

All three of these temptations toward propaganda intensify with a captive, supportive audience—the danger in relegating religious books to religious bookstores and spiritual books to "spirituality" sections within chain bookstores. When we no longer have to win people over to our point of view, realism can become an impediment. The religious subculture will applaud books in which every prayer is answered and every disease is healed, but to the degree those books do not reflect reality they will become meaningless to a skeptical audience, as unconvincing as a Scientology tract or a *Daily Worker* newspaper.

For a positive model of these three guidelines of artful communication, as a Christian I need only follow the example of the Creator. God took into account the audience's ability to perceive in an ultimate sense, by flinging aside divine prerogatives and becoming the *Word*, one of us, with all the limitations of a human body. In all major revelations—creation, Jesus the Son, the Bible—God gave only enough evidence for those with faith and desire to follow the deductions to truth, yet without overwhelming human freedom. And as for being sincere, has a more earthy, realistic book ever been written than the Bible?

A friend of mine, a hand surgeon, was awakened from a thick sleep by a three a.m. telephone call and summoned to an emergency surgery. He specializes in microsurgery, reconnecting nerves and blood vessels finer than human hairs, performing meticulous twelve-hour procedures with no breaks. As he tried to overcome his grogginess, he realized he needed extra motivation to make it through the marathon procedure facing him. On impulse he called his pastor, also awakening him. "I have a very arduous surgery ahead of me, and I need something extra to concentrate on this time," he said. "I'd like to dedicate this surgery to you. If I think about you while I'm performing it, that will help me get through."

Should not that be the Christian artist's response to God—an offering of our work in dedication to the Giver of all good gifts? If so, how dare we produce propaganda without art, or art without meaning?

The selections you will read in this volume merit inclusion for a variety of reasons: original thought, fluent expression, vivid personal experiences. Each walks its own tightrope between art and propaganda, and in the process each strives for sincerity, for an integrity of approach and development, and for effective communication. Of all the spiritual writings in the past year, these stand out for their achievement.

When expressed well, the spiritual message lifts sights beyond the normal run of celebrity gossip, global headlines, and daily tasks. Looking back on T. S. Eliot's life, Russell Kirk said, "He made the poet's voice heard again, and thereby triumphed; knowing the community of souls, he freed others from captivity to time and the lonely ego; in the teeth of winds of doctrine, he attested the permanent things. And his communication is tongued with fire beyond the language of the living."

PHILIP YANCEY

The Best
Spiritual Writing 2012

STEPHEN M. BARR

Fearful Symmetries

FROM *First Things*

SINCE THE TIME OF NEWTON, SCIENCE HAS ADVANCED BY A STRATEGY rightly called "reductionism." This method, which explains things by analyzing them into smaller and simpler parts, has yielded a rich harvest of discoveries about the natural world. As a means of analysis, then, reductionism has certainly proven its value. But many wonder whether science is reductive in a more radical and disturbing way—by flattening, collapsing, and trivializing the world. For all its intellectual accomplishments, does science end up taking our sense of reality down several notches? One could well get that impression from perusing the writings of certain scientists. Francis Crick famously asserted that human life is "no more than the behavior of . . . nerve cells and their associated molecules." Marvin Minsky, a pioneer in the field of artificial intelligence, once described people as "machines made of meat." Neuroscientist Giulio Giorelli announced that "we have a soul, but it is made up of many tiny robots." And biologist Charles Zuker has concluded that "in essence, we are nothing but a big fly."

This tendency to downgrade and diminish reflects a metaphysical prejudice that equates explanatory reduction with a grim slide down the ladder of being. Powerful explanatory schemes reveal things to be simpler than they appear. What *simpler* means in science is much discussed among philosophers—it is not at all a simple question. But to many materialists it seems to mean lower, cruder, and more trivial. By this way of thinking, the further we push toward a more basic understanding of things, the more we are immersed in meaningless, brutish bits of matter.

The philosopher Georges Rey has written, for example, that "any ultimate explanation of mental phenomena will have to be in *non*-mental [i.e., *sub*-mental or material] terms or else it won't be an *explanation* of it." Of course, the logic of this could be turned around. One could just as well say that any ultimate explanation of the material world must be in nonmaterial terms. But for materialists the lower explains the higher; and *lower* does not just mean *more fundamental* but instead suggests a diminished ontological status. The presumption is that explanations move from evolved complexity to primitive *stuff*.

At first glance, the history of the cosmos seems to bear this out. Early on, the universe was filled with nearly featureless gas and dust, which eventually condensed to form galaxies, stars, and planets. In stars and supernovas, the simplest elements, hydrogen and helium, fused to make heavier ones, gradually building up the whole periodic table. In some primordial soup, or slime, or ooze on the early earth, atoms agglomerated into larger and more intricate molecules until self-replicating ones appeared and life began. From one-celled organisms, ever more complicated living things evolved, until sensation and thought appeared. In cosmic evolution the arrow apparently moves from chaos to order, formlessness to form, triviality to complexity, and matter to mind.

And that is why, according to philosopher Daniel Dennett, religion has it exactly upside down. Believers think that God reached down to bring order and create, whereas in reality the world was built—or rather built itself—from the ground up. In Dennett's metaphor, the world was constructed not by "skyhooks" reaching down from the heavens but by "cranes" supported by, and reaching up from, the solid ground.

The history to which the atheist points—of matter self-organizing and physical structures growing in complexity—is correct as far as it goes, but it is only part of the story. The lessons the atheist draws are naive. Yes, the world we experience is the result of processes that move upward. But Dennett and others overlook the hidden forces and principles that govern those processes. In short, they are not true reductionists because they don't go all the way down to the most basic explanations of reality.

As we turn to the fundamental principles of physics, we discover that order does not really emerge from chaos, as we might naively assume; it always emerges from greater and more impressive order already present at a deeper level. It turns out that things are not more coarse or crude or unformed as one goes down into the foundations of the physical world but more subtle, sophisticated, and intricate the deeper one goes.

Let's start with a simple but instructive example of how order can appear to emerge spontaneously from mere chaos through the operation of natural forces. Imagine a large number of identical marbles rolling around randomly in a shoe box. If the box is tilted, all the marbles will roll down into a corner and arrange themselves into what is called the "hexagonal closest packing" pattern. (This is the same pattern one sees in oranges stacked on a fruit stand or in cells in a beehive.) This orderly structure emerges as the result of blind physical forces and mathematical laws. There is no hand arranging it. Physics requires the marbles to lower their gravitational potential energy as much as possible by squeezing down into the corner, which leads to the geometry of hexagonal packing.

At this point it seems as though order has indeed sprung from mere chaos. To see why this is wrong, however, consider a genuinely chaotic situation: a typical teenager's bedroom. Imagine a huge jack tilting the bedroom so that everything in it slides into a corner. The result would not be an orderly pattern but instead a jumbled heap of lamps, furniture, books, clothing, and what have you.

Why the difference? Part of the answer is that, unlike the objects in the bedroom, the marbles in the box all have the same size and shape. But there's more to it. Put a number of spoons of the same size and shape into a box and tilt it, and the result will be a jumbled heap. Marbles differ from spoons because their shape is spherical. When spoons tumble into a corner, they end up pointing every which way, but marbles don't point every which way, because no matter which way a sphere is turned it looks exactly the same.

These two crucial features of the marbles—having the same shape and having a spherical shape—should be understood as *principles of order* that are already present in the supposedly chaotic situation before the box was tilted. In fact, the more we reduce to deeper explanations, the higher we go. This is because, in a sense that can be made mathematically precise, the preexisting order inherent in the marbles is *greater* than the order that emerges after the marbles arrange themselves. This requires some explanation.

Both the preexisting order and the order that emerges involve symmetry, a concept of central importance in modern physics, as we'll see. Mathematicians and physicists have a peculiar way of thinking about symmetry: A symmetry is something that is *done*. For example, if one rotates a square by 90 degrees, it looks the same, so rotating by 90 degrees is said to be a symmetry of the square. So is rotating by 180 degrees, 270 degrees, or a full 360 degrees. A square thus has exactly four symmetries.

Not surprisingly, the hexagonal pattern the marbles form has six symmetries (rotating by any multiple of 60 degrees: 60, 120, 180,

240, 300, and 360 degrees). A sphere, on the other hand, has an infinite number of symmetries—doubly infinite, in fact, since rotating a sphere by *any* angle about *any* axis leaves it looking the same. And, what's more, the symmetries of a sphere *include* all the symmetries of a hexagon.

If we think this way about symmetry, careful analysis shows that, when marbles arrange themselves into the hexagonal pattern, just six of the infinite number of symmetries in the shape of the marbles are expressed or manifested in their final arrangement. The rest of the symmetries are said, in the jargon of physics, to be *spontaneously broken*. So, in the simple example of marbles in a tilted box, we can see that symmetry isn't popping out of nowhere. It is being distilled out of a greater symmetry already present within the spherical shape of the marbles.

The idea of *spontaneous symmetry breaking* is important in fundamental physics. The equations of electromagnetism have a mathematical structure that is dictated by a set of so-called gauge symmetries, discovered by the mathematician and physicist Hermann Weyl almost a century ago. For a long time it seemed that two other basic forces of nature, the weak force and the strong force, were not based on symmetries. But about forty years ago it was found that the weak force is actually based on an even larger set of gauge symmetries than those of electromagnetism. Because the symmetries of the weak force are spontaneously broken, however, they do not manifest or express themselves in an obvious way, which is why it took so long to discover them. (The strong force is based on a yet larger set of gauge symmetries, but this fact was obscured by a quite different effect and also was not discovered for a long time.)

This history illustrates a general trend in modern physics: The more deeply it has probed the structure of matter, the greater the mathematical order it has found. The order we see in nature does not come from chaos; it is distilled out of a more fundamental order.

Symmetry is just one kind of order. In the case of the marbles in the box, other principles of order were also at work, such as the principle that caused the marbles to seek out the configuration of lowest energy. This is an aspect of a beautiful mathematical principle, called the principle of least action, that underlies all of classical physics. When physicists investigated the subatomic realm, however, they discovered that the principle of least action is just a limiting case of the much more subtle and sophisticated path integral principle, which is the basis of quantum mechanics, as Richard Feynman showed in the 1940s. The lesson is the same: The deeper one looks, the more remarkable the mathematical structure one sees.

The mathematical order underlying physical phenomena is most easily observed in the motions of the heavenly bodies. Even primitive societies were aware of it, and it inspired not only feelings of religious awe (many expressions of which are found in the Bible itself) but also the earliest attempts at mathematical science. And when scientists began to study the solar system with more precision, they discovered unsuspected patterns even more beautiful than those known to the ancients.

Four hundred years ago, for example, Johannes Kepler discovered three marvelous geometrical laws that describe planetary motion. So impressed was he by the beauty of these laws that he wrote this prayer in his treatise *Harmonices Mundi* (The harmonies of the world): "I thank thee, Lord God our Creator, that thou hast allowed me to see the beauty in thy work of creation." Decades later, Newton succeeded in explaining Kepler's laws—but he did not explain them *down*, if by down we mean reducing what we observe and experience to something more trivial or brutish. On the contrary, he explained them by deriving them from an underlying order that is more general and impressive, which we now call Newton's laws of mechanics and gravity. Newton's law of gravity was later explained, in turn, by Einstein, who showed that it followed from a more profound theory of gravity called general relativity. And it is now generally believed that Einstein's theory is but the manifestation of a yet more fundamental theory, which many suspect to be superstring theory. Superstring theory has a mathematical structure so sophisticated that, after a quarter of a century of study by hundreds of the world's most brilliant physicists and mathematicians, it is still not fully understood.

It is true that science seeks to simplify our picture of the world. An explanation should in some sense be simpler than the thing it explains. And, indeed, there is a sense in which Einstein's theory of gravity is simpler than Newton's, and Newton's theory of planetary motion simpler than Kepler's.

As physics Nobel laureate Frank Wilczek notes, however, Einstein's theory is "not 'simple' in the usual sense of the word." Whereas Kepler's laws can be explained in a few minutes to a junior-high-school student, Newton's laws cannot be fully explained without using calculus. And to explain Einstein's theory requires four-dimensional, curved, non-Euclidean space-time and much else besides. And yet, once we know enough, Einstein's theory does have a compelling simplicity greater than Newton's theory. The simplicity to which scientific reductionism leads us, then, is of a very paradoxical kind. It is a simplicity that is by no means simpleminded. It is not at all jejune, but deeply interesting and intellectually rich.

The same paradox can be found in many fields. The chess world champion Capablanca was admired for the purity and simplicity of his style. But to understand his moves one must have an understanding of the game that can be acquired only by years of experience and study. A later world champion, Mikhail Botvinnik, wrote of him, "In this simplicity there was a unique beauty of genuine depth." Another world champion, Emanuel Lasker, observed that "[in Capablanca's games] there is nothing hidden, artificial, or labored. Although they are transparent, they are never banal and are often deep." Wilczek had just the right term for this kind of simplicity, which is also found in the fundamental laws of physics: *profound simplicity*.

Profound simplicity always impresses with its elegance, economy of means, harmony, and perfection. This perfection, as Wilczek notes, is such that one feels that the slightest alteration would be disastrous. He quotes Salieri's envious description of Mozart's music in the film *Amadeus*: "Displace one note and there would be diminishment. Displace one phrase and the structure would fall." Applying this to physics, Wilczek says, "A theory begins to be perfect if any change makes it worse. . . . A theory becomes perfectly perfect if it's impossible to change it without ruining it entirely."

Symmetry is one of the factors that contribute to profound simplicity, both in the laws of physics and in works of art. Paint over one petal of the rose window of a cathedral, remove one column from a colonnade, and the symmetry is destroyed. Each part is necessary for the completion of the pattern.

The symmetries that characterize the deepest laws of physics are mathematically richer and stranger than the ones we encounter in everyday life. The gauge symmetries of the strong and weak forces, for example, involve rotations in abstract mathematical spaces with complex dimensions. In other words, the coordinates in those peculiar spaces are not ordinary numbers, as they are for the space in which we live, but complex numbers, which are numbers that contain the square root of minus one. Grand unified theories—which combine the strong, weak, and electromagnetic forces into a single mathematical structure—posit symmetries that involve rotations in abstract spaces of five or more complex dimensions.

Stranger and more profoundly simple are supersymmetries. There is much reason to think that supersymmetries are built into the laws of physics, and finding evidence of that is one of the main goals of the Large Hadron Collider outside Geneva, Switzerland, which has recently begun to take data. Supersymmetries involve so-called Grassmann numbers, which are utterly different from the ordinary numbers we use to count and measure things. Whereas ordinary numbers (and even complex numbers) have the common-sense property that $a \times b = b \times a$, Grassmann numbers have the bizarre property that $a \times b = -b \times a$. A simple enough formula, but hard indeed for the human mind to fathom.

Esoteric symmetries also lie at the heart of Einstein's theory of relativity. These Lorentz symmetries involve rotations not just in three-dimensional space but in four-dimensional space-time. We can all visualize the symmetries of a sphere or a hexagonal pattern, but Lorentz symmetries, supersymmetries, and the gauge symmetries of the weak, strong, and grand unified forces lie far outside our experience and intuition. They can be grasped only with the tools of advanced mathematics.

Physicists have found beauty in the mathematical principles animating the physical world, from Kepler, who praised God for the elegant geometry of the planets' orbits, to Hermann Weyl, for whom mathematical physics revealed a "flawless harmony that is in conformity with sublime Reason."

Some might suspect that this beauty is in the eye of the beholder, or that scientists think their own theories beautiful simply out of vanity. But there is a remarkable fact that suggests otherwise. Again and again throughout history, what started as pure mathematics—ideas developed solely for the sake of their intrinsic interest and elegance—turned out later to be needed to express fundamental laws of physics.

For example, complex numbers were invented and the theory of them deeply investigated by the early nineteenth century, a mathematical development that seemed to have no relevance to physical reality. Only in the 1920s was it discovered that complex numbers were needed to write the equations of quantum mechanics. Or, in another instance, when the mathematician William Rowan Hamilton invented quaternions in the mid-nineteenth century, they were regarded as an ingenious but totally useless construct. Hamilton himself held this view. When asked by an aristocratic lady whether quaternions were useful for anything, Hamilton joked, "Aye, madam, quaternions are *very* useful—for solving problems involving quaternions." And yet, many decades later, quaternions were put to use to describe properties of subatomic particles such as the spin of electrons as well as the relation between neutrons and protons. Or again, Riemannian geometry was developed long before it was found to be needed for Einstein's theory of gravity. And a branch of mathematics called the theory of Lie groups was developed before it was found to describe the gauge symmetries of the fundamental forces.

Indeed, mathematical beauty has become a guiding principle in the search for better theories in fundamental physics. Werner Heisenberg wrote, "In exact science, no less than in the arts, beauty is the most important source of illumination and clarity." Paul Dirac, one of the giants of twentieth-century physics, went so far as to say that it was more important to have "beauty in one's equations" than to have them fit the experimental data.

At the roots of the physical world, therefore, one does not find mere inchoate slime or dust but instead a richness and perfection of form based on profound, subtle, and beautiful mathematical *ideas*. This is what the famous astrophysicist Sir James Jeans meant when he said many decades ago that "the universe begins to look more like a great thought than a great machine." Benedict XVI expressed the same basic insight when in his Regensburg lecture he referred to "the mathematical structure of matter, its intrinsic rationality, . . . the Platonic element in the modern understanding of nature."

Modern science does not directly imply or require any particular metaphysical theory of reality, but it does suggest to us that the picture presented by Daniel Dennett and Richard Dawkins is false because the picture is only partial. In the terms of Dennett's metaphor of cranes constructing complexity, one sees what is built from the ground up; but delving beneath the surface, one finds an astonishing, hidden world—the underground mechanisms of the cranes, as it were.

It is true that the cosmos was at one point a swirling mass of gas and dust out of which has come the extraordinary complexity of life as we experience it. Yet, at every moment in this process of development, a greater and more impressive order operates within—an order that did not develop but was there from the beginning. In the upper world, mind, thought, and ideas make their appearance as fruit on the topmost branches of an evolutionary tree. Below the surface, we see the taproots of reality, the fundamental laws of physics that shimmer with ideas of profound simplicity.

To describe people as machines made of meat is as scientifically unsophisticated as to think of the sun as a heat-emitting machine made of swirling gas. It ignores the reasons why the machines function as they do—reasons that the explanations of modern physics reduce to simplicities as elegant as they are elusive. Peering into the hidden depths, we see that matter itself is the expression of "a great thought," of ideas that are, as Weyl said, "in conformity with sublime Reason." And we begin to discover that matter, although mindless itself, is the product of a Mind of infinite profundity and infinite simplicity.

JOHN BERGER

The Company of Drawings

FROM *Harper's Magazine*

for Marie-Claude

I'M DRAWING SOME IRISES THAT ARE GROWING AGAINST THE SOUTH wall of a house. They are about one meter tall, but, beginning to be in full bloom, they are somewhat bent over by the weight of their flowers. Four to a stalk. The sun is shining. It's the month of May. All the snow at altitudes less than 1,500 meters has melted.

I think these irises are of a variety called Copper Lustre. Their colors are dark crimson-brown, yellow, white, copper: the colors of the instruments of a brass band being played with abandon. Their stalks and calyxes and sepals are a pale viridian.

I'm drawing with black ink (Sheaffer's) and wash and spit, using my finger rather than a brush. Beside me on the grass, where I'm sitting, are a few sheets of colored Chinese rice paper. I chose them for their cereal colors. Maybe later I will tear shapes from them and use them as collage. Who knows? I have a glue stick if need be. There is also on the grass a bright-yellow oil pastel, taken from a pastel kit made for schoolkids with the trade name Giotto.

The drawn flowers look as though they're going to be half life-size. You lose your sense of time when drawing. You are so concentrated on scales of space. I've probably been drawing for about forty minutes, perhaps longer.

Irises grew in Babylon. Their name came later from the Greek goddess of the rainbow. The French *fleur de lys* was an iris. The blossoms occupy the top half of the paper, the stems force their way upward through the bottom half. The stems are not vertical, they lean to the right.

At a certain moment, if you don't decide to abandon a drawing in order to begin another, the looking involved in what you are measuring and summoning up changes.

At first you question the model (the seven irises) in order to discover lines, shapes, tones that you can trace on the paper. The drawing accumulates the answers. Also, of course, it accumulates corrections, after further questioning of the first answers. Drawing is correcting. I'm beginning now to use the Chinese papers; they turn the ink lines into veins.

At a certain moment—if you are lucky—the accumulation becomes an image. That is to say, it stops being a heap of signs and becomes a presence. Uncouth, but a presence. This is when your looking changes. You start questioning the presence as much as the model.

Where is it asking to be changed so as to become less uncouth? You stare at the drawing and repeatedly glance at the seven irises to look not at their structure this time but at what is radiating from them, at their energy. How do they interact with the air around them, with the sunshine, with the warmth reflected off the wall of the house?

Drawing now involves subtracting as much as adding. It involves the paper as much as the forms drawn on it. I use razor blade, pencil, yellow crayon, spit. I can't hurry.

. . .

I'm taking my time, as if I had all the time in the world. I do have all the time in the world. And with this belief I continue making the minimal corrections, one after another and then another, in order to make the presence of the seven irises a little more comfortable and so more evident. A small snail, who likes the leaves of a nearby black-currant bush, is examining the circle of my implements laid out on the grass. All the time in the world.

In fact I have to deliver the drawing tonight. I have made it for Marie-Claude, who died two days ago, age fifty-eight, of a heart attack.

Tonight the drawing will be in the church somewhere near her coffin. The coffin will be open for those who want to see Marie-Claude for the last time.

Her funeral is tomorrow. Then the drawing, rolled up and tied with a ribbon, will be placed with live flowers in her coffin and be buried with her.

We who draw do so not only to make something visible to others but also to accompany something invisible to its incalculable destination.

Two days after Marie-Claude's funeral I received an email telling that a small drawing of mine—an eighth the size of the drawing of the Copper Lustre irises—had been sold in a London art auction for £4,500. A sum of money such as Marie-Claude would never have dreamt of having in her hands during her entire lifetime.

The auction was organized by the Helen Bamber Foundation, which gives moral, material, and legal support to people begging for asylum in Great Britain, people whose lives and identities have been shattered by emigrant traffickers—the contemporary equivalent of slave traders—by armies that terrorize civilian populations, and by racist governments. The foundation appealed to artists to give them a work that could be sold to raise funds for its activities.

Along with many others I sent a small contribution: a little portrait in charcoal of the Subcomandante Marcos that I had made in Chiapas, southeast Mexico, around Christmas 2007.

He, I, two Zapatista comandantes, and two children are taking it easy in a log cabin on the outskirts of the town of San Cristóbal de las Casas.

We've written letters to each other, Marcos and I, we've spoken together from the same platform, but we have never before sat face-to-face in private. He knows I'd like to draw him. I know he won't take off his mask. We could talk about the Mexican elections or about peasants as a class of survivors, and we don't. A strange quietude affects us both. We smile. I watch him, and I have no sense of urgency about drawing him. It's as if we've spent countless days together, as if everything is unremarkably familiar and requires no action.

Finally I open my sketchbook and pick up a stick of charcoal. I see his low brow, his two eyes, the bridge of his nose. The rest is concealed by ski mask and cap. I let the charcoal, held between my thumb and two fingers, draw, as if reading by touch some kind of braille. The drawing stops. I blow fixative onto it so it won't smudge. The log cabin smells of the alcohol of the fixative.

In the second drawing his right hand comes up to touch the cheek of his mask, a large hand splayed out, with pain between its fingers. The pain of solitude. The solitude of an entire people during the last half millennium.

Later, a third drawing starts. Two eyes examining me. The presumed undulation of a smile. He is smoking his pipe.

Smoking a pipe, or watching a companion smoking a pipe, is another way of letting time pass, of doing nothing.

I fix the drawing. The next drawing, the fourth, is about two men looking hard at each other. Each in his own manner.

Maybe the four are not proper drawings but simply sketch-maps of an encounter. Maps that may make it less likely to get lost. A question of hope.

It was one of these maps that I gave to the Helen Bamber Foundation.

Apparently the bidding for it was prolonged and fierce. The bidders were competing to give money to a cause in which they believed, and, in exchange, they hoped to get a little closer to a visionary political thinker sheltering in the mountains of southeast Mexico.

The money the drawing fetched at the auction will help to buy medicines, care, counselors, nurses, lawyers for Sara or Hamid or Gulsen or Xin . . .

We who draw do so not only to make something observed visible to others but also to accompany something invisible to its incalculable destination.

Now, a drawing I started two weeks ago, and every day since I've worked on it, crept up on it to take it unawares, corrected it, erased it—it's a large charcoal drawing on thick paper—hidden it away, displayed it, reworked it, looked at it in a mirror, redrawn it, and today I think it's over.

It's a drawing of María Muñoz, the Spanish dancer. In 1989, with Pep Ramis, the father of their three children, María founded a dance company called Mal Pelo. They work in Girona in Catalonia and perform in numerous European cities. Five years ago they invited me to collaborate with them.

Collaborate how? I'd watch them for hours improvising and rehearsing, singly, together, in couples. And sometimes I'd suggest a twist in the story line or a word or two or an image that might be projected. They could use me as a kind of narrative clock.

I watched them preparing meals, talking round a table, comforting children, mending a chair, changing clothes, exercising and dancing. María was by far the most experienced dancer, but she did not direct; rather she set an example, often by showing how to take risks.

The bodies of dancers with their kind of devotion are dual. And this is visible whatever they are doing. A kind of Uncertainty Principle determines them; instead of being alternately particle and wave, their bodies are alternately giver and gift.

They know their own bodies in such a penetrating way that they can be within them or before them and beyond them. And this alternates, sometimes changing every few seconds, sometimes every few minutes.

The duality of each body is what allows them, when they perform, to merge into a single entity. They lean against, lift, carry, roll over, separate from, conjoin, buttress each other so that two or three bodies become a single dwelling, like a living cell is a dwelling for its molecules and messengers, or a forest for its animals.

The same duality explains why they are as much intrigued by falling as by leaping, and why the ground challenges them as much as the air.

I write this about the company, Mal Pelo, performing, because it is a way of describing María's body.

One day watching her, I started to think about the late Degas bronzes and drawings of nude dancers and, in particular, one called *Spanish Dance*. I asked María if she would pose for me. She agreed.

Let me show you something, she suggested. It's a preparatory position we take on the floor. We call it the Bridge, because our weight is suspended between our left hand palm down on the floor and our right foot also flat on the floor. Between those two fixed points the whole body is expectant, waiting, suspended.

Drawing María in the Bridge position was like drawing a coal miner working in a very narrow seam. María's body was highly feminine, but what was comparable was its visible experience of exertion and endurance.

Its duality was evident in its calm—her relaxed left foot lay on the floor like an animal asleep—and in the grid of forces in her hips and back ready to challenge every dead weight.

Finally we stopped. She came to look at the drawing. We laughed together.

Then the days of working at home on it. The image in my head was often clearer than the one on the paper. I redrew and redrew. The paper became gray with alterations and cancellations. The drawing didn't get better, but gradually she, about to stand up, was more insistently there.

And today, like I said, something has happened. The effort of my corrections and the endurance of the paper have begun to resemble the resilience of María's own body. The surface of the drawing, its skin, not its image, makes me think of how there are moments when a dancer can make your hairs stand on end.

We who draw do so not only to make something observed visible to others but also to accompany something invisible to its incalculable destination.

ROBERT BLY

The Ant

FROM *The Atlantic*

The ant moves on his tiny Sephardic feet.
The flute is always glad to repeat the same note.
The ocean rejoices in its dusky mansion.

Often bears are piled up close to each other.
In their world it's just one hump after another.
It's like looking at piles of many melons.

You and I have spent so many hours working.
We have paid dearly for the life we have.
It's all right if we do nothing tonight.

I am so much in love with mournful music
That I don't bother to look for violinists.
The aging peepers satisfy me for hours.

I love to see the fiddlers tuning up their old fiddles,
And the singer urging the low notes to come.
I saw her trying to keep the dawn from breaking.

You and I have worked hard for the life we have.
But we love to remember the way the soul leaps
Over and over into the lonely heavens.

PETER J. BOYER

Frat House for Jesus

FROM *The New Yorker*

ONE MIDWINTER NIGHT IN 2008, SENATOR JOHN ENSIGN, OF
Nevada, the chairman of the Senate Republican Policy Committee,
was roused from bed when six men entered his room and ordered
him to get up. Ensign knew the men intimately; a few hours earlier,
he had eaten dinner with them, as he had nearly every Tuesday eve-
ning since he'd come to Washington. Now they were rebuking him
for his recklessness. They told him he was endangering his career,
ruining lives, and offending God.

The men leading this intervention considered themselves En-
sign's closest friends in Washington. Four of those who confronted
Ensign—Senator Tom Coburn and Representatives Bart Stupak,
Mike Doyle, and Zach Wamp—lived with him in an eighteenth-
century brick row house on C Street, in southeast Washington, a
short walk from the Capitol. The men regarded themselves in part as
an accountability group. Despite their political differences—Coburn
and Wamp are Republicans, Stupak and Doyle are Democrats—they
had pledged to hold one another to a life lived by the principles of
Jesus, and they considered the Tuesday supper gatherings at C Street
an inviolable ritual.

The regulars at the dinner included the nine men who lived at
the house, along with half a dozen colleagues and friends who were

non-residents. Every Tuesday evening, they would convene in the first-floor living room of the C Street house, a large space furnished with a long leather sofa and stuffed chairs. A bookshelf was filled with political biographies and James Patterson novels, and paintings of hunting scenes and sailing vessels hung on the walls, suggesting the atmosphere of a men's club, or, as Coburn put it, a fraternity house. (Some of the private bedrooms upstairs, including his, were usually in a state of collegiate disarray.) After some small talk and friendly ribbing, the group broke up, and the men took their places in two narrow, adjoining dining rooms down the hall.

The meals were prepared by a volunteer host couple who lived in the house, and were served by a team of silent young men, also volunteers, who were part of the group's mentoring program. At mealtime, the tone turned more serious, but the subject of conversation was rarely politics. Spiritual issues and the most intimate personal matters were discussed, with the assurance of absolute confidentiality.

Coburn, the senior man in the house, enjoyed these sessions, but at dinner that Tuesday night in 2008 he was plainly troubled. Finally, he spoke out. "Guys," he said, "we've got a problem in the house."

One day some weeks earlier, Coburn said, he had learned that John Ensign, who was married, was having an affair with Cynthia Hampton, the wife of one of his aides, Doug Hampton, and there had been an immediate intervention that same day. Meeting in an upstairs room at the C Street house (a room that was occasionally used for marriage counselling), Doug Hampton, accompanied by Coburn and three lay ministers who manage C Street, had confronted Ensign about the affair. The encounter was filled with recrimination and tears, and culminated in Ensign confessing and vowing to repent. Coburn returned to the Senate, but the others remained with Ensign, handing him a pen and paper and dictating a letter to Cynthia Hampton declaring his intention to end the affair.

"Cindy," the letter began. "This is the most important letter that I've ever written. What I did with you was wrong. I was completely self-centered + only thinking of myself." Ensign wrote that God wished for the two marriages to heal, and for the two lovers to "restore our relationships to Him." The letter was put in a FedEx envelope, and addressed. The three ministers—Marty Sherman, Tim Coe, and David Coe—drove with Ensign to a FedEx station, and watched as he slipped the letter into the drop-box.

Hearing of this weeks later, the men at Coburn's table were astonished. Ensign, a handsome, silver-haired conservative, was a Republican with national prospects. He and Doug Hampton had been extremely close, attending religious retreats together, and even buying houses in adjacent Las Vegas neighborhoods. Cindy Hampton had been Ensign's campaign treasurer. Ensign's Pentecostal faith, embraced when he was in graduate school, had been a central part of his public identity. An active member of the evangelical group Promise Keepers, he had publicly pledged himself to a life of "spiritual, moral, ethical, and sexual purity."

According to Doug Hampton, Ensign, after mailing the letter and shaking his escorts, had telephoned Cindy Hampton and begged her to disregard the package he had just sent. He soon met her again, in Las Vegas, where they resumed the affair.

Coburn's group lingered until well after the men in the adjoining dining room, including Ensign, had said their benediction and dispersed. Ensign had gone to his room, at the far end of the basement. At last, Steve Largent, a former Republican congressman and N.F.L. star—and one of the original C Street residents—spoke up. "Let's go wake him up, right now," he said.

Coburn, Largent, Stupak, Wamp, Doyle, and Sherman went downstairs and roused Ensign. This second intervention ended with Ensign sitting at the foot of his bed, weeping. "You're right," he told his friends. "I'm going to end this craziness."

Some in the C Street group wanted Ensign out of the house, but the prevailing view was that he should stay. Dealing with the affair seemed to pose a test of the group's very purpose: in the fevered atmosphere of an election year, could the men of C Street cope with the situation privately? Looking back, Coburn believed that the Ensign case was a C Street success story. A year after that midnight confrontation, word of Ensign's affair had not leaked, and Ensign and his wife, Darlene, had reconciled.

Doug and Cindy Hampton were together, too, but Doug Hampton was still angry at Ensign. He believed that Ensign had destroyed his life, and, with the help of powerful friends, had got away with it. In June, 2009, after Ensign learned that Hampton intended to reveal the affair, he publicly confessed, and resigned his Republican leadership position. The tawdriness of the double betrayal, of wife and close friend, produced a wave of sex-scandal stories, but the damage was confined to Ensign. Then, a week later, the Republican governor of South Carolina, Mark Sanford, made his own public confession, a rambling tale of the "impossible love" that he had found with a woman in Argentina. Sanford spoke of an inner struggle over the betrayal of his marriage vows, and mentioned that he had sought the counsel of some of his old circle in Washington. "I was part of a group called C Street when I was in Washington," he said. "It was, believe it or not, a Christian Bible study—some folks that asked members of Congress hard questions that I think were very, very important. And I've been working with them."

The press soon discovered that John Ensign lived at the C Street house. A month later, in the circuit court of Hinds County, Mississippi, Leisha Pickering, the wife of the former Republican congressman Chip Pickering, another resident of the C Street house, filed an alienation-of-affection lawsuit suggesting that Pickering had committed adultery while living there. A picture began to emerge of a boys-gone-wild house of pleasure. The men of C Street, pledged to silence, declined to respond to press inquiries, which only heightened interest ("THE POLITICAL ENCLAVE THAT DARE NOT SPEAK ITS NAME," a Washington *Post* headline read). Public records revealed little; the house was registered to an obscure evangelical youth group, and enjoyed the tax status of a registered church. Word spread that the tenants were paying below-market rents (about nine hundred dollars a month each), which prompted an inquiry by the Office of Congressional Ethics. Even if the residents had been inclined to talk about the house, some knew nothing more about it than the fact that they made out their monthly checks to "C Street Center."

The C Street house was known to be associated with a ministry called the Fellowship, a nondenominational entity that sponsored the annual National Prayer Breakfast. But the Fellowship's more significant work was its invisible ministry to political leaders, dating back to the New Deal era. Through the years, small Fellowship-inspired prayer groups have held weekly meetings in the Pentagon, in the Attorney General's office, in various congressional hideaways inside the Capitol, and in the White House itself. The Fellowship has offered succor to Bill Clinton and Al Gore, to Dwight Eisenhower and Marion Barry, and to many of the Watergate felons. D. Michael Lindsay, a Rice University sociologist who has studied the ways in which evangelicals have become part of the American élite, was astonished by what he discovered about the Fellowship. "They are the most significant spiritual force in the lives of leaders—especially leaders in Washington—of any entity that I know," he says. "They are mentioned more often in the interviews I've conducted than any other group. They have had a more sustained influence over the decades than any other entity. There is nothing comparable to them."

. . .

The Fellowship avoids publicity for its activities. Heath Shuler, a two-term Democratic representative from North Carolina who lives in the house on C Street and has attended a weekly prayer session sponsored by the Fellowship since he arrived in Washington, recently said, "I've been here the whole time, and there's talk about what the Fellowship is, but I honestly have no idea what they're talking about. I honestly don't know what it is." Tom Coburn acknowledges that influence and secrecy, two of the chief attributes of the Fellowship, make a provocative combination. "Everybody in this town, and probably in the media world, says, Well, if you're not out front, then you obviously have something to hide," Coburn says. One view of the Fellowship, with some popularity on the secular left, is of a sort of theocratic Blackwater, advancing a conservative agenda in the councils of power throughout the world. Secretary of State Hillary Clinton, a friend of the Fellowship, might dispute that view—if she spoke about the group, which she does not.

The Fellowship's participants (there is no official membership) describe themselves simply as followers of Jesus, an informal network of friends seeking harmony by modelling their lives after his. They are assertively nondoctrinal (eschewing even the term "Christian") and nonecclesiastical (denominations tend to be divisive), and although the core figures are evangelicals, they do not believe in proselytizing. I have spoken to Buddhists, Muslims, and Jews who consider themselves part of this network. The group rejects anything resembling a formal structure—there is no titled executive team, and even the name "Fellowship" is unofficial, an informal convenience. The business cards of those leaders who carry them list the individual's name at the top and addresses and telephone numbers at the bottom, with a blank space in between, where the name of the entity might go. A formal foundation does exist—a 501(c)(3) called the International Foundation, which oversees three hundred or so ministries associated with the Fellowship, and has a board of directors that approves a budget for the ministries (in the fifteen-million-dollar range) and the salaries of the parent entity's relatively few employees. The Fellowship's affiliated ministries vary widely in their missions, from operating a secondary school in Uganda to funding a program for inner-city youths in Washington, D.C. The core mission of the Fellowship, however, is interpersonal ministry to the powerful, meant "to turn their hearts to the poor."

For the past forty years, this mission has been largely driven by one man, a layman from Oregon named Doug Coe. Coe insists that he is not the leader of anything. He sat in on the weekly House and Senate prayer groups for fifty years, speaking only once in all that time. Coe generally avoids interviews and photographers; a few years ago, when *Time* named him one of the nation's most influential evangelicals, he tried to persuade the writer not to include him on the list, and, failing that, declined to provide a photograph of himself. His admirers describe him in terms that suggest a near-mystical visionary, with a powerful personal magnetism. "Almost everyone, from the moment they meet Doug Coe, they see he's somebody special," Don Bonker, a former Democratic congressman from Washington and a longtime associate of Coe's, says. In Hillary Clinton's memoir, "Living History," she wrote that Coe was "a unique presence in Washington: a genuinely loving spiritual mentor and guide to anyone, regardless of party or faith, who wants to deepen his or her relationship to God."

In May, I travelled to Arlington, Virginia, where I met Doug Coe. The setting was a Revolutionary War-era mansion called the Cedars, which, since 1978, has served as the Fellowship's home base. The house sits on seven acres, which rise to the high point of the Potomac palisade, near the Key Bridge, and is secluded by thick woodlands. The Cedars is used as a place for prayer meetings and meals (served by volunteers, as at the C Street house), and as a refuge for friends of the group. It was where William Aramony, the former director of United Way, went when he learned that he was about to be indicted as a swindler, and where Lee Atwater, the Republican political operative, retreated when he learned that he had a brain tumor. Michael Jackson and his family stayed at the Cedars when he came to Washington for a 9/11 memorial concert.

Coe greeted me in the front parlor, and escorted me to a side library. Coe is eighty-one now, and had recently undergone angioplasty, but he did not seem infirm. He was dressed in khaki trousers, a polo shirt, and a sport coat. Sliding into a leather chair, he said, "Tell me your story"—his standard opening with a stranger. Then, in a looping, elliptical narrative, he told me his.

Coe was reared in Salem, Oregon, in a home that valued education (his father was the state superintendent of schools) and the methods of John Wesley. His mother spent hours on her knees in daily prayer and fretted about the soul of her son. Coe, who preferred playing ball to practicing religion, parted from the Church at his earliest opportunity, when he left home for Willamette University to study math and physics. "For me to think that a baby born two thousand years ago to a fifteen-year-old girl in Bethlehem created the solar system—that didn't make any sense to me," he said. Other tenets of the faith gave him pause, too. "I just couldn't figure out a God that would send everybody to Hell except a few of my friends, and my mom and my dad," he says.

Then one night, alone in his room at Willamette, Coe had a religious experience. He describes it, as many born-again Christians do, as an almost corporeal encounter. He found himself promising to give his life to God's work—as long as he didn't have to evangelize, or spend too much time in prayer. He set out to test the efficacy of prayer by composing a list of desirable outcomes, having nothing to do directly with himself, and determined to try to pray them into reality by a certain date. One of the items on his list, he says, was that his favorite professor at school, a political-science instructor, would have a personal experience with Jesus. As the deadline neared, the professor, Mark Hatfield, told Coe that he had "met the Lord." Coe and Hatfield became close friends and prayer partners, and remained so when Hatfield entered electoral politics, winning a seat in the state legislature, and eventually becoming governor and a U.S. senator. Coe travelled with Hatfield throughout the state, the two of them talking about Jesus as if he were present with them. (As one of the Senate's most liberal Republicans, Hatfield opposed the Vietnam War, the Reagan tax cuts, and the Gulf War.)

When the big preachers came through Oregon in the early nineteen-fifties, Billy Graham among them, they all stopped by to visit Hatfield, and Coe began to develop a network of important connections. One who made a lasting impression was a Norwegian immigrant named Abraham Vereide, a Methodist preacher who had created a unique ministry that existed outside the organized churches and aimed to change the world by changing the hearts of leaders.

Vereide had arrived in America, which he called the "land of the unchained Bible," in 1905, at the age of eighteen, with a burning zeal and uncommon drive. He soon made his way from preaching a horseback circuit to a prominent pulpit in downtown Seattle. On his recommendation, the city's civic leaders created the program that came to be known as Goodwill Industries, putting people to work at reclaiming and reselling surplus goods. In 1934, in a meeting with nineteen of the city's civic leaders, Vereide proposed that they try to order their lives according to the principles of Jesus. They met again the next week, and the next, with the understanding that the gatherings were utterly secret. "This was an intimate circle," Vereide wrote, according to "Modern Viking," a privately published authorized biography by Norman Grubb. "We didn't dare tell anybody what was going on, or even include anyone else," Vereide continued. "It was a sharing fellowship." Vereide began to hear from men across the country (Fiorello LaGuardia sought him out on a trip West), and what had evolved into the prayer-breakfast idea became a national movement. At Vereide's instigation, a prayer group was started in the House, and then in the Senate, and they continue today. In 1953, Vereide's friend Senator Frank Carlson, of Kansas, invited the new President, Dwight Eisenhower, to attend a prayer breakfast. It was the first instance of what has become the National Prayer Breakfast, attended annually by every President since.

The real work of the movement, though, was in the small groups of top men (as Vereide described his mission field) which proliferated across the country. Sam Shoemaker, the New York Episcopal priest who helped to devise the Twelve Step program for Alcoholics Anonymous, in the nineteen-thirties, was Vereide's close friend and adviser, and made key connections for him in New York and in Washington. Thomas Watson, of I.B.M., summoned Vereide to discuss his groups, as did Marvin Coyle, the president of Chevrolet, and J. C. Penney. Prayer groups were spreading overseas, and, by the end of the nineteen-fifties, with Vereide in his seventies, the core group of men around him decided to bring younger blood into the leadership circle. Doug Coe was recruited into the organization, which was then called International Christian Leadership, as field director, in 1959, and when Vereide died, a decade later, Coe effectively became his successor.

Coe's flock consisted of a quarter of the members of the House and the Senate, and a wide international network of parliamentarians, potentates, military brass, and business executives. He had no pulpit and no title, and although he was called the "stealth Billy Graham," he was no preacher. (A video of a talk he once gave to a group of evangelicals shows him prone to disjointed narrative and given to bizarre analogy, suggesting that Christians could use the sort of blind devotion that Maoists, Nazis, and the Mafia understood.) But Coe had a vision for the prayer-group movement that matched Vereide's, and, in some ways, eclipsed it.

Under Coe, the Fellowship's work became more focussed on an intensely personal, "relational" ministry to leaders, many of them public leaders, which made absolute trust paramount. What some saw as obsessive secrecy, Coe says, was a necessary privacy. "We're not being secretive, it's just that no one advertises that we've got a guy here who's an atheist and is having a problem with his life, or maybe stole money from his country's treasury," he said.

The other change under Coe was a refining of the brand of faith that animated the Fellowship. Coe distilled that faith down to the raw teaching of Jesus, as presented in the Gospels—Matthew, Mark, Luke, and John—and in the first few chapters of the Acts of the Apostles. This approach conformed with Coe's youthful rebellion against the idea of a God who would condemn all but a particular brand of believer. "They tell Jewish friends, You can't go to Heaven unless you're a Christian," Coe says. "Well, the facts are, if that is true, Isaiah could never go to Heaven, Mary could never go to Heaven, Jesus could never go to Heaven. It's crazy."

But there is also a strategic value to this insistently nondoctrinal approach: anybody, of any faith, can admire Coe's Jesus. Rabbi Jack Bemporad, who works in the field of interreligious relations, met Coe on a trip to Iran several years ago. "He wants to have a way of presenting Jesus so that whoever he's talking to will find a way of accepting it," Bemporad says. "He's not dogmatic and saying, 'You've got to believe in the Trinity,' or 'He's the son of God.'" Bemporad became a friend of Coe's, and has visited the Cedars to speak about Jesus as a teacher of Judaism.

Coe also finds spiritual communion with the Dalai Lama ("the Dalai Lama loves Jesus"), and recently sent me a book of the Dalai

Lama's meditations on the Gospels. Along with a note, Coe slipped in a small tract titled "A Follower of Jesus," which amounted to a summation of the Fellowship's creed. The Followers of Jesus, it said, seek "a 'revolution of love' so powerful that the division and animosity separating people and nations will be greatly eliminated or replaced by the spirit of forgiveness and reconciliation as modeled by Jesus of Nazareth."

"I can tell you that critics to his right think that Doug is just doctrinally soft and confused," Michael Cromartie, the vice-president of the Ethics and Public Policy Center in Washington, and a friend of Coe's, says. "It's one thing to be an admirer of Jesus the man, but there are people in the more orthodox world who want to say that Jesus did more than just walk around and teach; he actually did something in history, on the Cross, that is crucial to everything."

Coe shrinks at the thought of trying to convert anyone. His gift, those close to him say, is for acting as a sort of spiritual adviser. In 1982, when Ed Meese, the White House counsellor, was inconsolable after his son, Scott, was killed in an automobile wreck, a friend in the White House, Herb Ellingwood, suggested that Meese consider trying a small prayer group. The next morning, at six-thirty, Ellingwood and Meese met on the steps of the Pentagon, where they were joined by Doug Coe, whom Meese did not know. They went inside, into the office of another member of their group, General Jack Vessey, who was the chairman of the Joint Chiefs of Staff. Meese was surprised; he had sat across from Vessey at national-security meetings, and had no idea that he was even a Christian. The group met every week at the Pentagon, until Vessey's retirement, when the prayer sessions moved to the Department of Justice, where Meese was by then presiding as Attorney General. When Meese left the government, the prayer group relocated to the Cedars, where it meets every Tuesday morning.

"It has meant a great deal to me," Meese told me. "All of us have had family problems, personal problems. It's a place where you can discuss these problems. You come together in the name of Jesus, so you have a natural kind of bond. And the group dynamics are such that you have total confidence that nothing you are going to say is going to make you vulnerable through your colleagues, which is rare in Washington."

Meese later got an idea of the Fellowship's pervasiveness while on a trip to Japan. Coe had told him that a prayer group was meeting at a particular hotel, and Meese, searching the lobby billboard's long list of events and meetings, finally found a listing for "Small Group," giving a room number. Meese went to the room, and found the prayer group he was looking for—a group begun years earlier, according to Doug Coe, at the suggestion of Al Gore and James Baker.

In the Coe era, the Fellowship's international outreach intensified, with an emphasis on a private, faith-based diplomacy that scored several quiet triumphs but also invited a darker interpretation of the Fellowship's motivations. The prevalent critique of the prayer movement's overseas involvement was chiefly advanced by the journalist Jeff Sharlet, whose 2008 book, "The Family: The Secret Fundamentalism at the Heart of American Power," painted an evocative portrait of a cultlike vanguard movement that "recasts theology in the language of empire," and facilitated a right-wing American foreign policy. (A second book, "C Street: The Fundamentalist Threat to American Democracy," will appear later this month.)

Those involved in the Fellowship's activities abroad insist that this critique vastly overstates the group's influence, and misrepresents its motivation. One practitioner of the Fellowship's private diplomacy is a former federal bureaucrat named Bob Hunter, who was an official in the Department of Housing and Urban Development under Jimmy Carter.

Hunter was a consumer advocate in the Ralph Nader mold. (Indeed, Nader was a friend and colleague, and Hunter marched against the Iraq war carrying a sign reading "The Emperor Has No Clues.") When he met Doug Coe, in 1978, he had experienced a midlife religious conversion that he credited with saving his marriage, and he was looking for some way to channel his new zeal when a minister friend arranged a visit to the Cedars. Hunter had a liberal's take on the Gospels. "I was new, I was a blank slate, I didn't have any biases," he recalls. "Jesus basically says that helping the poor is the goal. Reach out and help the least among us. I took that seriously. I wanted to know what Jesus was calling me to do." Coe gave Hunter the prayer test. He urged him to meet in a small group with his new friends in faith, and to start to pray. "He said, 'You need to try to find something to pray for that's bigger than yourself. Something that you guys can't do, because then you can't take the credit for it, when you start to see these things happen. And they will happen. I would suggest you pray for a place. You can pray for a place, or an idea, something. Places are easier, somehow. Maybe you ought to pray for the District of Columbia—they could use it—or the state of Virginia, or Brazil. Or even a whole continent, like Africa.'"

Hunter had no particular interest in foreign affairs at the time, but he and his friends began to pray for Uganda, a place that came to mind, he told me, because Idi Amin was in the news at the time. Soon, they met an Anglican missionary from Uganda, and launched a fund-raising campaign for the Mengo Hospital, in Kampala. Hunter continued to pray, and one day, at an airport, he met a young woman who turned out to be the daughter of Andrew Young, then the U.S. Ambassador to the United Nations. She introduced him to Young, who helped open many doors in Africa, and eventually Hunter was so well connected that he became an intermediary in getting Nelson Mandela to preside over peace talks for Burundi in 2000.

Hunter brought Yoweri Kaguta Museveni, the former African rebel who became Uganda's President, and other key Ugandan leaders into prayer groups. When Uganda's Parliament took up a bill last year that would have punished some homosexual acts with death, Hunter and his friends in the Fellowship felt they had the standing to urge the proposed measure's defeat. Museveni appointed a commission that studied the matter and then recommended that the bill be withdrawn. Using similar connections, in 2001 the Fellowship arranged a secret meeting at the Cedars between the warring leaders Joseph Kabila, the President of the Democratic Republic of Congo, and Paul Kagame, the President of Rwanda, who later signed a peace agreement.

Even friends of the Fellowship, however, acknowledge that the group has made itself vulnerable to unfriendly assessments, because its insistent secrecy and Coe's indiscriminate outreach to leaders of all kinds raise legitimate questions of accountability. An old friend of Coe's, the late Washington lawyer Jim Bell, a key figure in the early Fellowship, once said of Coe's willful political naïveté, "Doug has chosen to be a political eunuch," a posture that enabled him to befriend, in the name of Jesus, such men as the Somalian dictator Siad Barre.

Coe met Barre in 1980, and in 1983, when he arranged a multi-nation Africa trip for several Fellowship associates, he put Somalia on the itinerary. Coe thought it would be helpful to include a member of Congress in the entourage, and, at the last minute, he asked Chuck Grassley, then a new Republican senator from Iowa, to join. Kent Hotaling, a Coe associate who was on the trip, says that Grassley asked Coe, "What do you want me to do when I get there?"

"Just talk about the Senate group that you're part of, and how people meeting around Jesus, it helps them work out their differences, and that we're coming in the name of Jesus for friendship," Coe told Grassley. Hotaling says that Grassley said just that, and nothing more. "There was nothing from Doug that instructed him to talk politics. He didn't talk politics." But Hotaling acknowledges that Barre almost certainly inferred a political meaning in the visit. Somalia had been a client state of the Soviet Union, until a Soviet-backed coup in neighboring Ethiopia shifted the East-West balance in the Horn of Africa and left Somalia without a patron. No U.S. senator had ever visited Somalia, and the fact that Grassley had been sent by Doug Coe rather than by Ronald Reagan was a distinction Barre was unlikely to make. History hardly required Doug Coe's intervention—Somalia and the United States believed they needed each other at the time—but Coe cannot be surprised at the accusation of complicity in the devastation that Barre later brought to the country. "Somalia wanted guns," Sharlet wrote, and the Fellowship "helped it get guns."

In 1997, Coe travelled to Sudan with a former Republican congressman named Mark Siljander, and met with the country's notorious President, Omar al-Bashir. The Clinton Administration had broken diplomatic ties with Bashir, who had declared Sharia law and undertaken a program of religious cleansing which killed two million Christians and animists, and made refugees of four million more. According to the evangelical magazine *World*, Siljander may have taken Coe's Jesus-only, no-questions-asked ecumenism too seriously. Siljander wrote a book called "A Deadly Misunderstanding: A Congressman's Quest to Bridge the Muslim-Christian Divide," in which he asserted that Bashir was "a bad man" in the eyes of the West, but "in the eyes of God, as near as I could understand it, he was just another human being, with frailties and failings like the rest of us." In 2005, the F.B.I. began to investigate Siljander's work for a Sudan-based Islamic charity with terrorist ties, and this July Siljander pleaded guilty to felony counts of acting as an unregistered foreign agent and of obstruction of justice. He faces a possible fifteen-year prison sentence.

Just a few minutes after I met Coe that first evening at the Cedars, he told me, "Most of my friends are bad people. They all broke the Ten Commandments, as far as I can tell." He went on to cite the crimes of such Biblical leaders as King David and the apostle Paul, which was his way of saying that judgment is God's work, not his. That is his explanation, or rationalization, for the spiritual friendships that he and others in the Fellowship have formed over the years with such men as Indonesia's Suharto, or General Gustavo Álvarez Martínez, the Honduran strongman. On one occasion, the Fellowship decided to invite Teodoro Obiang Nguema Mbasogo, the President of Equatorial Guinea, to the annual National Prayer Breakfast. Obiang, who came to power in 1979 by leading a coup that resulted in the execution of his tyrannical uncle, has been called the worst dictator in Africa. When a State Department official asked why the Fellowship would be inviting such a tyrant to a prayer breakfast, Coe says, the answer was "That's why we invited him." In the event, Obiang did come to the breakfast, but little in his record suggests that his association with the Fellowship has moderated his authoritarian style. Holding others accountable for their actions is a tenet of Christian duty as old as the Church, but Coe says that he does not judge. "Jesus even met with the Devil," he said.

Members of the group concede that some people may seek their fellowship for reasons other than a wish to grow in Jesus. In the early nineteen-nineties, a Russian media entrepreneur named Vladimir Gusinsky, who'd had a falling-out with Vladimir Putin, was looking West for new opportunities. He hired the public-relations firm APCO, which specializes in crisis management, to help introduce him in the United States. One of the APCO executives handling Gusinsky was Don Bonker, the former Democratic congressman, and an established figure within the Fellowship. Bonker brought

Gusinsky, a secular Jew, to the Cedars to meet Doug Coe. "We emerged from that meeting, and we were walking to the limo, and Gusinsky stopped me," Bonker recalls. "He said, 'That is an amazing man. I want to come back here and see him again.'"

Gusinsky attended the Prayer Breakfast the next year, and has missed only one of the events in the years since. In 1998, when Coe and a group of his close associates made a whirlwind trip through the former republics of the Soviet Union, meeting with leaders introduced by friends in the international network, Gusinsky provided a 727 with a full crew to transport them. It is impossible, ultimately, to know the motivation of someone like Gusinsky, who comes from a political culture in which proximity to power is everything. The Fellowship meant entrée to a rarefied circle, and the prospect of shaking hands with a President. "There's this whole Washington phenomenon, related to access to power and the aphrodisiac of power," Michael Cromartie, of the Ethics and Public Policy Center, says. "You bring an oligarch over to the Cedars and he says, 'Ah, these are my kind of people. They have pictures on the wall of all these Presidents, they seem to be in touch with power, they know people with money, this will help my business.'"

If international dignitaries view the Prayer Breakfast as a reliable means of unofficial access, some Presidents—most notably, Bill Clinton—have been more accommodating than others. "Bill and Hillary got it," says Doug Burleigh, who is Coe's son-in-law, and a key figure in the Fellowship. "They came early, they'd meet with the groups early and do a photo op with 'em, hug 'em. They got what this was about." George W. Bush, on the other hand, made it clear to Coe and the others from the start that he'd show up at the Prayer Breakfast but not to expect much more. "George came late, and left early—he did every year," Burleigh says. "Now, I appreciate his honesty. He told Doug, 'You know, this isn't my thing.'" "After Bush's first, perfunctory appearance, Clinton telephoned Coe to console him. "He didn't badmouth Bush, he gave it the best spin," Burleigh recalls. "He said, 'Hey, Bush'll get it. He doesn't understand what this thing's about.'"

In 1984, Coe was introduced to a man named Michael Timmis, a wealthy recent convert, eager to do God's work, who had heard that Doug Coe was the man to see. Timmis was a hard-charging overachiever from a working-class Irish Catholic family in Detroit, who had made a fortune in high-risk business transactions. Along the way, he had alienated his wife and two children, and his born-again experience had not helped matters at home. Coe told him that he needed to go back to Detroit and learn how to love his family. Timmis was a bit put off, but the two men stayed in touch, and Coe eventually offered to "disciple" Timmis—to become his spiritual mentor.

One morning a year later, Timmis found his seventeen-year-old daughter, Laura, dead in the garage of the family's Grosse Pointe home. She had committed suicide, after an argument with her parents about skipping school. Timmis's grief was compounded by his fear of also losing his son, Mike, Jr., a troubled college senior whose estrangement seemed irreparable. Coe met the young man during an Easter visit to Grosse Pointe, and got him to promise to visit the Cedars and help to computerize the Fellowship's records. After graduation, his parents held him to his promise, and Mike, Jr., reluctantly headed to Arlington for a week's stay. Four days later, Coe telephoned Timmis to tell him that Mike, Jr., had found the Lord, and was determined to become a missionary in Africa. Timmis and his son reconciled, and Timmis offered Coe any sum he named. No need for that, Coe said, but he added that there was a ministry in Washington that could use some help. "Why don't you help those guys?" Coe asked.

"Those guys" were Coe's sons, David and Tim, and their friend Marty Sherman. The Coe brothers and Sherman had been schoolmates at James Madison University, where they were part of a fraternity for believers, and tried to model themselves after the early Christians described in the Book of Acts. After graduating, they apprenticed with the Fellowship, and saw a chance to branch out when the house on C Street became available.

The place had been built as a convent for St. Peter's Catholic Church, in 1880, and had taken on many incarnations since, most recently as an outreach center for a Hawaii-based ministry called Youth with a Mission (known as Y-WAM), which was looking for a buyer. The house was technically owned by a Y-WAM entity-of-convenience foundation called the C Street Center, and Timmis acquired the house by purchasing the foundation. The District of Columbia allowed the new owner to keep the C Street Center name on the city records, which is why, when the scandal broke, reporters couldn't determine the property's real owner.

The lay ministers used the place as a base for their contact work on the Hill, which became a significantly richer mission field when the Republican revolution of 1994 brought a huge crop of Christian conservatives to town. Among them was Steve Largent, the new congressman from Oklahoma, who was greeted by Tim Coe and Sherman soon after he moved into his office in the Cannon Building. A friendship developed, and, when Largent heard about Sherman's frat house for Jesus, he was curious. When the rules governing congressional travel allowance were changed, enabling weekly commutes to the home district, senators and congressmen scrambled for part-time quarters in Washington, some sharing apartments with other members, some bunking in their offices. The C Street house, with its dormlike rooms upstairs, suggested itself as an obvious option.

Largent, Coburn, Wamp, and Doyle were the first to move in, and they were soon joined by Bart Stupak. (Over the years, the roster of residents included Republican Senators Sam Brownback, John Thune, and Jim DeMint, and Kansas Representative Jerry Moran, as well as John Ensign.) Prospective housemates were usually recruited from the prayer groups. Until the recent scandals, wives of the C Street residents were generally enthusiastic supporters of the living arrangement. "My wife doesn't live here in Washington, she lives at home, and she loves the fact that I'm surrounded by a group of men that know her," Coburn says. "She knows that if I start wandering, Marty or Mike Doyle or Bart Stupak or Heath, they're gonna say, 'Hey, what's the deal?'"

The Tuesday supper was the only formal meal served to the residents, although Jim DeMint could be found most mornings making his way downstairs, in pajama bottoms and T-shirt, to fetch his breakfast of tea, Oreos, and dried cranberries. The men's private quarters were strikingly modest. Stupak had one of the better rooms, a corner space on the third floor, with a private bath, but DeMint slept in a space just big enough for his bed, and hung his clothes in a closet down the hall.

There was shoptalk, but politicking was avoided, a custom that proved useful during moments of peak partisanship on the Hill, such as Bill Clinton's impeachment or last year's health-care debate. "It's hard to hate somebody that you're praying with," Coburn says. Heath Shuler says, "This is really the only time that I see the barriers completely knocked down between the two political parties. They love one another, they care about one another. Now, sometimes, that changes. They'll walk out the door and get on C-SPAN and try to win an Emmy, and that changes. But, truly and sincerely, there is that love there."

Much of the talk in the house was deeply personal. Chip Pickering spoke of his unhappy marriage, and made it clear that he meant to end it, even as he was reminded (vainly) of his marriage vows. Mark Sanford never lived at the house but did pray with the group often enough that his wife, Jenny, sought the group's counsel when she learned of her husband's affair. Those cases became famous failures, but the men at C Street contend that their support group has mostly worked, as on the morning in the spring of 2000 when each of them received an urgent summons to Stupak's home in Menominee, Michigan. Stupak's youngest son, Bart, Jr., had shot and killed himself after a high-school graduation party at the family's home. "There was no decision to be made. I mean, we had to get to Bart and just be there to support him as soon as we could," Largent says. Tom Coburn was at Stupak's side when he viewed his son's body, in the mortuary, and other C Street men helped to repair the damage to the wall caused by the bullet. "We had a contingent of ninety members of Congress come to that funeral," Coburn recalls. "And what they got to see was something that they hadn't seen in a long time: Here's three Republicans and two Democrats lovin' a brother through a problem. They came because they knew what we had."

Soon after the Pickering story broke, an exodus from the C Street house began. John Thune, the Republican from South Dakota, who is said to have Presidential aspirations, was the first to leave, in July of 2009. A group of congresswomen who used the house for a Wednesday-morning prayer session found a new venue, and a moderate Democrat who had been considering a move into the house pulled back. John Ensign asked his housemates' forgiveness, and left, but the taint remained. Stupak and Doyle, pressured by constituents and the press, had moved out by the end of the year. That left only Coburn, DeMint, Wamp, Shuler, and Moran—conservatives who were in little danger of being punished by voters for staying. The Justice Department and the Senate Ethics Committee were said to be scrutinizing Ensign's dealings with Doug Hampton for possible impropriety. The House Office of Congressional Ethics, however, had decided that the residents' rental rates were appropriate for the boarding-house arrangement, and did not recommend that any action be taken. District officials revised the house's tax status, removing much of its exemption.

This spring, a group of core associates gathered at the Cedars and debated whether the time had come to alter the Fellowship's rigid policy of secretiveness. Some in the group had long argued for greater transparency and accountability, if for no other reason than to counter the darker conjectures about the movement. By most accounts, this view prevailed, despite Coe's reservations. Change will almost certainly be minor, and come slowly. A Web site has been designed, and is scheduled to be launched this month.

Marty Sherman and the Coe brothers attended the meeting, and began by apologizing for the embarrassment their program had caused. There has been talk of closing down the C Street house, and even of selling it. "If it has reached the point where the reporting on C Street has been so negative that it becomes how people identify what we do, and what we stand for, then, yeah, it should shut down," Don Bonker, the former Democratic congressman, says. "I've just never thought it was a good idea for people to take up residence. And now, with the negative reporting, I think that is having an injurious effect on the whole movement, on the Fellowship, and what it represents." Closing the place would be easy enough to do, given that Mike Timmis and Marty Sherman sit on the board of the foundation that owns it.

In the meantime, when Congress is in session the Tuesday-night gatherings continue, still attended by members who no longer live in the house. During the supper accountability session, according to Tom Coburn, "a question that'll be asked about every four weeks is, Is anybody here having an affair?"

KATHARINE COLES

All Souls Night

FROM *The Gettysburg Review*

Why not shatter a night with snow—so early—
Or watch a half-moon laze
Back on her bed of clouds, the glitter

Of stars half-crazed by time? Even those
Clouds shred by so fast the moon is left

Hanging onto the night. Planted
On our own ground, we have
The barest sense of each other's bodies

Slipping away. No wonder
We can hardly bear our bliss, pouring

Onto us without a moment's notice—
A tap on the shoulder, a touch, a kiss.
So it fills us up. So it will pass.

BILLY COLLINS

Gold

FROM *The Gettysburg Review*

I don't want to make too much of this,
but because the bedroom faces east
across a lake here in Florida,

when the sun first rises
and reflects off the water,
the whole room is suffused with the kind
of golden light that might travel
the length of a passageway in a megalithic tomb
precisely at dawn on the summer solstice.

Again, I don't want to exaggerate,
but it reminds me of a brand of light
that could illuminate the walls
of a hidden chamber full of treasure,
pearls and gold coins overflowing the silver platters.

I feel like comparing it to the fire
that Aphrodite lit in the human eye
so as to make it possible for us to perceive
the other three elements,

but the last thing I want to do
is risk losing your confidence
by appearing to lay it on too thick.

Let's just say that the morning light here
would bring to anyone's mind
the rings of light that Dante
deploys in the final cantos of the *Paradiso*
to convey the presence of God
while bringing *The Divine Comedy*
to a stunning climax and leave it at that.

ANDREW COOPER

The Debacle

FROM *Tricycle*

I WAS STANDING IN THE BACK CORNER OF THE WELL-APPOINTED front room of the San Francisco Zen Center Guest House. My pants were down around my ankles, and I was davening—rocking back and forth in the rhythmic movement that traditionally accompanies Jewish prayer—as I recited from the copy of Philip Roth's *Portnoy's Complaint* that I held open before me. In the center of the spacious room, near the high bay windows that look out from the renovated Victorian's second floor, four tall, fair-skinned Zen Center priests in golden robes stood, erect and dignified, conferring intently in hushed voices. Noticing my presence, they turned, and each fixed a stern gaze upon me. I felt that I should stop, but I couldn't. In fact, flushed with self-consciousness, my davening became more rapid and my chanting louder, until, frantic, my voice was no longer recognizable as my own.

That was when I awoke. It was nearly pitch black, and I was in a strange bed. I couldn't recall where I was. The scent of the sandalwood soap on the nightstand and the brushing of the branches against the windows were the first clues, and in a minute it came together. I was in the same guest house I had been dreaming about, though in a different room. It was the second day of the Vietnamese Zen master Thich Nhat Hanh's first teaching tour of American dharma centers, a tour that I had spent much of the previous year organizing and on which I was now, in the spring of 1983, accompanying him as his assistant. I sat up in bed, clammy with sweat, and to the surrounding darkness, the chilly San Francisco night, and to myself, I for some reason muttered, "I'm Jewish."

This was obviously an odd thing to say, and I'm still not really sure why I said it, but it had the calming effect of bringing me back to myself. I certainly needed that kind of help on that particular night. Although I was *at* San Francisco Zen Center, I was *in* extremis. The previous June, at an interfaith conference on nuclear disarmament in New York City, the Zen Centers abbot, Richard Baker Roshi, had met Thich Nhat Hanh and invited him to come from his home in France to San Francisco to be a guest teacher at Zen Center. I had attended the conference as well, and at its conclusion, I was introduced to Nhat Hanh, or as I learned to call him, Thay, an affectionate Vietnamese Buddhist term for a respected teacher. I spent a good part of the next week with Thay Nhat Hanh, and after we had spent several days together he told me of Baker Roshi's invitation, which he was all but certain he would accept. Then he said that he wanted me to organize the visit.

This last thing really threw me for a loop. Up until then, I had thought he was, more than anything, just thinking aloud, with me as a sounding board. Talking with him that way was pretty terrific, actually. Thich Nhat Hanh was, is, an extraordinary man: an eminent Buddhist teacher, a figure of considerable stature in Vietnamese literature, and a man renowned internationally for his work for peace and social justice. He was fascinating, congenial, challenging, funny, and unpredictable, and everything had been going so well until he brought up this business about organizing his visit to San Francisco Zen Center. I just didn't know what to make of *that*.

As Thay knew well, I was a student of Taizan Maezumi Roshi at the Zen Center of Los Angeles. I told Thay that, since Baker

Roshi had invited him, it would be highly irregular for me, as someone from ZCLA, to have anything to do with organizing the visit. Thay assured me that there would be no problem, but I was not very assured. When I pointed out that Baker Roshi would likely not understand the reasons for my involvement—and why would he, since I didn't understand them myself?—and might therefore find it intrusive, Thay simply said that I just needed to explain that this is what he, Thay, wanted, and then everything would be fine. I voiced my doubts, but Thay insisted. Either he didn't get it or he didn't care. Or maybe he did. I had no idea.

I thought perhaps Thay was asking me to plan things because I was outside the S.F. Zen Center orbit and he wanted the trip to include visits to other Buddhist groups. Or maybe it was because I was an organizer of the then-nascent Buddhist Peace Fellowship (BPF) and he hoped to reach out to Buddhist social activists. I asked him about these reasons, and he was amenable to pursuing both directions, but it was in a casual "If you think that's best, then go ahead" kind of way. So that's what I did: I went ahead.

After the disarmament conference, word of Thich Nhat Hanh's upcoming visit spread quickly, and I was back at the Zen Center of Los Angeles only a short time before I began to receive calls and letters from around the country asking for, and occasionally demanding, a place in the itinerary. Within a few months, Thay's two-week visit to San Francisco Zen Center had turned into a six-week cross-country teaching tour, with additional stops in Los Angeles, Minneapolis, Rochester, upstate New York, and New York City. I arranged for BPF to sponsor the trip, which in the short run gave me some organizational cover and in the long run would provide a structure for those interested in Buddhist activism to connect with each other. It was a monster to plan, taking up my nights and weekends for the better part of eight months. But it was marvelous.

Things at the Zen Center of L.A., however, had not been going particularly well for me, though I prefer to think this was not related to my involvement with Thich Nhat Hanh. For well more than a year, I had been bumping heads with several in the center's leadership, and a few days before I was to leave to meet up with Thay in San Francisco at the start of the trip, I was summarily fired from the ZCLA staff. I hadn't a clue what I would do when I got back. Or if I would go back. Or what.

So with the tour I'd been responsible for organizing about to begin, and the course of my life after it ended now up in the air, I was feeling a bit, you know, out of sorts.

The day after my dream, a documentary film crew was scheduled to come to the San Francisco Zen Center Guest House to film a discussion between Daniel Ellsberg and Thich Nhat Hanh. Joanna Macy, who was then just coming into her own as a voice for Buddhist activism, and her husband, Fran, a leader in the citizen diplomacy movement, were also to participate, but it was inevitable that the focus was going to be on Ellsberg and Nhat Hanh. Ellsberg, who had famously and courageously leaked the Pentagon Papers during the Vietnam War, epitomized the Western ideal of the political actor as a man of conscience. Thich Nhat Hanh helped pioneer—indeed, in the West his name was virtually synonymous with—the emergence of engaged Buddhism. How could one pass up an opportunity for such a meeting of the ways?

At least that's what I thought when the idea was pitched to me about two months earlier by a documentary filmmaker. It sounded great, and even though Thay had been clear that his main interest for the visit was in teaching the dharma to committed students, I thought the idea worth running past him. In his letter back to me, Thay agreed to the proposal, though he betrayed no discernable enthusiasm.

I called the filmmaker and told him I had gotten Thay's approval but that I now had to make sure it was okay with the people at San Francisco Zen Center. I also asked for and received his assurance that things would be kept simple and in every way not an imposition on Zen Center's hospitality.

Taking this proposal to Zen Center was a delicate matter. The previous September, three months after the disarmament conference, I had flown up to San Francisco to meet with Baker Roshi about Thay's visit. Early in our meeting, I said that I recognized the awkwardness of the situation and that during the San Francisco part of the trip I would, with a couple of specific exceptions indicated in a letter Thay had sent me, just try to stay out of the way. Baker Roshi accepted this, and while his displeasure with my involvement was palpable, we had come to what seemed a fair working agreement: while Thay was a guest of San Francisco Zen Center, the planning of his activities would be up to Baker Roshi. Now, in proposing this filmed discussion, I was breaking the agreement, kind of. Technically I had exceeded no boundary, but I was the one shuffling things along.

I ran the proposal up the Zen Center ladder, and word came down to proceed. As the day of Thay's arrival drew near, new wrinkles began to appear in the plan for the filming. One camera would not be enough—would a second one be okay? More lighting would be necessary. A second assistant, and then one more than that, would be needed. The crew would need more time to set up. Each time I passed on a new request, I felt my ineffectualness once again confirmed. By the day of the filming, the whole thing had snowballed to comprise a six-hour block of time, a four-person crew, Zen Center support staff to help with the overloaded electrical circuits and other problems that had arisen and were bound to arise, and so forth. I had said that I did not want to be intrusive or disruptive, but I had succeeded in being both. I had fallen for the promise, and the thrill, of being part of a big event, and it had gotten the better of me. Still, while I might have screwed up, the event itself might, I hoped, set things aright.

That the anxious imagery of my dream had assumed a specifically Jewish caste was, I knew, connected to a contrast in how I perceived San Francisco Zen Center and the Zen Center of Los Angeles. I was not alone in this—others at ZCLA and even some visitors from other Buddhist groups had made mention of the same thing: San Francisco Zen Center had about it a very gentile feeling, and ZCLA was, in a word, very Jewish. I am not here talking about demographics— there were a lot of Jews at both places, as there were at most of the meditation-oriented Buddhist communities. Nor am I speaking in a religious sense, as few Jews at ZCLA were observant, and I imagine the same was true at SFZC. I am referring to something similar to what Lenny Bruce was getting at in his famous routine "Jewish and goyish."

"If you live in New York or any other big city, you are Jewish. It doesn't matter if you are Catholic. If you live in New York, you are Jewish. If you live in Butte, Montana, you are going to be goyish, even if you are Jewish."

According to Lenny, Count Basie was Jewish, although he wasn't, and Eddie Cantor was goyish, even though he was a Jew. Lime soda is goyish; black cherry soda is Jewish. And so it goes.

Jewish, in this sense, is not a matter of membership in a particular group but a placement in a string of binary oppositions plucked from an amorphous cluster of associations. But whereas Lenny's binaries reflect his own Jewish partisanship, I mean nothing of the sort. It's just that something about SFZC made me feel less like I'd come there from another Zen center than like I'd been driven up from Flatbush Avenue in Brooklyn in a cheap suit, carrying a suitcase full of fabric samples and deposited in some Episcopal enclave in Greenwich, Connecticut.

Back then at least, the atmosphere at San Francisco Zen Center was far more contained than that at ZCLA. Practice was more formal, people were more reserved, and they were far more proficient in the elaborate protocols of Zen practice. ZCLA, on the other hand, was embarrassingly sentimental, maddeningly argumentative, and we seemed never to meet an idea so harebrained as to not be worth pursuing. Just like my family.

Thich Nhat Hanh's talk in June 1982, on the third and final day of the Reverence for Life Conference in New York City, was something remarkable. Even while he was still being introduced, Thay began walking, at a snail's pace—which I soon learned was his normal cruising speed—up to the speaker's podium. Rather than stand behind the podium, however, he stopped in front and spoke from there. He spoke gently, in lyrical cadences, yet there was steel in his words. There was a similar pairing in the commanding presence he projected—light as a feather yet solid as rock. Within minutes the audience was transfixed.

He expressed himself in delicately accented, down-to-earth language, only occasionally citing explicitly Buddhist sources. He used stories and personal anecdotes to illustrate his points, he casually posed brief contemplations, and he read several of his own poems to stunning effect. At the heart of his talk, however, was a well-known passage from the Pali canon:

> When this is, that is.
> This arising, that arises.
> When this is not, that is not.
> This ceasing, that ceases.

This is the most succinct formulation of the Buddhist teaching of *paticcasamuppada*, or dependent origination, one of Buddhism's core ideas. Starting with this most simple of expressions—When this is, that is—Thay explicated dependent origination as a vision of radical interdependence, or what he called "interbeing," in which all beings support and are in turn supported by all other beings. This elaboration of paticcasamuppada encompassed the foundation, the practice, and the fulfillment of spiritual life.

In the film *Shakespeare in Love*, there is a crucial moment immediately following the conclusion of the debut of *Romeo and Juliet*, the play set within the movie. After the final words are spoken, the audience, held in the thrall of a play that has shown "the very nature and truth of love," is struck silent for a second or two before erupting into applause. That's how I remember the brief, spellbound silence immediately following Thay's talk. It was a cinematic moment. He had, one might say, *shown* the nature and truth of interdependence.

During the conference, I had struck up a friendship with two of Thich Nhat Hanh's disciples, his longtime co-worker Cao Ngoc Phuong (who now is known by her monastic name, Sister Chan Khong) and his niece Nguyen Anh-Huong. Shortly after Thay's talk, they told me he had asked to meet me that night, after the closing ceremony. They didn't say why, and I, glad for the opportunity, didn't ask.

After the conference's closing ceremony, Sister Phuong led me through the crowd milling about on the granite steps outside the church where the conference had convened. When we found Thay, he and I greeted each other with short bows. Then he reached out as though to shake my hand, but instead he simply held it and peered up at me. He had warm brown eyes and finely articulated features. I held his gaze and waited, uncomfortably, for him to say something, which he did not. After maybe five or six seconds—real seconds, not writers' ones—he tucked my hand under his arm, turned, and began walking down Park Avenue. We walked slowly and silently, and it took me an embarrassingly long time to figure out—Oh, I get it!—that I was supposed to be doing walking meditation. Sister Phuong and Sister Anh-Huong preceded us, at a similar pace, by about ten yards. At some point, Thay informed me that we were going back to the apartment at which they were staying to talk and have tea. Their guest digs were not that far away, but it took us forever to get there.

The apartment was huge and expensively furnished and obviously had been lent to the conference organizers by someone extremely wealthy. Everyone disappeared for a few minutes while I tried not to get lost as I explored the vast reaches of the living room. Soon Thay returned and seated himself cross-legged on a long green sofa. Sister Phuong brought tea, and then she and Sister Anh-Huong said goodnight. From his perch on the sofa, Thay patted the cushion right beside him, indicating for me to sit. It was close quarters. Then, without preamble, he locked me in his sights and asked, "Are you happy?"

This was definitely not small talk. In fact, it didn't exactly fit any category of talk I was familiar with. It had some of the flavor of a Zen master's demand to "Show me your original face," but it was also quite different. Nor was it the same as talking with a friend, being interviewed for a job, working with a therapist, or being interrogated by the Special Branch, though it had elements of each of these. Still, for some reason I felt I had a sense of the spirit of the question, and so I gave my best answer.

"Yes," I said, my usual chattiness in abeyance for the moment.

Thay seemed to chew on that for a few seconds. So did I. Then I explained a bit more, but not much, and Thay took it in without comment. He then asked, "Have you ever thought about suicide?" I told him I had, when I was nineteen and had sunk into deep melancholia. Again he simply heard me out, then asked another question. This is how things went for the next hour or two. Thay would ask a question ("What's the most important thing for two people in love?" "What do you like to do for fun?"), and I would answer as best I could. Occasionally he would remark briefly on what I'd said, but usually he'd just listen.

I was, of course, aware of how weird the whole thing was, but I sensed nothing threatening about it. The very strangeness of the exchange made it all the more intriguing. And there was this: in some way I couldn't really pin down and despite appearances, I felt that the communication was mutual, that it emerged from a shared, unspoken recognition of an underlying affinity.

Eventually, Thay seemed satisfied that he had learned what he needed to know, or maybe he just ran out of questions. In any case, he asked me if there was anything else I wanted to say. I felt obliged to come clean about a perplexing personal trait that I had long struggled with and that had caused more than a little trouble in my life as a Buddhist.

"I should tell you," I said, "that I can be very stubborn."

"Stubborn is good," he said. Then he stood up, stretched, and said, "OK, the interrogation is over." We both laughed at that.

It was very late, and as I readied myself to leave, Thay said he would like me to come upstate with the three of them for a few days. I figured they needed a driver, and I was happy to help out. Then he said, "If we are going to work together, there has to be more to it than just that you have something I want and I have something you want." This seemed a reasonable, albeit peculiarly abstract, proposition, and I nodded my agreement. It was while we were upstate that he asked me to plan his visit to the States the following year.

About an hour before the discussion with Daniel Ellsberg and the Macys was to start, Thay asked me if I could suggest something they might talk about, and after giving it some thought, I said I could. In the mid-1970s, when tens of thousands of Vietnamese began fleeing their country by sea, many of those in the U.S. who had once worked together in the antiwar movement became bitterly divided over how to respond to these "boat people." Some viewed them as mere economic refugees who were seeking new opportunity or attempting to regain the privilege they had enjoyed under U.S. patronage. Others considered them political refugees who were escaping the programs—forced labor zones, re-education camps, mass imprisonment and torture—of an oppressive regime. Many boat people drowned or starved in overcrowded and unseaworthy vessels; many were preyed upon mercilessly by pirates. Eventually they numbered in the hundreds of thousands, and most of them languished in refugee camps.

Some of Thay's former allies in the American and international peace movements had criticized his actions on behalf of the boat people as politically naive, questionable in motive, and worse. It was an ugly episode for a lot of people, and a bitter one for Thay and Sister Phuong.

Some months earlier, I'd heard Daniel Ellsberg speak about issues in the aftermath of the war. Thay and Ellsberg seemed to be in fundamental agreement about the boat people, yet they had arrived at their conclusions in very different ways, and I felt this could make for a fruitful discussion. I thought that by addressing this specific issue, they might bring greater understanding to some of the perennial problems that crop up when political concerns collide with moral ones, and in the process perhaps they might heal old wounds that in some quarters still festered. Thay thought it a good idea, and to tell the truth, I was pretty pleased with myself for coming up with it.

The discussion was being filmed in the front room of the Zen Center Guest House—the very room I'd dreamed about the night before. The room was packed with film equipment, electrical wires, and maybe thirty people, who filled in every inch of space that was left. In the center of the room, Daniel Ellsberg sat stage right, the Macys were in the middle, and Thich Nhat Hanh completed the arc. Thay got the ball rolling.

"I want to ask Daniel Ellsberg: Why does the American peace movement have no compassion?" That's what he said. He might have said it a little differently; he might have said a little more; but that was pretty much the crux of it.

My guess is that no one there, except me and maybe Ellsberg, knew what this was about. But everyone recognized the peculiar note that had been struck. I just cringed: *Oh no. Oh no. This is not what I meant. This is not what I meant at all.* A knot began to form in the pit of my stomach.

I hoped that Ellsberg would find a way past this. Not that it would be easy. He had just been blindsided, targeted unfairly with one of those questions one can't possibly answer because the premise itself is so askew. But if anyone knew how to think on his feet, it was Daniel Ellsberg. Maybe he could set this thing aright.

What happened next, however, couldn't have been worse: Ellsberg took Thay's question personally and responded defensively. He answered the unfortunate challenge with a few of his own, in particular, he challenged Thay's passing judgment on who was and who was not compassionate. From there, the nastiness and absurdity just accelerated. Here they were, two great and good men, arguing like kids on the playground, about compassion—who had it, who had the right to talk about it, who really understood what it was. It was their pain talking, and neither seemed able to see it or admit it or get a handle on it.

Every so often, Fran or Joanna would jump in to try to change the subject, but Ellsberg and Thay weren't about to fall for *that.* They were Ali and Frazier, LaMotta and Robinson, just waiting between rounds for the bell so they could get back to pummeling each other. There was no stopping them; they were going to go the distance.

Finally, and mercifully, it was over, and there followed another cinematic moment, but one very different from what had followed Thay's talk at Reverence for Life. This was like the audience response to the performance of the jaw-droppingly awful musical number "Springtime for Hitler" ("We're marching to a faster pace/ Look out, here comes the master race!") in the play within Mel Brooks's movie *The Producers*: stunned silence and disbelief.

Soon people began slowly to file out of the room, but in a kind of daze, much like they were walking away from a pileup on the interstate. Joanna approached me and in a shaky voice asked, "What about paticcasamuppada?" It's not often one gets to be part of an unqualified and incomprehensible debacle.

Needless to say, I was feeling just horrible about my role in the whole thing. I had pushed the event through, and I had suggested the starting topic, and while it was true that I had no control over the turn the discussion had taken, there was no getting away from the fact that my judgment had been just abysmal. But oddly enough, I also felt a sense of relief. For while that part of myself represented by those upright Buddhist priests was glaring down at me more harshly than ever, that davening Jew had hitched up his pants and stepped out of his corner and was ready for action. One must, after all, move ahead from where one is, not where one would like to be.

Everybody, even the best of us, will sometimes behave ingloriously, and to think otherwise is to be hemmed in by vanity. As sad sinners wandering through samsara, one of the few things we can count on is that we are on occasion going to screw up miserably. For those of us who are exceptionally reliable in this regard, it is nothing less than a saving grace, is it not, that in our guise as bodhisattvas, falling down on the job is the biggest part *of* the job, and sometimes, somehow, failure, if allowed to do its work, can actually be surprisingly emancipatory. It can even help make us whole. We have to try to be better—wiser, kinder, more generous—people, but mostly there's no getting away from our embarrassing, maddening, harebrained selves. There's a joke that is a good reminder of that.

One day, in the middle of service, the rabbi calls out, "Oh Lord, I'm nothing, nothing. I'm nothing." As the rabbi continues, the cantor joins in: "I'm nothing, oh Lord, nothing." In the back of the synagogue, the *shamus*—something like a temple janitor—broom in hand, is so inspired by this display of humility before the Almighty that he too joins in: "I'm nuttin', Lord, I'm nuttin'." The rabbi looks up and eyes the shamus disapprovingly. He then turns to the cantor and says, "So look who says he's nothing."

While it's true that spiritual aspiration is an inestimable good, sometimes there's nothing better for the soul than falling flat on your face. You have to work with what you've got, and what you've got is who you are, and there's no way around *that*.

KATE FARRELL

The Search

FROM *Harvard Divinity Bulletin*

But then the moon
comes up after all and with
a glow bright enough to wake
you through the bedroom
curtains,
            the night outside, one
vast luminous room beside which
indoor rooms seem to belong to
a preliminary, rudimentary
dimension,
            and her there shining—
mother daughter friend *anima mundi*—
so still and low that it's almost as though
you hadn't broken every vow you ever
made in the wayside tabernacles
of the universe.
            This time you go
back to bed, close your eyes and head
far into the dark, try to find a place to set
up shop, see things only in the light

love throws, doing away with
mental fuss.
                    Soon you're walking
down an unfamiliar road in a nighttime
countryside, hoping to come across a local
acquainted with the lesser known
lunar writings.
                    Houses are few;
everyone is asleep; the air suffused
with a beautiful half-light whose source
you can't place. You're strangely
unafraid and in no hurry.

EAMON GRENNAN

World As Is

FROM *The Hudson Review*

Between the old stone man in his limestone greatcoat
and the small white house on the hill; between the pale green waves
     and the high notes of the plovers as they arrow away
from the sand and my solid figure striding there; between the foal
     sheltering under his mother's flank from the slanting rain
and the blackbird at dusk singing and bringing the fixed stars out
     lies what bond, I wonder, as I trudge head down, bent
into the protection of hedges, what *delicate machine* makes its presence
     felt in the world of spent tabernacles and rattled nerves
we inhabit? Or is it something in the nature of *the evanescent symmetries*
     lets this bee—that has banged against the window
and jack hammered there in raging indignation at the irreversible logic
     of the fact of glass—be scooped into the soft dark
of the napkin I've wrapped it in, through which I can feel
     what we would call its anger, its despair, still quick to the end
it must sense is happening, till I open the cloth outside

and after a second or two of stillness as daylight
envelops it again it lights out and floats off in the free air,

at one again with what makes simple sense to it: the world
as is: things in their exquisite, absolute, inexpressible

balance: work to be done, direction chosen, anything can happen.

A. G. HARMON

In Nomine

FROM *Image*

ACROSS THE HIGHWAY ARE A TACO BELL, A COMFORT INN, AND A freestanding building that houses a Chinese buffet. A Case tractor company is nearby, and what looks to be an old service station, deserted, with orange-and-tan panels on the garage door and wild grass sprouting through the asphalt. Somewhat disconcerting is an abandoned Wal-Mart, a modern-day Arkansas standard. The ghosts of its letters hang on the wall above the empty storefront.

As a child, I was fascinated by stories of old towns that had lost their hold upon the clay bank and then slipped—stone floor and housetop—into the Mississippi River. I imagined their uncorrupted churches, rot-free homes and schools, as lying at the bottom of a silty floor, a park for scuba divers and catfish. But now the towns along the river disappear in less dramatic ways. The most vital part of such places is the interstate, which slowly loosens the grip of the desiccated societies. In time, they slough their skins, begin their slide toward the asphalt channels that bring whatever life they have, then pull whatever life they give, toward the larger, more attractive places further down the way.

I sit on the hood of my car in a parking lot, killing time. It's not a bad choice, this spot—quiet, except for the trucks soaring down the divided four-lane road. Later, I'm expected at a bookstore to read from a novel I've written, the last of many trips over the past year. But there's an hour or more to go yet; fearing I might underestimate the drive to Blytheville, I have arrived far too early.

I'm glad I have my book, not only for the obvious reason that I will read from it, but also because it will help to introduce me, without confusion. For soon I will need to speak my name, and my name is easier seen than said, read than understood. I often have to repeat it—"A.G. It's initials. A.G."—and watch as the listener's eyes blink, sometimes registering, sometimes flitting away as though I've assigned an algorithm to compute. The phenomenon has made me self-conscious, at times annoyed, at others defensive. But if I were to add apologetic, I would immediately answer myself with a solid rebuke. I'm the fourth to bear these initials, the latest to carry them, and as I was often told, "None of the others were ever anything but proud."

And that fact, my name, these two letters, is why there is a significant line between this place and me. Nearly sixty years ago, just across the highway, the cotton fields, and the long wide river that runs a seam down the middle of this country, a boy that I never knew, died. I know his face, though. I know stories of his wit and bravery and skill. I do not know his voice, though I might have, had my mother as a child not purposefully broken the only record made of it because my grandmother could not bear the possibility of ever having it played within her hearing. I have some of his things: his wallet—the one he might have had at the time of his death, as there are dark stains on the leather, perhaps blood—and inside it, pictures of his motorcycles, of him in his Navy uniform, and cards from his club memberships—a high school fraternity comes to mind. I have his cowboy boots—caramel-colored leather, with white stitching and finger holes on the sides to pull them on. There are also things that I had once, but lost—like the silver bracelet he made in shop, carelessly left at a hotel; and his military jacket, worn for farm work and ruined completely. I have his boyhood spectacles. I have his diary, which includes only fourteen entries (*January 1, 1938: I have been a good boy and have had a bad cole today*). He could not spell very well.

I have these things, have lost those, and above all, I bear his name.

I was never asked or expected to fill a place left open by my uncle's death, but I have taken it as an unspoken challenge. The name has been something I wanted to be worthy of, and when I have not done so—as I have not always done so—I have been ashamed of failing more than myself. Because when a child is given a name like mine, an old name that was others'—many others'—he feels responsible; at least, I did. There is a legacy in being a namesake that cannot be overlooked, and though pathologies might be attributed to this view, I find them all invalid. I do not live with ghosts in my subconscious, or feel particularly burdened by my history—certainly not in some unhealthy way. Obligations are not always burdens, and even so, it is not always bad to carry them. I prefer to think of the name as something left to me—like land, or a house, or any other bequeathed object—things you may sell, dismiss, ignore, or tend.

Certainly, there have been times when my name was a labor, not because it was my uncle's, and my grandfather's, and my great-grandfather's, but because of its own peculiarity. Confusions are common. It seems the mind is not mapped for the configuration of A and G, but for A and J, and even people who have known me for years will make the occasional slip. It also takes up a good deal of time to explain, most tiresomely in situations when a name must be given only for quick and disposable reference—such as waiting for a table, or making reservations. Sometimes it's easier to offer a fabrication (on the phone, after a bewildered pause at the other end, I have more than once been asked to spell A.G.). "Ted" usually works; "Lon" is not bad either, and is at least a derivative of my full first name—Alonzo.

In addition to confusions, there have been disappointments, mostly from childhood. I could never find my name on the revolving stand full of miniature license plates at Stuckey's, or on the cheap key rings or notepads sold at the beach-side convenience stores. As my first name is obscure, I would have to settle for my second—George—but it was never satisfactory by itself. Neither name alone would have been, in fact. I went by my initials, and somehow the two full names, whether separate, together, or in conjunction with my other middle name (Alonzo George Moore) would not suffice. I was A.G., for better or worse.

The initials have also been provocative. Once it is understood that I do in fact answer to them, it is often wondered what they "stand for"—what meaning the cryptic shorthand is designed to hide, and what precisely is being hidden. The tactless usually assume—once they learn my real name—that I have chosen the shorter form for myself, unwilling to go by names so old and out of fashion. But the truth is that the three who went before me also used initials, and though my great-grandmother was once told she might as well have named her son "One-Two" as "A.G.," none of the subsequent bearers were particularly dissuaded from continuing the tradition.

But the idea of the letters as name—as symbols that stand for something deeper—brings to the fore what interests me most. Any name, even the most commonplace, suggests more than the utilitarian convenience of distinguishing one child from the other. However much or little thought is put into the process, the name itself stands for something substantive—virtue, idea, notion—that the parents found inspiring, auspicious, or if nothing else, beautiful. The additional aspect of names like mine, and the qualitative difference I claim for all like me—those named for someone—is that the name has not only its semantic significance, but also a concrete referent in the form of the person for whom one is named. The name-sake "Gabriel" is not only "strong man of God," but also "strong man of God in honor of the strong man of God who was my mother's father"—hence a name that is both concept and tribute. And while any name can be either scorned or valued—or even changed, for that matter—the child named for another also has the knowledge that he or she is accepting or rejecting bone and blood, the mighty deeds or lovely gestures of some worthy soul whose shade mingles with his own shadow.

After the reading, I make my way back across the river, driving home. I had not planned on stopping in Caruthersville, but no one is expecting me any time soon. It is doubtful I will pass through here again; a side trip will not put me far out of my way.

The town is off the interstate, which may have been old Highway 51 that ran up through the Delta. I don't know for sure, and Mother doesn't either, if A.G. rode his motorcycle all the way up here from Mississippi, or whether they pulled the bikes on a trailer behind a car. A boy named Butch came too—an old man by the time I met him at my grandmother's funeral; some others may have gone as well, but that part of the story is unclear.

I drive in on the road he must have traveled himself, as there is only one way to the town from the west. Long fields stretch out on either side, longer for the tilt of the sun, and a *Welcome to Caruthersville* sign greets me as I approach. Little could have changed between what he saw then and what I am seeing now, though fifty-seven years have gone by. On the right is a huge cemetery, which I cannot help but feel is a bleak coincidence, then on until I meet the road that leads to town.

I'm searching for something that looks old enough, some place where they could have raced motorbikes. As of twenty years ago I know it was still there, because my brother married a girl whose grandparents lived nearby; one time, like me now, he visited the place out of curiosity. But I didn't know I would be coming here today, so I didn't think to ask him what to look for. For now, I have to find my own way.

I pass a high school, a stretch of stores, a church—Sacred Heart, where I say a prayer for my uncle—then on to the close of the street at the river's edge. At the end of that street, I come to the water, where a faux riverboat is permanently moored. I cut back in a few streets.

There are some places that could, possibly, be it. A recreation center looks too new, but it could have been renovated. I have always imagined it as an inside track—grandstands and flashing lights and sepia-colored dirt—though I was never told that was the case. A place next door looks old and big enough—an unmarked warehouse of some sort with small windows at the top. I pull into the parking lot, content that this is as close as I'll come.

It's important for me to get out of the car and stand, as I've never felt I was actually in a place until I got out and set my feet on the ground. It's a Saturday; no one is around as I stare at the building.

It's hard to mark death in a public place. There are statues and monuments and brass plaques, surely, but those on the whole are meant to honor heroes of good wars or martyrs of good causes—recognized by government decree and set off from the common path. But when a private citizen dies in a public place, it becomes awkward. The modern phenomenon of roadside crosses is perhaps the successor to stone cairns, and only a little more shabby, inadequate, and temporal in its attempt to hallow the place of passing. But not every such place can be marked in even this inadequate way, and what you are left with in such a case is simply standing still, curiously still to any lookers-on, as something is thought of or prayed for nearby.

This must be a common desire, to be where it happened, born of the absurd but powerful notion that somehow, despite time and circumstance, we are belatedly making those we have lost feel less alone, in some years-late communion with their last acts. So I stand near where I think A.G. raced and died, staring at the orange stripes of a newly painted parking lot as I consider again what has been considered before, often, by those who loved him.

They were beautiful Harley-Davidsons, his motorcycles, one black and one white; polished, large, and heavy, the way all old machinery seemed to be. My grandfather, the A.G. my uncle was named after, bought the bikes for him right after he came back from the war. But neither was the one he was riding that day.

They had known so little of the event—even that he had planned to race. Of all things, it was my mother's confirmation day—so I suppose a Sunday?—and the rest of the family was down in Jackson. Why was he not asked to attend, I wonder? Even when my grandparents were alive, no one would have dared ask, and I suppose everyone is dead now who would know the answer. But I also wonder if he had told them he was going to a race all the way up here, in Caruthersville, Missouri. It seems like an awfully long way to drive from Mississippi. How would he have even known of the race, way down there? And if he had told the truth about not planning to race, when did he change his mind? And why? Why would he have brought this bike instead of the others? Perhaps they were not the kind you raced.

They say that he was going to win the event—held around a circular, fenced track—and that it was almost over when it happened. In another strange, almost unbelievable irony, one of my own father's college roommates was a boy who was in that very race with A.G., and told him of it when he learned he was dating my mother. Somehow—from this boy? from A.G.'s friend Butch?—the story has come down that the bike had not started right, that it stalled in some way, and that he was making up for lost ground at the end.

It must have been loud there, the sound of all those motors, revving like chainsaws gnawing through timber—and the people cheering and all the lights burning, as I imagine it, lights on poles and lights on stands and the flashing lights of cameras.

He was coming down the home stretch (how hard that is to think of—dying on the home stretch, within sight of the end—the shock and pity of it) when something happened that made him spin out. The one thing they are certain of is that he was thrown off, tossed up in the air, and impaled on an iron fence pole. They say that when they got to him, he was trying to lift himself off; he was almost strong enough to do it. He was very strong.

For a little while, he had raccoon tails on each of his handlebars, which I think was the fashion then. He also put a knob on the steering wheel of his car, so that he could spin it around easily with one hand; my grandfather made him take it off. He could ride any horse, however wild, and would make them rear up just to show you. He could go back in the woods and build carts out of slender tree trunks. Once in high school, when he was thirsty and needed water, a schoolteacher tried to block the door to keep him from getting a drink at the fountain, so he picked him up and moved him right out of the way. Next to his yearbook picture—curly brown hair and hazel eyes and dimples—it says he had "personality plus." All the boys admired him, called him "Tarzan," and he dated all the prettiest girls—there was one named Betty with blonde hair, and another named Eleanor with dark. In the Navy, he rescued pilots from crash landings and pulled them from wreckage still raging with fire. Once, he walked on an airplane's wing, balancing on the tip as it flew along, way up in the air—"high as the clouds," they always said. High as the clouds.

. . .

To name is to limit, to set apart, to draw lines around for identification and understanding. The act both differentiates and restricts, necessarily giving the child the beginnings of an identity while also limiting what he can be. And for the namesake there is an additional consideration. The usual semantic limitation exists in the act of assigning a name, but so does what would seem the very converse of that limitation: a semantic extension, in that the name points both to the present bearer and back to the subject of testament. In this sense, the old way of explaining a namesake as "called for" his father, grandfather, etc. is literally true.

I suspect the inherited name is not as pervasive as it once was. In the past, it was an expression of long lineage, of clansmanship and tribe, a means by which time and death were transcended, an emblematic bond between the living and the dead. While it is not the fashion now, the act of naming took on ceremonies and built modalities that revealed the importance society attached to the deed. Rubrics made certain names the stock of the family, and to repeat them was somehow to reinforce who a family was, and perhaps to claim a timeless continuation of those merits: "Yes, that John is gone, but here is another; that Mary has passed, but this next is made from her, out of the same cloth." Two hundred years ago, the British had a systematics of honoring: the first son was to be named after the father's father; the first daughter after the mother's mother; the second son, the mother's father; the second daughter, the father's mother. Not until the third pair were the parents themselves honored. So the oldest were celebrated first, to revive and refresh their connection to the familial consciousness, to keep them from slipping from the table of kindred memory. To jump the system required a good excuse, and even so would be worthy of remark and no small surprise: Luke records the consternation of the community towards Elizabeth and Zachariah when they proposed to call their new son John, as none in their family bore such a name; only an angel could make it all right.

Even when the name was not meant to memorialize another family member, it was often given in respect of a saint with whom the family had close association. By naming the baby after a particular patron, the child was not only provided with an immediate protector and mediator, but also given a history to emulate. In the christening there came a set of instructions, a life pattern to guide the shaky steps of the fresh, bewildered newborn—"Your name is Mark, after the Mark of old, and therefore. . . ." The name became something to live up to, something that must be kept good, not sullied or "run through the mud." These metaphors brought out the near materiality of the name, integrated with the soul in such a way that the name too was capable of falling from sanctity, of being brought into disgrace.

This early practice reveals a conception of naming and names as a mystical act, both potent and dangerous. It is an understanding as old as it is pervasive, and finds its source in the fundamental belief that to speak a name is to summon one who has power over us, or to seek power over one whose name we speak. God's name is unspeakable—Jewish words for him are all indirections (Adonai, Elohim, El Shaddai), and even spelling "God" fully is forbidden to a Jew. One aspect of exorcism is to require the demon to speak its name, as Jesus Christ demanded of the "legion" that tormented the man in the country of the Gadarenes. Egyptians went by sobriquets, keeping their hidden names secret in order to retain their power and protect them from slipping into their enemy's use. This existential reverence found its way into mystical names for children, either predicting the child's future (Bonaventure) or symbolizing some aspect of God's praise (Amadeus). When Protestants took the fore, hortatory names (Increase, Resolve) and grace names (Purity, Chastity) carried forth the same basic ethos, if not the same theology. Naming practices too had the odor of mystery. Students of onomastics speak of children programmed for the monastery by being named Benedict or Agnes; in a practice frowned upon and ultimately forbidden by the church, boys could be named by assigning a disciple to each of twelve candles: the name of the last one burning became that of the child.

Different too from modern practice was the old taste for repetition, not novelty. The ancient Romans had a cache of given names, the Praenomen, barely over sixty in number, and even then only about a fifth were actually used. The Anglo-Saxons were prone to pass on whole names, or at least their elements (—*fried*, —*wulf*). The prominence of certain names that we today consider traditional—James, John, Mary, Anne—showed an affinity for solidarity and establishment.

This propensity is of course the opposite of today's, when disassociation from the masses is so highly valued. Maybe this is a natural outgrowth of American modernistic thinking; there is no longer much need to acknowledge or memorialize the family in the act of naming, but rather a tendency towards the individual concept—an intention to encapsulate an idea. Even so, the originality so yearned for is not all that far removed from the naming customs of the past. Old hortatory names—Constance and Prudence—gave over in the sixties to Sunshine and Willow, but there was but a worldview between them. The Romantics of the nineteenth century gave us Daisy and Hyacinth, and they live on in the Heathers and Ambers that run about kindergartens now. The commercial culture too has made its mark, but it always had a certain place: there were Jewels, Rubys, and Pearls in the past; Tiffanys have only made them into a chain. Boys' names are not without their counterparts; the patience of Job has been replaced by the bling of Mercury and Marquis, and the birth of a Lexus has been reported. The old feminine name Mercedes may come back soon, though long detached from its relation to mercy.

It is the idea of the patron, the mediator available for invocation, that has most struck my personal fancy. But a parallel concept also moves me: the old practice of naming to assuage. Often, a newborn was given the name of his deceased older brother or sister, or that of an older relative who had died prematurely. This was especially so when the relative had died by violence. There was some thought that the deceased were recovered or fulfilled in this way. And true to form, children would often grow into the roles of the names given. Like the child christened after a saint, the name became a mandate for right living, which strikes me as a uniquely generous thing to be given.

It is questionable whether you can rectify anything for those behind you: "He made such and such a mistake, so don't you. Let his life be a warning"—are admonitions heard in all families, but with more direct application for the namesake. It is somehow implied that his mistakes are more likely to be yours as well. Is it because when we learn our context, the breadth of meaning behind our names, those things do in fact become more likely? All I know for sure is that in sharing my uncle's name, it was as though his fate had become a caution to me—not to die, not to be reckless, not to get myself killed. Rash behavior and careless acts were met with "I guess you won't survive your boyhood—it seems all the A.G.s are prone to . . . ," which did, in fact, have its intended effect; it brought me to heel. But not only out of fear; more out of compulsion. I wanted of course to live, but not just for me; for him too, and for my grandfather, who had lost his own namesake. His line had run out and had to be grafted onto that of my father. I could not squander myself; it was his last chance.

I would later learn my idea was wrong—that the racetrack was outside, not inside, and was perhaps once an old horse track, converted.

My brother corrects me when I ask, and my mother is not sure where I could have gotten the impression that I have always entertained. So I have not, in fact, been exactly where he died, though within the close vicinity. In the end, what I have indulged myself with in Caruthersville has been conjecture, an imagination of what A.G.'s death was like. But that strikes me as familiar, as I and others have always, and will always, imagine what his life was like, and more irresistibly, what it would have been like had he lived.

It is easy to make too much of things, but would he have married Eleanor? She came to his funeral. And my grandfather had planned to buy him a tractor company in Hazelhurst; would that have been his occupation? When his old diary is consulted, are there portents in it, signs of what was to be and what might have been? For example: *1/14 Today I went to the show and saw* Submarine D1. *I liked it very much. A.G. Moore.* I looked it up; it was a war movie that featured a young, uncredited Ronald Reagan. Was that my uncle's first fascination with the Navy, and why he joined when the time came? Or this one: *1/13 Today Miss Laura told me to get a Bible book so I did. It cost $2.00. Spot cash. No credit.* I hear my grandfather in that—the jargon of a horse and cattle trader. A.G., to his disappointment, was not as good an auctioneer as my grandfather; you could hear that on the record they made of him trying, the one my mother destroyed. Still, I think he would have been a shrewd businessman. In that respect he was like his father, whom he so wanted to please; he wanted to be his father, in truth, and though their relationship was a stormy one, his idolization comes through: *1/6 Tonight Daddy will be home; 1/7 Tonight Daddy said I was a good boy.*

For some reason, he was taken to another town after the accident and died there. Someone brought him back to Mississippi, following the path of the river home. A long, long ride.

Though I had been wrong about most of the day, the part that was undeniably true occurred to me as I left, in the very act of leaving the town itself. For in doing so, I was seeing what he never got to: the town from the other side, from the west, as the sun set and the day and place were put behind him. Had things gone differently, that day and town might have been casually remembered, remarked upon from time to time, forgotten in favor of all the other living that had been done, and all that was yet to be. Instead, in leaving it, I was living the rest of his tale. *Thank You for Visiting Caruthersville. Come Again.*

It is a small name. Very small; and the questioner is right to ask what it means: the letters do in fact stand for more, a deposit of blood, a trove and horde of lives lived behind my own.

But mostly they stand for him, and for those like him who were cut short, laid waste, pulled down before their proper end; for all the souls ascended, for the confluence of the ages.

I have stood within miles of his death, more than a half century past, and within the air of the last life that he lived. I have stood at the foot of the river, as the delta of all that he was, and in me, of all that he remains. And I stand here still; in his name.

TONY HISS

Wonderlust

FROM *The American Scholar*

ONE SPRING MORNING, WITH NOTHING ON MY MIND WHILE I WAS walking home on East 16th Street, a quiet New York residential block near Union Square Park in Manhattan, after dropping my son off at school, I saw three people staring wide-eyed at an apartment building fire escape overhead. Blue and white feathers drifted slowly toward the sidewalk. A peregrine falcon—the cliff-dwelling hawk known to birders as the "embodiment of freedom"—was plucking and eating a pigeon. Peregrines, with fierce black eyes, blue-gray backs, and white bellies, can fly 200 miles an hour when swooping to kill. They are crow-sized; this one looked enormous.

Above the fire escape I could see puffy white clouds and a pale blue sky, as I had a minute before. When I looked down again, however, the concrete sidewalk and the asphalt street looked suddenly insubstantial, no more than a paper-thin, makeshift, temporary cover—like a throw rug, almost, or a picnic blanket—hiding the island's original underpinnings, dirt and boulders, that have been a continuing presence at least since the last glaciers retreated. I seemed connected to a different "now," a longer time frame, peregrine time, so to speak, an uninterrupted, postglacial present moment more than 10,000 years old that dated back to the peregrines' arrival in the New York area. DDT spraying after World War II almost eliminated peregrines from the region, but captive breeding programs have restored them. With Manhattan's endless supply of pigeons, peregrines now accept local skyscrapers as cliffs for nesting. The bird I saw probably lived near the top of the 700-foot-tall Met Life Tower on 23rd Street; the pigeon it ate probably came from Union Square Park.

My expression for moments like this is *deep travel*. In an instant, our sense of the here and now that we're a part of expands exponentially, and everything around us is so vivid and intensely experienced that it's like waking up while already awake. Deep travel has a distinctive taste, and people who like it tend to look for ways of getting more of it. It often surprises us, stealing over us unawares. But it can be sought out, chosen, practiced, remembered, returned to. That's because, as I've come to realize, it's an ancient though under-appreciated human ability built into all of us, one of the bedrock components of human intelligence. In my own deep travel, I've found that, once I reactivate it, even a long-familiar route—like a walk through nearby streets—exists within such a fullness of brand-new or never-before-considered details and questions that I wonder how I ever had the capacity to exclude this information from consideration.

Many who write about travel have noticed that the word itself, in its original Old French form, *travaillier*, had only harsh meanings, such as *toil*, *trouble*, and *torment*, and seems to trace back to an even older Latin word, *tripalium*, the name of a three-staked Roman instrument of torture. Modern travel, the movements of hundreds of millions of people day by day, also includes the extraordinary, often tortuous circumstances of millions of migrants and refugees, many of whom are in motion only involuntarily, fearing for their lives. Ordinary 21st-century travel itself has been accompanied by an undercurrent of fear since its first year, when 9/11 forced us to realize that any vehicle at all, even a passenger plane, can be used as a bomb. Sometimes the feeling of vulnerability fades, but its vibration is never quite stilled; and there are times when, even without a head-line, we can feel it stealing back over us like some thickening of the air, a small, dark cloud or a patch of fog or mist, shifting, change-able, and capable, even when not directly overhead, of shadowing landscape and landmarks, draining off light and color, blurring clarity.

These ugly realities add to the difficulty of the urgency of get-ting it right. Travel already confers so many blessings—moving goods and foods around and spreading ideas and innovations, light-ening our load, extending humanity's reach, bringing people to-gether who might never otherwise meet, challenging stay-at-home thinking. As we set our sights even higher and restore travel's extra, innermost dimension, we will welcome it, seek it out, rely on it at any moment of any day, confidently, routinely, implicitly, as an ever-present opportunity, a built-in launch pad and catapult for lifting the wings of the human spirit.

What are the pathways that lead back into deep travel? I've been exploring a few of them. Wonder, it's frequently said, is a feel-ing that is alive in children but has dried up in adults. There are fa-mous sayings about wonder—Descartes called it "the first of the passions"; Plato celebrated it as "the only beginning of philosophy"; Ralph Waldo Emerson saw it leading to a different passion—"Men love to wonder, and that is the seed of science." But how do you isolate or amplify the flavor of it? A friend suggested looking at a small book on the subject by Rachel Carson, *The Sense of Wonder*. Carson, now revered as a founder of modern environmentalism, brought out only four books in her short lifetime—three about the sea and *Silent Spring*, the famous bestseller about the dangers of DDT and other pesticides. She died at the age of 56, and *The Sense of Wonder*, originally a magazine article titled "Helping Your Child to Wonder," was published posthumously.

Carson agrees with the widespread and almost despairing assumption that wonder is perishable and too easily outgrown:

> A child's world is fresh and new and beautiful, full of wonder and excitement. It is our misfortune that for most of us that clear-eyed vision, that true instinct for what is beautiful and awe-inspiring, is dimmed and even lost before we reach adulthood. If I had influence with the good fairy who is supposed to preside over the christening of all children I should ask that her gift to each child in the world be a sense of wonder so indestructible that it would last throughout life, as an unfailing antidote against the boredom and disenchantments of later years, the sterile preoccupation with things that are artificial, the alienation from the sources of our strength.

The hope the book offers is almost a hope against hope—she thinks parents can, in effect, teach their children to stay aloft and in the process regain an ability to fly, which they themselves may already have lost. Buoyancy, she thinks, can be both rescued and regained once wonder is focused on the natural world: "If a child is to keep alive his inborn sense of wonder without any such gift from the fairies, he needs the companionship of at least one adult who can share it, rediscovering with him the joy, excitement and mystery of the world we live in." The book has many pleasures, among them a story of first offering this gift to her 20-month-old great-nephew: she wraps him in a blanket and carries him down to the Maine seashore on a stormy fall night. "Out there, just at the edge of where-we-couldn't-see, big waves were thundering in, dimly seen white shapes that boomed and shouted and threw great handfuls of froth at us. Together we laughed for pure joy—he a baby meeting for the first time the wild tumult of Oceanus, I with the salt of half a lifetime of sea love in me. But I think we felt the same spine-tingling response to the vast roaring ocean and the wild night."

In *The Sense of Wonder*, there's a quiet lament about neglecting nature, thoughts brought on by walking outside and seeing the stars one summer night in southern Maine. "If this were a sight that could be seen only once in a century," Carson writes, "this little headland would be thronged with spectators. But it can be seen many scores of nights in any year, and so the lights burned in the cottages and the inhabitants probably gave not a thought to the beauty overhead; and because they could see it almost any night perhaps they will never see it."

Here was an entrance I was looking for. It wasn't that the value of the stars had dimmed or that their supply had in anyway diminished. It was that certainty had triumphed over scarcity. What had dried up and disappeared from the mind's riverbed was the flow of attention. Because with certainty can come the complacency of pseudo-certainty. It's a matter of confusing some *thats* with a *what*. Knowing from repeated experience that we can count on the stars to be there and that their continuing presence is not an immediate threat, we begin to think we can say with the same level of confidence that we know what they are. Attention is withdrawn and moves in a different course. Some people know a great deal about the stars, others next to nothing. There is always more to find out. But habituation—not noticing something that seems unchanging and harmless—can cloak both knowledge and ignorance with the same mantle of indifference: "Oh, yes, the stars." Something we have a word for.

Bringing this one realization back into your mind, elementary as it is, I've since found, can bring you straightaway into deep travel. It could be called the "wonder induction"—a simple matter while you're moving around or looking at a scene or at anything at all, perhaps something as humble as a fire hydrant, and saying to yourself that, however many times you've seen it or one like it, you don't know exactly what it is. Or at least that there's a lot you haven't found out so far. Such as how it works, and what it's connected to, and where it came from, and who thought of it, and how many people are responsible for it, and when it might next be used, and why it looks the way it does, and how and when it got there. And having thought such thoughts, attention surges back, the world opens up again, and the immensity of the not-yet-known and the still-to-be-explored returns and beckons. Even after infrequent contact or what feels like a long absence, "wonder" hasn't vanished. It's constantly only a single thought away from making a fresh appearance.

The life of Jean-Henri Casimir Fabre, considered the father of modern entomology, and praised by Darwin as an "incomparable observer," seems to exemplify Emerson's observation about wonder growing into science. Fabre, who died in 1915, at the age of 87, made many of his pioneering 19th-century discoveries about bees, wasps, beetles, grasshoppers, and crickets while peering through a magnifying glass as he walked around the two-and-a-half "worthless" acres he had owned for 36 years in Provence. I've kept for 25 years in my small "Wonder" file of clippings a short appreciation of this "marvelous old man." It was written by the American essayist Edmund Fuller, who had spent part of a May day wandering through Fabre's small garden, and then quoted from what Fabre had written about his "laboratory in the open fields": "I go the circuit of my enclosure over and over again, a hundred times by short stages; I stop here and I stop there; patiently I put questions and, at long intervals, I receive some scrap of a reply. . . . This is what I wished for . . . a bit of land, oh, not so very large . . . an abandoned, barren, sun-scorched bit of land, favoured by thistles and by Wasps and Bees. . . . I observe, I experiment, I let the facts speak for themselves."

Fabre's "best instruments," Fuller wrote, "were 'Time and Patience.' In a difficult period, closing the third of his ten volumes, he wrote: 'Dear Insects, my study of you has sustained me in my heaviest trials. I must take my leave of you for today. . . . Shall I be able to speak to you again?' He did, again and again."

Perhaps age-old moral injunctions, such as "pride goeth . . . before a fall," have parallel uses that apply to our access to perceptions. Maybe "pride" is a deadly sin or a vice (the original Latin word means "failing" or "defect"), and maybe—less judgmentally—it's a technical description of a specific kind of fragmentary perception, or should it perhaps be called a restricted information flow, like an artery unable to pump enough blood? A state people can get stuck in without realizing it. Something that, along with, say, anger or greed, can deaden sensations that might otherwise reach you. A tendency to be preoccupied by a "love of one's own excellence"—St. Augustine's definition of pride—would leave little room for wonder. Whether being humble (the "holy virtue" that, according to Dante, acts as an antidote to pride), or at least being more forthright and honest about what you know and don't know, will make you a better person, it can certainly restore a far wider range of awarenesses.

When I told another old friend about the wonder bridge into deep travel, he said, "Oh, there's an even easier way than that. What you're calling deep travel brings with it, you say, a remembrance that you don't know nearly what you could about what you're passing through if you open yourself up to it. But what about those times when your ignorance is total and you don't even know where you are? Those are the off-balance moments when I think everyone is projected headlong into deep travel. You slow down, you may stop altogether. You're lost. You've *got* to find, and soon, some way to proceed, and so your senses are wide open and, for the time being, everything and everyone is a potential source of information. But that's not what I'm suggesting—getting lost. That's the situation behind the idea I use."

This friend works at the Metropolitan Museum of Art in New York. "I call it the 'Warsaw induction,'" he said. "All you have to do is look around you"—we were having a sandwich in a crowded coffee shop on Madison Avenue—"and say to yourself, 'What would I notice, what would I want to know more about, what would I find compelling and be fascinated by if we were having lunch in Warsaw right now, instead of New York?' I say 'Warsaw,' of course, just to mean some place I've never been; if you've been to Warsaw, try Cairo instead, or Cape Town or Ulan Bator.

"Suddenly there is no way of knowing whether what you're seeing has been there for a long time or was only just put there, and you don't know, either, whether what's happening goes on all the time or is something brand new. Everything around you has a question inside it, and the answer may have something unusual or exceptional to tell you, not just about how to fit yourself into Warsaw patterns but about how to live your life anywhere, although if that's the case, you probably won't know about it until later. Why is there a picture of the Bay of Naples on the wall behind us? Why was there a bowl of pickles on the table before we even sat down? Does the noise in here mean that lunch is a celebration, the high point of a day? Or is it in hours the farthest away from home that people get, the other end of an orbit that's about to swing back?

"I should add that there are a couple of ways to play Warsaw—in 'Warsaw Lite' you assume you speak 'Polish.' Meaning that if you're in New York and can understand the conversations of the people at the next tables, then that's extra information that's available to you to help you figure out where you are and what's going on. In 'Intense Warsaw' you don't know 'Polish,' so you try to ignore the words you're overhearing to let yourself be guided only by the tone of voice or the gestures that accompany it, maybe a stare or a smile or a frown."

Deep travel is not so much the enemy of the ordinary as it is an understanding that when you start to look closely there is no ordinary. Because the answers to questions like "What would I think about the street I'm walking down if I had no idea where I am?" or "What if I knew this would be the only chance I'll ever have to see the sky the way it looks tonight?" are by their very nature open-ended. "The greatest of all the accomplishments of 20th-century science," Lewis Thomas, then chancellor of New York's Memorial Sloan-Kettering Cancer Center, said almost 30 years ago, "has been the discovery of human ignorance." He later added, "Each time we learn something new and surprising, the astonishment comes with the realization that we were wrong before." Finding ourselves in the presence of the unknown, or the not-yet-known, or the unknowable can be an uncomfortable encounter or a thrilling one, depending on circumstances. But because of the way our minds have been assembled, the extra dimensions of deep travel and the rewards they bring are readily available. Sometimes deep travel will assert itself with no warning. But when that doesn't happen, these riches can be ours for the asking. It's a choice that often has far-reaching consequences. "Two reeds drink from one stream," said the 13th-century Persian poet Jalaluddin Rumi. "One is hollow, the other is sugar-cane."

JOE HOOVER

A Figure in Black and Gray

FROM *The Sun*

THERE IS A NUN HERE AT THIS CATHOLIC RETREAT CENTER WHO wears a gray pinstriped skirt, a white blouse, and a black habit and I think is French, or maybe Spanish. She is old and small and moves slowly and has a wide forehead, and she stands right up close to the tall reading-room clock to see the time. She stands there and stares and then adjusts the hands on the white plastic clock she carries in her purse. She moans while she does this, frightening and sepulchral and tender.

This retreat house is, like many others, quiet and a little unreal, its flowers almost too bright and fluttery amid fresh mulch. Outside, the lawn is profoundly green and rolls downhill to a cliff overlooking the Potomac River. There is a woods and a Stations of the Cross and a fine chapel for prayer. As a Jesuit in training, moving toward priesthood, I am delighted to spend my eight required days here in this spiritual fantasyland, and I don't know if I could take one minute beyond that.

There are also icons and statues and tabernacles and altars, and yet perhaps the most profound image I can contemplate is this nun, who herself is mournfully contemplating the time on a clock twice her size. I want her to pray for me. I want to come up with some reason to need help, so she will offer prayers to God on my behalf. I almost wish upon myself a vocational crisis—some bright, spiritual girl in a distant college town, or in the too-frequented outskirts of my dreams, intruding into my somber meditation here on the river. I almost wish for this so that the nun may pray to keep me strong, and I will feel the effect of her prayers like poured concrete around this life I have chosen.

I don't believe it is just a romantic notion that leads me to ascribe such power to this sister. I am fairly certain her power is real. First of all she is old, which means she has stayed in the order. She has *stayed*. Why? I don't know. Duty. Obligation. Not wanting to let people down. Resting in the Lord. Bliss, service, fear, harmony, fulfillment. Whatever the reason, she is here.

And, as my dad said more than once when sizing up the prom date of one of his fidgeting, slick-haired sons, "She has an open face." The nun's face is not radiant or pleasant or cheery. It is just open. It hides nothing: a face that fits into its surroundings cleanly and is easy to look into from all sides.

She walks as if she commands any room she enters, because she does. Her humility inversely dominates any space she is in. I am certain she would be appalled at the thought that she could or would dominate a room, which only makes her more dominant.

She wears a brown nylon over her right hand, giving the impression it has been broken or is deformed or for some reason is out of commission at this time and maybe will be until she dies. Because her hand is hidden in this unmajestic way, it almost seems as if she were hiding a sacred wound, some lesser stigmata she is too humble to reveal to a world anxious to pounce on any sign of the freakishly mystical.

Is it unfair to heap all this grandeur on such a woman? Maybe she was fierce and brutal in some classroom. Maybe she didn't call home enough. Perhaps she kited funds from a retirement account or spent a good part of her days avoiding the sisters she couldn't stand.

Maybe she gardened poorly. Who knows? I can't imagine any of it. Whatever she did or didn't do, she has left it all behind. She is just this. And what is this? Perhaps the best I can say is: she just sends something out.

And lastly I am certain of her powers because of the way she allowed me, when we met at the beverage station one day at lunch in what was perhaps the high point of my retreat, to open the little creamer for her and pour it into her coffee. Then she let me open a second creamer and pour it for her. When she reached for a sugar packet, I started to take that too, and she said to me in English, "I can pour the sugar myself," and walked away.

So I want this sister to intercede for me. But what shall she pray for if there is no vocational crisis? (And there isn't, except in the way that any religious vocation is a kind of crisis.) Maybe she can pray for what I do. As part of my training—"formation," the Jesuits call it—I work at a high school on an Indian reservation, where I'm the campus minister and also teach religion and help put on plays. But when people ask what my job is, I usually say that I drive a bus. Because I do drive a bus. Many of the teachers do, taking the kids all over the Dakota prairies. I drive a school bus down the gray roads, and sometimes I say the rosary while I drive and imagine that the snow covering the stubble in the cornfields is like the Virgin Mary protecting the world, protecting me. Or I notice that the cows in a pasture, though spread out over acres and acres, are all facing the same way, every last one with its back to the road, and it feels meaningful, as if they were all staring in awe at something, confounded; as if they were praying in pious formation. But they are not praying. They are just cows. It is I who am praying, driving the yellow bus to a junior-varsity basketball game. I feel maybe this nun, in her overpowering humility, would appreciate all of that and offer her own prayer. The kids need to get there on time, she might say, and point to her white clock.

Or, better yet, maybe I need her prayers for "interior freedom," as my Jesuit teachers call it: being free to live out of the Holy Spirit and not the lower spirits of envy, comparison, and pride. I need her prayers so I won't go around in the shadow of the Jesuits who've come before me, the ghosts of many wonderful priests and brothers I've heard about: *Such a great listener! You never felt so listened to! He made everyone—all the kids, the faculty, everyone—feel like they were incredibly important! Even kids he was disciplining, as he was disciplining them, knew they were loved by this man.* I need the freedom to find my own way of doing this, despite all the wonderful departed priests crowding my darkened brainpan.

Now I am on this retreat, after a year at the high school, to chew on the work and the life. I am here to let prayer and silence fill the hollow places inside me, so that teaching sixteen-year-olds on the plains doesn't become a thin and fleeting experience but somehow etches itself deeper into me. I am here so my life will get soaked more thoroughly with the deluge of the past year. The hope is that my actions may become somehow more real to me, more deeply felt in looking at them than they were even in the doing, like emotional moments in movies — in particular, films about gutsy, underdog high-school sports teams.

I am here with Jesuits from all over the country, all of us in the middle stage: no longer novices but not yet priests, working for a spell "in the vineyard," as some might say. (Officially we are called "regents"—a term used by the Society of Jesus that means, roughly, "You will teach high school.") I am proud of these regents, these vinedressers, these men. If you are looking for an exposé by a discontented seminarian, you will have to look elsewhere. I like being in this outfit. They are for the most part "regular guys," which is a somewhat prideful way we talk about ourselves: Regular guys who lift weights, write blogs, and make mix CDs of songs by famously unknown bands. Guys who won't be caught in a chapel every minute of the day (said usually with a hint of bravado). Guys who can knock back a few. And it's true, I like that we are men composed of flesh and blood and doubt and beating hearts, and not merely incense and smoke and wordy Thomistic propositions. Regular guys afflicted with a passion for reading who, when there is free time, head to isolated corners with magazines or newspapers. Solitary men who may have to rehearse once or twice before saying to another brother, "Hey, want to take a walk?" Regular guys in a bookish sort of way. But still.

One was an army sergeant who fought in the Gulf War and then became a medical doctor before joining the Society of Jesus. Another used to clothe and feed the mentally challenged. Another played a lot of ultimate Frisbee. One man wrote speeches for a congressman, and another entered the order at age twenty-one and on his bio, under "work experience," wrote, unironically, that he'd had a paper route. What they all have in common is a weakness: an inability to say no to a deeply imprinted call—a call to poverty, chastity, and obedience, strange virtues that had to be flushed out from their hiding places, shown to us, and somehow made desirable. We're men who, for the most part, had good jobs and degrees but were brought low by something many of us hadn't really asked for, and to which we all eventually yielded. In the end concession and surrender may be our greatest accomplishments.

I want all of these men to stay, but many don't. Their weakness leaves them, I guess. I don't really know. Most of us on this retreat are six years into a decade-long journey toward priesthood, and many of our brothers have left us along the way. When someone departs, it seems those left behind hunker down and wonder if they, too, can bear out this life—which is maybe why I said a religious vocation is always a kind of crisis. A number of those who've departed were my good friends. They are now married or have partners. They work as youth ministers, study law, teach kids, run retreats, fight for the poor.

They are good men doing good things, often in the Church, but they've left our brotherhood. I'd like a little pity for this, but who has pity to share regarding such matters when there are so many far more tragic stories of people leaving? A freshman once told me that, during her eighth-grade graduation, her father had sat in the car in the parking lot and drank. Geographically he was not far from the ceremony, but by all appearances he had long ago left the precious, fractured territory of his daughter. And now she, at fifteen, was beginning to drink heavily, to leave herself by the same soaked, numb path that her father had left her.

So I try not to spend a lot of time carping about the departures of my dear Jesuit brothers. Staring at the nun in gray, on the other hand, baffled by the simple fact that she is still here—this is something I could, or maybe should, spend a great many hours doing.

I hope she discerns that we unfinished Jesuits are worth her prayers—not because we are going to go out and do mighty things for the Lord and set the world on fire, nor because we are mortified holy men who pray with discipline and deep reverence. I want her prayers because we were all taken by the hand and led on this odd, precarious path—with good healthcare and fine schooling—and none of us who remains has had it in him to wrest free and run in the other direction. But we need help. I don't know how to put it any more simply. I am tempted to go up to the nun and grab her by the shoulders and bark into her guileless face, *Out with it! What is your secret? Why do you stay? How did you get the way you are? Where does the peace come from? Name the coordinates, the latitude and longitude of where you stood to be drenched by God with such grace, to have this serenity, to be able to overpower a room with the nothingness of you.*

I am afraid she would merely say, *I prayed. I worked. I tried to give my life to God.* These things I already know about. I fear that they are all it is: holding out, keeping on, building a bridge to the holy ether stone by stone.

I don't always subscribe to prayer as a cure for everything. Perhaps I am not mortified enough to do so. I do know, however, that other people believe prayer is the answer—this sister probably being one of them. If we become what we look at, then perhaps I may be given a truer purpose simply by watching this nun; staring confounded, like the mysterious cattle all turned in one direction; comparing myself not to the priests in the cemetery but to the wounded bird of her, a figure in black and gray filled with what I don't have but what I at least can see.

One day at lunch, after putting her empty tray away, the nun came back to her place at the table and prayed silently. I assume she gave thanks for her meal. I expected it to be a ten-second rote, though sincere, prayer. But she stayed longer: moment after moment, really praying, likely in thanks for that cup of corn chowder, the cold white macaroni salad, the BLT, the ice water, maybe even for the little packets of apple jelly. This prayer was serious business: her hands folded, head lowered, eyes closed. A heavy prayer poured on the minor affair of the meal like buckets of water on a tiny garden plot. And me watching, hoping it would not end.

PICO IYER

A Chapel Is Where You Can Hear Something Beating Below Your Heart

FROM *Portland*

GIANT FIGURES ARE TALKING AND STRUTTING AND SINGING ON enormous screens above me, and someone is chattering away on the mini-screen in the cab from which I just stepped. Nine people at this street-corner are shouting into thin air, wearing wires around their chins and jabbing at screens in their hands. One teenager in Sacramento, I read recently sent 300,000 text messages in a month—or ten a minute for every minute of her waking day, assuming she was awake sixteen hours a day. There are more cell-phones than people on the planet now, almost (ten mobiles for every one at the beginning of the century). Even by the end of the last century, the average human being in a country such as ours saw as many images in a day as a Victorian inhaled in a lifetime.

And then I walk off crowded Fifth Avenue and into the capacious silence of Saint Patrick's. Candles are flickering here and there intensifying my sense of all I cannot see. Figures are on their knees, heads bowed, drawing my attention to what cannot be said. Light is flooding through the great blue windows, and I have entered a realm where no I or realm exists. I register everything around me: the worn stones, the little crosses, the hymn-books, the upturned faces;

then I sit down, close my eyes—and step out of time, into everything that stretches beyond it.

When I look back on my life, the parts that matter and sustain me, all I see is a series of chapels. They may be old or young, cracked brown or open space; they may be lectories or afterthoughts, hidden corners of a city or deserted spaces in the forest. They are as variable as people. But like people they have a stillness at the core of them which makes all discussion of high and low, East and West, you and me dissolve. Bells toll and toll and I lose all sense of whether they are chiming within me or without.

The first time I was asked to enter a New York office building—for a job interview twenty-eight years ago—I gathered myself, in all senses, in St. Patrick's, and knew that it would put everything I was about to face (a company, a new life, my twittering ambitions) into place. It was the frame that gave everything else definition. Ever since, I've made it my practice to step into that great thronged space whenever I return to the city, to remind myself of what is real, what is lasting, before giving myself to everything that isn't. A chapel is the biggest immensity we face in our daily lives, unless we live in a desert or in the vicinity of the Grand Canyon. A chapel is the deepest silence we can absorb, unless we stay in a cloister. A chapel is where we allow ourselves to be broken open as if we were children again, trembling at home before our parents.

Whenever I fly, I step into an airport chapel. The people there may be sleeping, reading, praying, but all of them are there because they want to be collected. When I go to San Francisco, I stay across from Grace Cathedral, and visit it several times a day, to put solid ground underneath my feet. Returning to the college I attended, I sit on a pew at the back, listening to the high-voiced choir, and think back on that shuffling kid who wandered the downy grounds and what relation he might have to the person who now sits here.

So much of our time is spent running from ourselves, or hiding from the world; a chapel brings us back to the source, in ourselves and in the larger sense of self—as if there were a difference. Look around you. Occasional figures are exploring their separate silences; the rich and the poor are hard to tell apart, heads bowed. Light is diffused and general; when you hear voices, they are joined in a chorus or reading from a holy book. The space at the heart of the Rothko Chapel is empty, and that emptiness is prayer and surrender.

In 1929 the British Broadcasting Corporation decided to start broadcasting "live silence" in memory of the dead instead of just halting transmission for two minutes every day; it was important, it was felt, to hear the rustle of papers, the singing of birds outside, an occasional cough. As a BBC spokesman put it, with rare wisdom, silence is "a solvent which destroys personality and gives us leave to be great and universal." Permits us, in short, to be who we are and could be if only we had the openness and trust. A chapel is where we hear something and nothing, ourselves and everyone else, a silence that is not the absence of noise but the presence of something much deeper: the depth beneath our thoughts.

This spring I came, for the first time, to the Chapel of Christ the Teacher at the University of Portland, to give a talk as the light was falling. Great shafts of sunshine stretched across the courtyard, catching and sharpening the faces of students returning to their rooms. Later in the evening, since this was Holy Week, an enormous cross was carried into the space, in darkness and reverence and silence. Now, however, people were walking in from all directions, leaving themselves at the door, putting away their business cards and gathering in a circle. They said nothing, and looked around them. The light through the windows began to fade. A scatter of seats became a congregation. And whatever was said, or not said, became less important than the silence.

·   ·   ·

Many years ago, when I was too young to know better, I worked in a 25th floor office four blocks from Times Square, in New York City. Teletypes juddered the news furiously into our midst every second—this was the World Affairs department of *Time* magazine— and messengers breathlessly brought the latest reports from our correspondents to our offices. Editors barked, early computers sputtered, televisions in our senior editors' offices gave us the news as it was breaking. We spoke and conferred and checked facts and wrote, often, twenty or twenty-five pages in an evening.

I left all that for a monastery on the backstreets of Kyoto. I wanted to learn about silence. I wanted to learn about who I was when I wasn't thinking about it. The Japanese are masters of not saying anything, both because their attention is always on listening, on saying little, even on speaking generically, and because, when they do talk, they are very eager to say nothing offensive, outrageous or confrontational. They're like talk-show hosts in a nation where self-display is almost forbidden. You learn more by listening than talking, they know; you create a wider circle not by thinking about yourself, but about the people around you, and how you can find common ground with them. The Japanese idea of a dream date—I've been with my Japanese sweetheart for 23 years and I've learned the hard way—is to go to a movie and come out saying nothing.

Perhaps I wouldn't need this kind of training in paying attention and keeping quiet were it not for the fact that I used to love babbling, and my colleges and friends in England and the U.S. trained and encouraged me to talk, to thrust myself forward, to assert my little self in all its puny glory. Perhaps we wouldn't need chapels if our lives were already clear and calm (a saint or a Jesus may never need to go into a church; he's always carrying one inside himself). Chapels are emergency rooms for the soul. They are the one place we can reliably go to find who we are and what we should be doing with our lives—usually by finding all we aren't, and what is much greater than us, to which we can only give ourselves up.

"I like the silent church," Emerson wrote, "before the service begins."

I grew up in chapels, at school in England. For all the years of my growing up, we had to go to chapel every morning and to say prayers in a smaller room every evening. Chapel became everything we longed to flee; it was where we made faces at one another, doodled in our hymn-books, sniggered at each other every time we sang about "the bosom of the Lord" or the "breast" of a green hill. All we wanted was open space, mobility, freedom—the California of the soul. But as the years went on, I started to see that no movement made sense unless it had a changelessness beneath it; that all our explorations were only as rich as the still place we brought them back to.

I noticed, in my early thirties, that I had accumulated 1.5 million miles with United Airlines alone; I started going to a monastery. It wasn't in order to become religious or to attend services in the chapel, though I did go there, over and over, as Emerson might have done, when nobody was present. The real chapel was my little cell in the hermitage, looking out on the boundless blue of the Pacific Ocean below, the Steller's jay that just alighted on the splintered fence in my garden. Chapel was silence and spaciousness and whatever put the human round, my human, all too human thoughts, in some kind of vaster context.

My house had burned down eight months before, and kind friends might have been thinking that I was seeking out a home; but in the chapel of my cell, I was seeking only a reminder of the inner home we always carry with us. To be a journalist is to be beholden to the contents of just now, the news the public need; to be a human—even if you're a journalist—is to be conscious of the old, what stands outside of time, our prime necessity. I could only write for *Time*, I thought, if I focused on Eternity.

I've stayed in those little cells in a Benedictine hermitage above the sea more than fifty times by now, over almost twenty years. I've stayed in the cloister with the monks; spent three weeks at a time in silence; stayed in a trailer in the dark, and in a house for the monastery's laborers, where I'd come upon monks doing press-ups against the rafters on the ground floor and planning their next raid upon the monastery computer.

Now the place lives inside me so powerfully that my home in Japan looks and feels like a Benedictine hermitage. I receive no newspapers or magazines there, and I watch no television. I've never had a cell-phone, and I've ensured that we have almost no Internet connections at all. We own no car or bicycle, and the whole apartment (formerly, population four, my wife and two children and myself) consists of two rooms. I sleep on a couch in the living room at 8:30 every night, and think this is the most luxurious, expansive, liberating adventure I could imagine.

A chapel is where you can hear something beating below your heart.

We've always needed chapels, however confused or contradictory we may be in the way we define our religious affiliations; we've always had to have quietness and stillness to undertake our journeys into battle, or just the tumult of the world. How can we act in the world, if we haven't had the time and chance to find out who we are and what the world and action might be?

But now Times Square is with us everywhere. The whole world is clamoring at our door even on a mountaintop (my monastery has wireless Internet, its workers downloaded so much of the world recently that the system crashed, and the monastery has a digital address, www.contemplation.com). Even in my cell in Japan, I can feel more than 6 billion voices, plus the Library of Alexandria, CNN, MSNBC, everything, in that inoffensive little white box with the apple on it. Take a bite, and you fall into the realm of Knowledge, and Ignorance, and Division.

The high-tech firm Intel experimented for seven months with enforcing "Quiet Time" for all of its workers for at least four consecutive hours a week (no e-mails were allowed, no phone calls accepted). It tried banning all e-mail checks on Fridays and assuring its workers that they had 24 hours, not 24 minutes, in which to respond to any internal e-mail. If people are always running to catch up, they will never have the time and space to create a world worth catching up with. Some colleges have now instituted a vespers hour, though often without a church; even in the most secular framework, what people require is the quietness to sink beneath the rush of the brain. Journalist friends of mine switch off their modems from Friday evening to Monday morning, every week, and I bow before them silently; I know that when I hop around the Web, watch YouTube videos, surf the TV set, I turn away and feel agitated. I go for a walk, enjoy a real conversation with a friend, turn off the lights and listen to Bach or Leonard Cohen, and I feel palpably richer, deeper, fuller, happier.

Happiness is absorption, being entirely yourself and entirely in one place. That is the chapel that we crave.

Long after my home had burned down, and I had begun going four times a year to my monastery up the coast, long after I'd constructed a more or less unplugged life in Japan—figuring that a journalist could write about the news best by not following its every convulsion, and writing from the chapel and not the madness of

Times Square—I found a Christian retreat-house in my own hometown. Sometimes, when I had an hour free in the day, or was running from errand to errand, I drove up into the silent hills and parked there, and just sat for a few minutes in its garden. Encircled by flowers. In a slice of light next to a statue of the Virgin.

Instantly, everything was okay. I had more reassurance than I would ever need. I was thinking of something more than an "I" I could never entirely respect.

Later, I opened the heavy doors and walked into the chapel, again when no one was there. It sat next to a sunlit courtyard overlooking the dry hills and far-off blue ocean of what could have been a space in Andalusia. A heavy bell spoke of the church's private sense of time. A row of blond-wood chairs was gathered in a circle. I knelt and closed my eyes and thought of the candle flickering in one corner of the chapel I loved in the monastery up the coast.

When I had to go to Sri Lanka, in the midst of its civil war, I went to the chapel to be still; to gather my resources and protection, as it were. I went there when I was forcibly evacuated from the house that my family had rebuilt after our earlier structure had burned down, and our new home was surrounded by wild flames driven by seventy mile-per-hour winds. In the very same week, my monastery in Big Sur was also encircled by fire.

I went there even when I was halfway across the world, because I had reconstituted the chapel in my head, my heart; it was where I went to be held by something profound. Then another wildfire struck up, and a newspaper editor called me in Japan: the retreat-house near my home was gone.

Where does one go when one's chapel is reduced to ash? Perhaps it is the first and main question before us all. There are still chapels everywhere. And I go to them. But like the best of teachers or friends, they always have the gift of making themselves immaterial, invisible—even, perhaps, immortal. I sit in Nara, the capital of Japan thirteen centuries ago, and I see a candle flickering. I feel the light descending from a skylight in the rotunda roof. I hear a fountain in the courtyard. I close my eyes and sit very still, by the side of my bed, and sense the chapel take shape around me.

If your silence is deep enough, bells toll all the way through it.

SAM JACOBSON

The Few, The Proud, The Chosen

FROM *Commentary*

THE FIRST WEEK AT UNITED STATES MARINE CORPS OFFICER Candidate School, our instructor platoon commander pulled me aside and asked whether I needed kosher meals. "Good evening, Sir. This candidate does not want the Platoon Commander to go out of his way for this candidate, Sir," I stammered, standing at stiff attention, still tentative with my candidate-speak. "I don't care what you want, Candidate. I'm just trying to find out if kosher meals are what you need."

I wasn't going to tell the captain that I grew up with a cut-and-paste Upper West Side-style Judaism, with friends who described themselves as "4-F peacenik yids." Nor did I tell him that I kept kosher at my dad's—on 96th and Columbus—but not at my mom's—on 96th and Broadway. That I never ate swine, sometimes ate shellfish, occasionally filtered my tap water to rid it of *treyf* crustaceans, and am still an on-again-off-again vegetarian. I wasn't about to tell the captain about my *mishigas* with Judaism. On the question of kosher meals, I believe I settled for a motivated (loud) and noncommittal, "Aye, Sir, good evening, Sir," about-faced, and double-timed back to formation.

A few weeks later, I did take advantage of the generous mood of religious accommodation and feared I was becoming the perfidious

Sheldon Grossbart from Philip Roth's "Defender of the Faith," who feigns orthodox observance to win special favor at Army boot camp in 1945. Once a week, our drill instructors marched us into a series of rooms for "Prayer and Praise." More than 200 funneled into the largest room, reserved for a generic Christian liturgy. A dozen chose the room for Mormons. A few made their way to the "no preference" room, and one, me, settled into a chair in a tiny office storage room set aside especially for the occasion of a religious outlier. Our class of almost 300 candidates started with three Jews. Two of them didn't make it more than a few weeks, so I was alone when the chaplain came in to drop off a Tupperware box of materials labeled "For Jewish Personnel in the Armed Forces of the United States." I flipped through a *siddur* and tried to remember what a good Jew would be doing on a Tuesday evening. But quickly I reverted to the only thing a Marine officer candidate knows how to do when left to sit in a room quietly, free from the screams of the gunnery sergeants. I slept, cheek mashed into the table, hands splayed out in front of me on the books and *kippot* and *tallitot*.

I woke to the sound of the door flying open and a sergeant instructor's query. "Is this part of your rituals, Jacobson?" Sleeping, as a matter of discipline, is strictly forbidden except during authorized hours, yet the instructor wasn't yelling as he usually would for such an infraction. I knew I was out of his jurisdiction, safe, for the rest of the hour anyway, in my office-room embassy. Abraham Joshua Heschel wrote that the Sabbath is a cathedral in time instead of space. Instead of a cathedral, that Tuesday evening *shabbes* hour was a fortified redoubt in time. Fridays and Saturdays we trained.

In that office room—in a Marine Corps building, in a Marine Corps camp, on a Marine Corps base—I was isolated from my fellow Marine candidates. It was my first experience with privacy since entering the Marines, and I didn't much care for it. It was as if I were AWOL and a civilian again. After that first night alone, nine short of a *minyan*, I chose to spend the rest of my Tuesdays alternating between the large Christian auditorium service and the "no preference" room.

The chaplain made his rounds at those Tuesday-night sessions, offering a prayer or that scarcest of boot-camp treatments—a smile and a kind word. Because there were no Muslim candidates, he had an unopened box of extra Korans. Still fantasizing that there would be time to read at Officer Candidate School, I asked for a copy and stowed it in my footlocker. One afternoon, after finding contraband in a candidate's locker—an old mealy apple smuggled from the chow hall—the sergeant instructors ordered an inspection. We 50 men stood at parade rest with our backs to the squad bay as the sergeants rifled through our trash, which is high Marine for "gear," which is Military for "belongings."

"Jacobson? JACOBSON, are you frickin Muslim, Jacobson?"

"No, Gunnery Sergeant."

"Are you a daggone frickin Muslim?"

"No, Gunnery Sergeant."

"Then why do you have this Koran in your foot locker?"

"This candidate was interested in reading it, Gunnery Sergeant."

"Are you frickin stupid, boy? You must be frickin stupid. Do I frickin care what frickin interests you?"

"NO, Gunnery Sergeant." After inspection, I found my Koran sitting alone in my footlocker, unharmed. The sergeant instructors had meticulously strewn everything else we owned in all directions. It took hours—of our designated sleep time, of course—to get everything back in its place.

A year and a half later, I began my service in Iraq as an infantry platoon commander, arriving with my unit in early September. For Kol Nidre, the military helicoptered all the interested Jews in Anbar

Province to Al Asad Air Base to form a *minyan*. Saddam Hussein had built the complex for his Air Force MiGs, alienating many Anbar Sunnis who believe it's holy ground. Within the base's barbed-wire perimeter is a small oasis pool and palm grove said by many local Bedouin to have been a rest and water stop for Abraham on his way through the desert to Canaan. Now under American control, the oasis is still off-limits to the populace.

Walking into the prefab chapel, surrounded by blast walls and barriers, I noticed a sign advertising "Jewish Movie Night" at Al Asad. I didn't need to see the movie. I was already in a Mel Brooks scene: from the as-yet-unreleased History of the World Part II. There were about 15 of us there for the service: a few airmen, sailors, civilian contractors, half a dozen soldiers, and a couple of Marines. The Kol Nidre service itself was unremarkable, which I think was only proper, since Jews have been saying Kol Nidre uninterrupted, by the waters of Babylon, for at least the past 1,500 years. That American Jews in Iraq now outnumber Iraqi Jews is one of the tragedies of this war. By last count, the Jews of Iraq, cloistered in a few Baghdad apartments, did not have sufficient numbers to form a *minyan*.

I spent Yom Kippur itself out on patrol in an oasis of Syro-Arabian desert. I managed to forgo my Meals Ready-to-Eat for the day, which wasn't hard given the nature of MREs. But I broke the fast early, drinking chai with some Bedouin, because I couldn't refuse the hospitality and because it's delicious. God knows mission has priority.

I had learned in the weeks before Yom Kippur that the Bedouin themselves often don't fast for Ramadan, because, so far as I could tell, the desert doesn't permit such luxuries. That night, the time of *Ne'ilah*, the concluding service of the holiday, like many other nights, we set up camp out in the desert, our humvees in a tight perimeter. Some Marines stood watch, posted with night-vision optics up in the turrets, others catching some sleep between their vehicles before the next patrol. I walked the lines for a couple of hours, chatted with the lance corporal on radio duty, and unrolled my sleeping bag for some rest.

My history in the Marines is a story of missed Fridays, and Saturdays, and holier days. For a Marine, the private sphere is so attenuated, and his public duties so large and ritualistically compelling, that religious observance becomes both more difficult and less desirable. Marines trade much of what goes by the name of individuality, or identity, for esprit. They love their rituals. And that includes the ritual hatred of the sometimes priggish sense of military propriety. The favorite straw man is the impeccably starched good-to-go march-in-step high-and-tight squared-away salty Sergeant Major straight out of central casting, who single-mindedly enforces the uniform standards and the archetype of the clean shave. This parody of the Sergeant Major is always ready with some canned false-motto: "How we doing Devil Dogs? Bunch a heart breakers and life takers. Are we motivated? Are we dedicated? Are we true to the colors? Oorah? Well let me hear it from your semper fi-aphragm!" We groan, but we love it. Even the OFP Marine—on his Own Frickin Program—needs the customs and courtesies to define himself against. The unit's rituals largely take the place of hard-to-accommodate religious customs. As an officer and platoon commander, I cannot imagine denying a Marine something so precious as the right to wear a *kippah* or other religious garb, but I also haven't heard of a Marine ever wanting to. The chain of command rarely makes religious accommodations, because they are rarely requested.

In the early 1980s, a rabbi turned Air Force clinical psychologist did request accommodation and was famously denied. When Dr. Simcha Goldman's superior officer at the March Air Force Base clinic instructed him not to wear a *kippah* with his uniform, he refused to comply and sued, claiming violation of his right to free ex-

ercise of religion. In *Goldman v. Weinberger*, the Supreme Court
rejected his claim, following the hands-off tradition of deference
to professional military judgment. Justice Brennan, in dissent, at-
tacked the Court's deference for being "absolute" and "uncritical."
He insisted that, at a minimum, the military must provide a rational
explanation for burdening a serviceman's free-exercise rights. But
explanations, like wars, are not always rational.

For better or worse, real or imagined, the military is one of the
few organizations that still attracts people looking for an alternative
to the "world of clerks and teachers, of co-education and zo-ophily,
of 'consumer's leagues' and 'associated charities,' of industrialism
unlimited, and feminism unabashed," as William James describes it
in his short essay "The Moral Equivalent of War." Martialism is one
such attempt at escape from that purblind bourgeois life. Observant
Judaism is another. Infantrymen are looking for a place where they
can indulge in anachronisms: love of glory, pugnacity, intrepidity,
severity, order, discipline, deprivation, devotion, exertion, hardihood,
risk, sharpness, precipitousness, contempt for life (whether one's
own or another's), conscription, the blood tax, honor, and, above all,
duty and self-forgetfulness. In this context, Dr. Goldman's language
of rights, of self-seeking—though never wrong—jars on duty-tuned
military ears. The old virtues—honor, courage, commitment—can't
always be communicated in court.

As the Goldman case worked its way through the judicial sys-
tem, Congress ordered the secretary of defense to form a study group,
which led to the military's new "neat and conservative" standard for
the wearing of *kippot* and religious paraphernalia more generally.
The DoD's "Accommodation of Religious Practices Within the Mil-
itary Services" seeks to systematize the standard. The revised 2009
edition stipulates that "a Jewish yarmulke may be worn with the
uniform" unless "prohibited by paragraph 5 or 7 of this enclosure." A
complete ban on wearing visible religious apparel is authorized when

requests for accommodation will have "an adverse impact on mission accomplishment, military readiness, unit cohesion, standards, or discipline."

Accommodation is almost always possible, but it also almost always has some consequence for unit cohesion and the maintenance of discipline. The willingness to tolerate such an effect is at the discretion of the chain of command, exactly as it was before the accommodation directive and *Goldman v. Weinberger*. Accommodation may be the default, but that default is a veneer behind which, as before, the commander's sense of readiness, cohesion, discipline, morale, and that catch-all, "military necessity," trumps all. Couched in the DoD directive's techno-bureaucratese is the possibility for the classic rejection of accommodation in favor of pugnacity, intrepidity, severity, deprivation, devotion, exertion, hardihood, sharpness, precipitousness, contempt for life, conscription, self-forgetfulness, and the blood tax.

Service and support-oriented units of the military, like Dr. Goldman's psychology clinic, are caught between worlds. On the one hand, they preserve at least the semblance of military decorum. Yet many enter these outfits as they would enter any trade, to learn a skill and earn a paycheck. This mixing of motives martial and civil, is what leads to breakdowns of understanding in the classic form of *Goldman v. Weinberger*. A rabbi turned clinical psychologist joins the Air Force to pay for school. Hilarity ensues.

In combat-oriented units of the military, where religious exemptions are both less possible and less desired, mix-ups are less frequent. The Marine Corps should only be so accommodating. A sweeping selflessness more akin to self-denial—or harder and broader, denial of the self—is the cardinal Marine virtue. It took me a long time to learn. Subordinate the self or risk insubordination. A Marine is a Marine first, and only secondly and peripherally a Buddhist or Jewish or Christian Marine. We want to be large, to contain multitudes, but we cannot be all things at all times. The pledge of *semper fidelis* precludes most observances, except perhaps a pared-down *sola fide* Protestantism. If the Marine Corps wanted you to have another religion, it would have issued you one. With a catechism that centers on the rifle, there is little room for other deities. The new credo: every Marine a rifleman. At boot camp and OCS, after lights out, recruits come to attention in their racks and recite their idolatrous creed:

This is my rifle. There are many like it, but this one is mine. It is my life. I must master it as I must master my life.

Without me, my rifle is useless. Without my rifle, I am useless. I must fire my rifle true. I must shoot straighter than any enemy who is trying to kill me. I must shoot him before he shoots me. I will . . .

My rifle is human, even as I am human, because it is my life. Thus, I will learn it as a brother. I will learn its weaknesses, its strengths, its parts, its accessories, its sights, and its barrel. I will keep my rifle clean and ready, even as I am clean and ready. We will become part of each other.

Before God I swear this creed. My rifle and I are the defenders of my country. We are the masters of our enemy. We are the saviors of my life. So be it, until victory is America's and there is no enemy, but Peace.

The trinity is changed. Father and Son become God and Rifle. It's hokey but vital. A Marine's weapon is by necessity the center of his new life, a life mostly inconsistent with the demands of halacha and Shema.

I'm not observant by civilian standards, but my small displays of Judaism are glaring. In the Marine Corps, after all, when you hear someone shout "JEW," you can be sure he's calling to a subordinate using the acronym for "Junior Enlisted Warrior." My bunkmate and fellow fire-team member at the Infantry Officer Course had attended the Citadel and never met a Jew before. He moderated his light Christ-killer jibing with no small admixture of esteem for the IDF and curiosity about my religion. He is still a great friend.

Jibing, like chewing tobacco, is a pastime in the Marine Corps. It is often caustic, mostly lighthearted, and always equal opportunity. Once, one of the corporals in my platoon wanted to get his squad excused from a particularly unpleasant duty and asked: "Sir, Don't you remember what it was like when your people were in bondage? Why won't you be our Moses?"

Before we left for Iraq, my platoon made the transition in training from conventional combined arms operations to more of a counterinsurgency—prior to that, hearts and minds meant "put two in the heart and one in the mind." The Marines decided I needed a nom de guerre, something strong, akin to "Lawrence of Arabia." They nixed Jacobson of Anbar Province and Hill 456 Sam. And I rejected Jewtenant Jacobson. As it turned out, some Iraqis came to know me as *Mulazim ibn 'Yakub*, literally, Lieutenant Son of Jacob, and later as *Mulazim Yusef*, Lieutenant Joseph, truly the Son of Jacob. Though they knew I was Jewish, they taught me the Iraqi girl's rhyming catchphrase for finding a husband: "*Lo mulazim, lo malazim*"—Either a lieutenant, or no one. When we returned home from Iraq, my commanding officer sat us down for a talk after an alleged incident of discrimination in another section of the battalion. "I treat you all as equals," he said. "Equally worthless."

After my noncommittal "Aye, Sir, good evening, Sir" with the captain at OCS, I'm glad the kosher food never materialized. What would I need it for? The standard Meal Ready-to-Eat is engineered to have just the right balance of nutrients to keep a Marine in the fight: vacuum-sealed pouches of carbohydrates, fatty acids, vitamins, minerals, and Tabasco. And eating those things, leaning against your pack, tired, dirty, hot, soaked and bullshitting with fellow Marines is a daily sacrament. I still stay away from the MREs that contain pig, like "Pork Rib, Boneless, Imitation" with "natural flavor, smoke flavor, grill flavor," though the man who named it is a genius of prosody (his other lyrical masterpieces: "Chicken Breast Strips, with Rib Meat, Chopped and Formed, with Chunky Salsa," and the Spartan "Spaghetti with Meat and Sauce"). I always trade my cheese spread w/bacon for the regular cheese-spread packet and do my best to convert the ubiquitous "Boxed Nasty" into something I can eat: open and remove ham from ham-and-cheese sandwich; attempt to prevent cheese from peeling off with ham; replace ham with Fritos; mustard to taste. Eat. Drink the Kool-Aid.

To retain too much of one's public religiosity, such as requesting kosher food, seems almost extravagant. How much ritual does a man need? At my graduation from the Infantry Officer Course, we each recited a quotation that is important to our lives. After a series of motivating Marine-isms and vigorous passages from Chesty Puller and Theodore Roosevelt, a fellow lieutenant stood and broke the formula with a line from the New Testament, to the accompaniment of confused looks in the crowd. For those who have a religion other than being a Marine, and many do, they mostly keep it to themselves, literally keep it in under their shirts. I was shirtless in the field one day, and a fellow lieutenant saw my dog tags up close for the first time. Religious Preference: Jewish. "I didn't know you were Jewish, Jacobson. It's good that it says it here. That way when you're captured, al-Qaeda will know to arrange for kosher meals."

MARK JARMAN

Bulgarian Icon of the Last Supper

FROM *The Hudson Review*

If they saw around his head and theirs the halos—
All would be known. And Judas without a halo
Would not fool anyone. This is true of all such paintings.
But why are the two white parsnips on the table
In the foreground? The upper room crowds in
With slotted windows, spindly pillars, under a small blue dome.
Everyone's dressed in the gold of holiness, even Judas.
And in Christ's halo, the letters of his fate are legible.
Anyone looking his way had to know. But those root vegetables,
There side by side, among the three-pronged forks—
They couldn't be more accurate, less stylized.
And in those loving cups—aren't those dumplings?
Everything else is flattened into the sacred.
All lineaments are red in the clothing worn, the faces
Long, lined, expressionless, are all alike.
Before each man, a scarlet triangle, like a place card,
Waits, perhaps, to be plucked up and hidden.
In Bulgarian, the words for "Last Supper," somewhat
        ambiguous,
Mean "holy or secret, enigmatic, mysterious meal."
Here, footnoted by dumplings. And a pair of parsnips.
As if to say: "Just as you eat at your house. Any night."

NOA JONES

Where the Buddha Woke Up

FROM *Tricycle*

SOME PILGRIMS, NOT JUST A FEW, PROSTRATE THEMSELVES ALL THE way from their villages in Tibet, crossing the Himalayas, risking banditry and crocodiles through India's most rogue state, Bihar, until they arrive in Bodhgaya.

Most are propelled by their devotion. I was propelled by a vague sense of duty and very little effort—I arrived by plane. The effort came only once I stopped busying myself with the outside world.

Things happen quickly in Bodhgaya, site of the Buddha's enlightenment. People say that karma cooks faster here. As if the Mahabodhi Temple is a hot plate and we pilgrims have just tumbled out of an egg carton. What has been hidden in the fragile shells of our egos comes sliding out. We fry. Our hearts are exposed. Another thing: Possessions disappear. The last time I came to Bodhgaya I was robbed blind en route on the night train from Varanasi. I arrived with no passport, no money, no practice materials. And the very day I arrived, my seemingly solid romance of one year ended. I'd been stripped of everything and sent back to the source. The navel of the earth. The Bodhi tree.

But I'm not thinking about that. I've got work to do. I enter the flood of pilgrims who cram the main mall outside of the temple. I call it the mall. It reminds me of the Pearl Street mall in Boulder, Colorado, with its brick promenade and open-air shopping opportunities. But where Boulder is fortified by Abercrombie & Fitch and Starbucks, here there is stand after stand selling dusty offerings— flowers, incense, gems, white ceremonial scarves (*katas*), Bodhi leaves, malas, everything a practitioner could need. Here there are beggars and hawkers, people with twisted limbs, blind men, *sadhus,* curious goats, everyone angling to impede us. A man is selling pomegranates covered in flies—a microcosm of the mall, which is crawling with red-robed monks and nuns who walk in clusters, all with black buzz cuts.

In the midst of all this, I stand a head above most others. I am pressed from all sides. I stumble over something on the ground. An adolescent girl lies on a piece of cardboard at the entrance of the temple, both legs amputated at the highest possible point. She is absorbed in the play of a twig she twirls; there is a single leaf attached, upon which she focuses her attention with the zeal that her Western legged counterparts might pour into texting. Maybe if she twirls the lopsided stick long enough someone will get the message.

I am body-checked by a hefty Burmese monk carrying a staff. Seven nuns dressed in white, faces behind masks, march by led by a monk chanting into a megaphone, one of the hundreds of megaphones cranked to the highest decibel level that contribute to the arpeggio of mantras and trumpets and "Madame! Flower? You need mala?" that surrounds me.

The Burmese monks wear rust-colored robes. Sri Lankan and Thai pilgrims come in bright white, their lamas in ochre. Zen practitioners from Japan, China, and Korea wear elegant gray, sometimes with a brown sash. There is a smattering of easy-to-spot Westerners, conspicuous in their funny pants, pants that billow, pants with a crotch that hangs below the knee MC Hammer-style, candy-striped pants. There is a *sadhu* in a patchwork quilt, a yogi with dreadlocks, pilgrims in traditional dress. There are robes the color of pumpkin and of neon plastic pumpkin. But today they are all a minority.

It is the Nyingma sect's Monlam. The Monlam is a Tibetan Buddhist prayer festival "for world peace" that draws tens of thousands of pilgrims to Bodhgaya each year. It's a rare congregation of the greatest living Buddhist masters, yogis, tulkus, and khenpos. They come, they pray. The gathering is also an opportunity for these great masters to meet and discuss the practical issues they face as lineage seat-holders and heads of ever-growing organizations. Each sect takes a turn reserving the temple grounds for their gatherings. Kagyü in December, Gelugpa in early January. The Nyingmapas are the largest gathering, the third week of January.

The Monlam makes sense. In ancient Tibet, people didn't register for teachings and book flights; rumor would spread that a lama had set up camp somewhere and pilgrims would gather, pitch a tent and spend a month receiving teachings. After the Chinese Cultural Revolution and the arrival of the Tibetan diaspora in India, there was chaos and a desperate effort at preservation. Prayer festivals were put on the back burner. The diaspora stumbled and struggled back to its feet. The first Nyingma Monlam, organized by Tarthang Tulku Rinpoche in 1989, was a sign that the exiles had regained their strength. Now tens of thousands of Buddhists come every year. These festivals have become the active and significant nucleus of Tibetan Buddhism.

The Monlam costs money. Orgyen Tobgyal Rinpoche tells me that thirteen thousand monks showed up for the free lunch the monastery is offering this year. Every day for ten days. Piles of offerings are given to the monks and practitioners who attend, thousands of dollars are given out in coin and in kind, *tsok* (offerings of food and drink for purification and merit), butter lamps, incense, food, *dana* (personal donations) and texts. Even Westerners find tea and biscuits and the occasional one hundred rupee note left on their cushions and prostration boards. The beggars watch hungrily, sometimes gathering in tribes and ransacking the tsok offerings while the security guards pretend to whack them with sticks.

The place is pulsating. It feels more wrathful than peaceful, not negative but not resting. It makes one wonder about the mechanism of bringing world peace. How do a bunch of monks sitting under the Bodhi tree affect the Middle East Peace process? Is their influence an abstract concept, or is there some global impact? I wonder.

I reach the gate that opens to the Mahabodhi temple and press through the pungent traffic of mala-swinging pilgrims circumambulating, four abreast, on the upper section of the temple complex. The main temple appears to be built on a sunken platform but actually the complex, which contains countless smaller stupas and temples, three levels of walkways, a lake, fountains and trees, is built upon the ruins of a once grand university. There is a debate about whether to continue Sir Alexander Cunningham's excavation work. But most practitioners are against it. This is a living temple, not an archaeological dig.

That night I have dinner with Gene Smith, who has just been honored by the entire Nyingma sect for his contributions to the preservation of the buddhadharma. It's to record the milestone of this ceremony that I have been summoned here. There is an entire story to be told, volumes of stories, about Gene alone. He deserves a great deal of attention. But the ceremony is over now, and in the morning Gene packs up the gong and is gone.

I have no return ticket, a last-minute decision that was made when I was otherwise engrossed and not thinking rationally. As I wave good-bye, I suddenly realize I am completely alone, with no real plan. I have been so focused on Gene—it was my job to accompany him on the flight over—for the past two days that I haven't even said a proper hello to the temple. It occurs to me that perhaps

I had no real purpose coming here. Instead I've been led to the temple by an egotistical sense of duty so that my ego could be struck down and given nothing to do but practice. A karmic trick.

I take one last good hot shower at the fake-fancy hotel where we've been hosted, watch some female professional wrestling on the television and eat some bonbons. An eleventh-hour luxury binge. I have a vague memory of what harshness the real Bodhgaya is capable of, like the memory of what lime pickle does to my salivary glands—powerful, but buffered by the soft quilt of time. I am about to get my first fresh taste. I check out of the hotel and find a place for a fraction of the price at the Burmese temple on the other side of town. I drop my bags in the cold concrete room filled with mosquitoes and head back out to greet the Mahabodhi.

One of the rickshaw drivers waiting outside the Burmese gate stares like he knows something about me. He gives me a look like we've got some shared history. Maybe he was the one who gave me a ride one night when I was sobbing with heartbreak. Maybe we had a moment about that back then. Or maybe he's just a pervert. So I avoid his eyes by looking up. The sky is the uniform periwinkle blue of flat places, the plains and the sea. It's the same color of the sky in the only photograph I have of my parents together, smiling on a windy day in front of the Statue of Liberty.

The Mahabodhi is a whole other kind of statue of liberty. It is breathtaking and simple, soaring into the sky from its recessed foundation. A monument of liberation. True liberation, no matter what color robes, at least we Buddhists agree on this. This is what we are working toward. And this is the best place to practice.

No one knows for sure who built it or when. King Ashoka came and erected something of some sort near a tree at this spot in the third century BCE. Most likely the current temple, intricate brickwork 55 meters tall, was built in the fifth or sixth century, during the Gupta period.

I wish I could travel faster than the speed of light, perch on a distant planet and look back on earth so that I could see back in time to the day when Siddhartha sat under a pipal tree in the sylvan fields of what was then known as Uruvela. I want to know exactly what happened, if there were witnesses to his enlightenment, what the weather was like, if there were wild hogs sipping from the river. Whatever the case, the place is saturated with thousands of years of practice. Think of a great cathedral like Chartres, then think of Auschwitz. These places have power because of what happened here. And what happened here is that a mortal man meditated very deeply and saw the true nature of mind. The exact spot of his enlightenment is known by Tibetans as the Vajrasana, the Diamond Seat. You have to come here to experience it.

"The Karmapa said that it's a hundred thousand times more powerful to practice here than any other place. Zopa Rinpoche said seven times more powerful," says Yogi Mike, who is my neighbor at the Burmese Vihar. "I don't know, one doesn't seem enough, one sounds a bit much." Mike has been here almost continuously since 1984. If you've been to Bodhgaya, you've probably seen him, the American guy sitting in meditation in the same spot night after night, clad in white, long beard, topknot. "But in the context of the Monlam, when there are so many great realized masters sitting there, and a whole sangha; in those key moments, it could be a hundred thousand times. That's why I'm here so many years."

Yogi Mike also answers my earlier question about world peace: "If there is a relation between transforming individuals' minds and the impact that has on the larger world, then there's definitely something major going on here."

In the incubating container of the temple, everyone can begin to seem slightly insane or needy or cross. I go to Mohammad's—Bodhgaya's most popular restaurant—to ground myself with some *momos*. A woman asks if she can join me. She begins forcefully signing and folding a stack of letters. She's leading a passionate environmental campaign to stop the use of plastic in Bodhgaya. She is from London but lives in Bodhgaya full time. She speaks fast. I ask her what we should do if we don't drink bottled water: can we trust the water fountains at the temple? "Drink hot water. That's what I do." Just as she finishes folding her letters, the waiter brings a plastic bag with two dinners packed in tinfoil and cardboard. She's ordered to go, and I must practice nonjudgment.

International sponsors have donated several UV filtration systems at the temple. Upkeep is integral. Last time I was here I drank only from the fountains, but this year I'm afraid. I ask the Management Committee Office where the water comes from. I'm told it's pumped from the river. The river is a drybed and polluted, as are many rivers in India. But the drinking water comes from 250 feet below the river and then chemicals are added, I am assured. No bacteria.

I will meet a beautiful swami who will tell me the story of that hidden river.

I go home and take a shower, after which I feel as though I've gone through a final rinse at the car wash. Slightly waxy. I dutifully fill my plastic bottle with the filtered water, and within a few hours I get sick. Really sick. I think I'm going to die here in my dark room. The mosquitoes sing. I am alone; I develop flu symptoms on top of everything else. Nobody knows or cares. I am not a survivor. Buddha was a survivor. How am I to follow in his path? I look at the Theravadins and I know I am not capable of the austerities they willingly endure. Nothing seems possible. Liberation is for greater souls than this one.

I am so incredibly congested, I cannot string two thoughts together. They call it Bodhgaya Blessing. "You must be purifying something," says a man next to me at Mohammad's where I've gone to get ginger lemon tea with honey. Here everything bad is considered good. Your lama is avoiding you? Mazal tov! You're losing your mind? Excellent news! Everyone gets the blessing. With all the pestilent snot flying directly from nose to pavement, all you can do is a little side-step dance and pray.

Yogi Mike affirms the virtues of suffering. "Especially during the season, I have the impression that the amount of purification and wisdom is far greater than what you could accomplish on your own," he says, stirring the embers of his smoke offering back at the Vihar. "The problem is, if you want to take the quick path, it means purification has to be quicker, which is inevitably harder. How can there be an increase in wisdom without purifying obstacles? Hardship is, I'm thinking, the greater of the two blessings. The purifying rather than the blissful, insightful ones that we all like. The ones that make it so hard you want to run away are perhaps the greatest blessing."

Even though I'm sick, I go to the temple. I practice all day long. When you come to Bodhgaya, you will see. You can't stay away. The tree is calling, the temple is calling. And once you get there, any direction you turn you end up bumping into a rinpoche or a *drupchen* or a five-thousand-person feast. So I just plop down somewhere, anywhere—I prefer dappled sunlight under the tree—and do my practice in the midst of it.

There is too much to look at, it's dizzying, so I just look at the feet of the circumambulating pilgrims for a while. No shoes allowed. What we get is lots of dirty athletic socks, calloused feet, mosquito-bitten feet, henna feet that look as if they have been dipped in pink ink, feet in plastic bags, knitted footies, Japanese two-toed tabi, a pair of slippers from the Hyatt Singapore, old pedicures, new pedicures, paws. Yogi Mike calls this inner section "the washing machine" when it gets crowded. The spin cycle. So many people. A Thai tour group in matching outfits and Mind Vacations baseball caps moves in with a megaphone, and the silence is pierced with call and response followed by a long nasal chant. It sounds like they are saying: "Someone no can pee pee so caca, why . . ." over and over again. I move around the corner and another group is chanting to the exact tune of the Smashing Pumpkins' song "Bullet with Butterfly Wings," which immediately imbeds itself in my brain.

It gets overwhelming, so I go back to my cool dark room and sit, febrile, amid the shadows. The mosquitoes describe the air above my bed with manic scribbles. Despite all my rage, I'm still just a rat in a cage replaying in my mind. The blood drinkers. They hover, hide, cling to the walls, lie in wait. A debate people here like to abbreviate and avoid is whether Mortein brand insect repellent actually kills them or just stuns them. Even the most devout Buddhists I encounter seem content with the connivance that despite the obvious derivation from the Latin *mortuus,* "dead," Mortein is harmless. I hear an Indian guide tell a tour group that Buddha sat under the Bodhi tree for a week without blinking. He demonstrates what that looks like. He looks like an Indian Don Knotts. And I think, if Buddha did that, he probably didn't swat away mosquitoes. So I try it. I sit, and I let them bite me. I feel the intensity of their bloodthirst. I feel sorry for them. And then one bites me in the ear and I think screw this and purchase some Mortein. I'm careful to plug it in only long enough so that the mosquitoes start to fly drunk, which makes it easier to catch them in my hand and release them outside. But then I accidentally kill one and freak out. And so in one afternoon, a lifetime passes.

I go to the temple with a question about this episode in mind, knowing that I will find someone with an answer. The question is: If I need this precious human body to attain enlightenment, then why should I sit and let mosquitoes who might have malaria or Dengue fever bite me? Why not swat? I understand *ahimsa* [nonharming]. But why the perfectly-still part?

The all-knowing rickshaw driver is standing outside the gate; I slip by him, deciding to walk the long way through the Indian village. There is a plot of land next to a school, covered in garbage, and in that garbage there stands a spavined mule crippled by disease and about ten geese. The geese have been painted fluorescent pink. "You have like this in America?" asks a man wearing a vest that looks as if it has been hewn from the pelt of a slain Muppet, Fozzie Bear, perhaps. "Sort of," I say. "Like this size or big size? Big size, or small size?" He shows me different sizes and I say, "Yes. No. Yes." He seemed very pleased with this answer. There are wild hogs, baby goats, naked children with lice leaping from their heads as garbage burns in small piles.

It is said in sacred texts that Bodhgaya is going to be the last place left on earth when the universe is destroyed. Even if I hang around here, I will be a goner. But these families living in tents, cooking with motor oil as fluorescent pink geese crap in the drinking water, might not even notice. Life is an apocalypse. I bow down to them. I am in awe. They have so much more than I do because they require so much less. I am probably painfully wrong about all of this.

I cut across the traffic on Bypass Road, wheezing against the particulates that fill the air, skirting past the mala sellers and beggars. I am speedy and then I come to a full stop, slammed back into practice mind by the sight of the temple. As always, magnificent, inviting.

Instead of finding an answer to the mosquito question, I find a swami. Just one look at his graceful stride and I realize how much pain I am in—the fever and chills and rickshaw rides and prostrations. I need yoga. He looks like he does yoga. I ask for an introduction. Swami Santoshananda of Gaya says he will teach me. I spend the next five evenings receiving his glowing instructions and start to feel like a human again. He tells me about the Niranjana River, how it was punished for lying. He shows me how to breathe. He tells me that if one is in meditation, one won't feel the mosquitoes. And anyway, they aren't doing it on purpose. They don't see me as a human, I'm just dinner. Have some sympathy.

It's a nice concept but difficult to put into practice. There is one Thai nun who comes with solar regularity and sits in what looks like mosquito-repellant deep meditation. Immoveable, even when the UV rays are burning down with midday ferocity. I ache to slather some SPF 30 on her. Instead, I take a photo of her covered in flies.

I start to feel better, and then I have to leave. I've lost ten pounds, I can see it in my face. Why is Buddha ever portrayed as chubby? I leave Bodhgaya in the middle of the night. A taxi to Gaya and then the Rajdhani Express. On the way to the station I feel an extreme shift. A pressure release. A too-heavy quilt lifted. But like when a quilt is lifted, the heat is lost. I could go on.

JILL NOEL KANDEL

Burial Cloth Removed

FROM *River Teeth*

TEN YEARS OF MY LIFE LIE HIDDEN. I MISSED THE 1980S ALTO-gether. When people talk about '80s TV shows, politics, or movies I hardly have a clue. Reagan went missing somewhere and I never really found him. A part of me went missing, too. I turned up later with a sort of confused amnesia. While I cannot say who won Os-cars, Super Bowls, or pennants, I can tell you other useless trivia. I can tell you about being mugged in Zimbabwe, being held at spear point in Lusaka, having army ants eat all my chickens and ducks—alive—down to the bone. I can tell you how the mist feels falling upward off of the magnificent Mosi-oa-Tunya Waterfalls, how an African fish eagle holds its heavy morning prey, about the pungent wild smell emitted by a herd a hundred strong of wildebeest.

I can tell you about being alone.

When Lazarus was sick unto death, Jesus knew and waited. He let Lazarus lie dead and cold for three days before He came. Before He wept. Does it matter what Lazarus missed those three days in the tomb? And when they pulled the cloth away—Mary and Mar-tha longing to see that beloved irreplaceable face again—was it the same as they remembered?

I love a God who is difficult to explain and hard to understand. He crushes what He loves. Take Joseph of the Old Testament. Joseph the good boy. Joseph the good man. There's not one sentence, not one word in the Bible that shows he ever did anything wrong, yet— beware of being too good—his brothers threw him in a pit, sold him as a slave, and told his father he was dead.

God hides His face from those He favors.

Hide Abby—Minnesota 2009

My youngest daughter, Abigail, has never lived outside of North Dakota and Minnesota. These are her boundaries. At the age of three, she liked to tell stories about Africa.

"Mom, the babies in Africa were all born with their eyes shut," she said to me.

"Abigail, you've never been to Africa."

"Yes, I have. The babies' eyes are shut. For five days. I've seen it. Just like my puppies."

She persisted not only in her made-up memories but also in her play. Her favorite game became Hide and Seek the Bear. It started while visiting friends in California. Their three big boys—all close to six feet tall and football built—hid her tiny brown bear in various rooms while she toddled around looking for it. The boys soon tired of the bear. Abby, little bigger than the bear herself, proved more appealing.

"Let's play Hide Abby," one of the boys called out.

And so they did. She was just a handful in those big palms.

"I'll hide her first," the oldest one said.

The others hid their eyes and he plunked Abby down inside an oval basket.

They hid her again and again, throughout the house for hours.

Hold Her—Zambia 1985

I am six months pregnant, and big. We are on our way home—back to Kalabo Village—from Lusaka, the capital city of Zambia.

My husband sits in the right-hand seat, driving. One-and-a-half-year-old Melinda plays between us.

We are driving through Kafue Game Park, on narrow, tall-grass roads. A bus, in front on the right, has stopped in the middle of the road. My husband slows down—ever the cautious driver. We're barely going twenty. He honks repeatedly and moves left to pass. We're exactly even with the bus, not able to see around it. There is less than a blur of movement. A thud sends a shudder through the truck. I see his knuckles; they are white.

A motionless girl, with one arm thrown across a pothole, lies on the cracked tarmac, sweet potatoes scattered all around. Her black hair hides her face and blends into the pavement. It is no different than the hair of all the young girls who stand looking down at her still form, clothed in its shabby dress. I thought there would be blood. There is not.

A crowd gathers.

I am a nurse. I watch her breathing and see something straight out of an intensive-care ward: Cheyne-Stokes. She sucks in a breath and stops breathing. A very long pause. A pause that says, "Oh, God. Oh, God. Oh, God." A rasp. She sucks another breath.

The pickup—stuffed with purchases from Lusaka, plants, seeds, fertilizer, and maps—reflects the hot sun, while my husband flings open the back doors and throws things, squashes them, ruins them.

Make room for her, for her grandfather who comes and kneels beside her, barefoot. His hair gray and speckled. The crowd full of torn shirts and missing teeth pushes tighter, yelling. People come running. They carry stained bundles, cassava roots, and hoes. They fill up the road with fear and noise. They fill my mind. I cannot think.

Pick up your child, Grandfather, pick her up and hold her in your arms. Carry her to the truck. Crawl in, scrunch up sideways, child on your lap breathing awfully.

I cannot think. I have seen this before. There is so much shouting in languages I cannot understand. I hear the sound of anger.

Melinda sits all alone, in the front seat. Go to her. Sit with her. Hold her in your arms, mother, never let her go.

I hear myself say, "Hurry. Hurry. We'll take her to the hospital!"

A young man stands next to the truck, dressed in clean, neat clothes; he's wearing shoes. He speaks to me in perfect English, "Roll up your window, Madame. It is good you have a child. It is good you are pregnant. The crowd is angry. Lock your door."

I look up at him in mute concentration. He points to the window making rolling motions with his hand. I bend down to reach the window handle and he is gone.

Finally an uncle, or possibly her father? We squish into the front, all four of us, reeking of cold sweat. It is thirty miles to the nearest hospital.

In What?

After we moved back to the states—to northern Minnesota—I tried to talk about Africa.

"I used to live in Zambia," I'd say to a new acquaintance.

"In what?"

"Zambia," I'd say. "A country in southern middle Africa."

"Oh, you lived in South Africa."

I changed tactics and told people we'd been living overseas.

"Were you missionaries?" they wanted to know.

"Well, we worked for a sort of Dutch Peace Corps thing. Doing agriculture."

Silence.

Once—at the grocery store of all places—a lady asked me where I'd lived.

"Where did you say you'd been? In Africa? I have a niece who lives there. She lives in, uhmm, what was it? Kenya? Uganda? No, Ethiopia."

"Hello," I replied. Only able to get one word inserted into her monologue.

"Oh, I can't remember but she's in Africa, you know, somewhere. I heard you were in, what was it, Zamboni?" she continued. "Oh, no," she laughed, "that's the name of those hockey machines that clean the ice isn't it?"

"Yes, it is," I replied.

"How nice," she answered. "I'll have to ask you about it sometime. Say, did your husband go deer hunting last weekend?"

A Moment Ago—Zambia

A moment ago we were happy. A moment ago I had been playing finger games with Melinda.

We drive fast and repeat words. "I didn't see her. Did you see her? I didn't see her." We repeat our words as if they will make everything go away, as if they can take the moment back and change it.

"I slowed way down. I pulled over. She didn't look."

At the hospital they tell us the doctor isn't in. He's at his home; its lunch time. The phone doesn't work.

Hold her, Grandfather, we'll find the doctor. Hold her. I hear someone say she is twelve years old.

We drive to the doctor's house. We race inside. We yell for the doctor. Why are we trying so hard to do everything fast, when all the world has slowed to a crawl? It seems like I'm up above the day and looking down. I watch myself. I am too skinny with a belly swaying in front of me, my face awful in its whiteness.

Stay at this unknown doctor's house with Melinda. Try to sit quietly, not to impose. Occupy your one-year-old as the day wears on hot and slow. Sit on the cement floor and play with LEGO. It's quiet as mourning. As if the day knows something that I do not.

I am hungry. My body relentlessly cares for its growing child. I'm embarrassed. I am ashamed. Wait through the afternoon with no lunch. Thirsty, nauseous with need, find the kitchen and the wife and ask for something to eat.

I see her looking at me. She moves her lips, "I didn't think you'd be hungry."

Enter the World

It's been years and years. My older children are adults now, and we all live in Minnesota.

But each morning when I wake up, I remember Africa. I think about those years. Years that hide away like my babies once hid in my womb. I feel those years kick inside my heart. Hidden and ever present they can still cause me to be short of breath. They grow and shape me. They will not be forgotten.

They want to enter the world and say: I did not live in Zamboni. I lived in a country with a name, just as special and wonderful as any other country on the globe. Zambia. Look at it. Say it. Spell it. Z-A-M-B-I-A. It lies in the southern part of Africa, landlocked and central. Color the borders of Zambia, fill them in with yellow or pink on a map of Africa, and you will see a butterfly. I lived in the western wing.

It was my home.

Maybe Someday—Zambia

He must tell his story to the police. He finds the station with its four officers whose English abilities are minimal.

"There's been an accident."

"Bwana, let us see the driving license. Yes, it is good. It is official Zambian. Now, the passport, Bwana. What country do you come from? Good, the Dutch passport, it is good. And the work permit? This you also have? Yes, it too is good."

"We brought her to the hospital."

"Bwana, you should not have stop. Why did you do this thing to stop? You must first come to police. The villagers they will be violent. They can take a revenge."

Notify the embassy in case troubles arise. Wonder about lawsuits. Worry about death. A court case. A night in jail. Prison. Talk with the police for hours. Who knows the implications?

Dear God, hold the little girl. Never let her go.

The officer sighs and looks down at his papers. He shakes his head.

"When will we teach our children to look?"

These are the words he says. They are only words.

Maybe someday they will help.

You Can Come Out Now

Abigail still loves to play Hide and Seek. She's small and limber and can curl up into almost any shape to hide in the most unlikely crannies. She possesses the uncanny ability to remain completely still and quiet.

When we play the game we take turns: hider, seeker. Abby likes to hide. After twenty minutes we're stumped. After thirty we're exasperated.

"Abigail! We can't find you," we call.

No answer.

"You can come out now!" We yell. She whoops with joy and emerges from the most unimaginable places. How did she ever get in there?

All Your Life—Zambia

My husband comes back.

"She's alive."

He cannot eat; I greedily consume.

Cling to the story. Jesus healed a twelve-year-old. Repeat the story over and over in your mind, your heart somewhere in your throat.

She takes a breath and doesn't take another.

Count the hours. From the moment you first saw her till she took her final breath: she lived twelve hours. She'll be with you all your life.

Pack up and continue toward home. You have two more days to journey. One day of travel on the main road. One day to cross the Barotse Floodplain, board the leaking pontoon, paddle across the Zambezi, and drive on, through the sand.

Later you are told it is Helen who takes the body back and it is Helen who attends the funeral. Helen. Single, elderly, and white. A missionary vulnerably alone in a village black with sorrow. A year later she will be dead herself, from cancer. You can't remember; did you ever see her again? Did you ever say thank you?

Sardines

As Abigail grows the game of Hide and Seek becomes more sophisticated. She calls it Sardines and plays it in the dark, the hide-and-seek components reversed.

There is only one hider. All the rest are seekers. When a seeker finds the hider he joins in and they hide side by side. The hiders increase in number and squish together till they resemble sardines in a can.

The last seeker to find the group starts the game over and becomes the hidden one.

I Know Nothing Of—Zambia

He never could forgive himself for that day. As if, unconsciously, he conducted his own court case, found himself guilty, and locked a piece of himself up in his own private prison. "I don't want to talk about it," he said, burying the story.

But the wind still blows the sand away. And sometimes it uncovers memories of a road called Kafue, beside a large and rusting bus.

I told one friend. She said, "That young man in the village was strange. He disappeared as quickly as he gave his message? He must have been an angel."

I had known it long before. I knew in that brief juncture I had been protected.

But where was *her* angel in that moment of time?

I think about it often. Some days I pretend that she lived, and I make up all sorts of horrible stories for her life. I see her die of AIDS, starvation, and misused by an evil older husband. She is his youngest wife, the one that he desires. The worse the ending I can contrive the better.

Some days I picture her as a hero. Other parents in the village take notice of her death and teach their own youngsters to look before they cross. She saves the lives of three other village children.

In the end, all I can do is tell what happened. I am tied for eternity to a village in Zambia, linked to a family whose name I do not even know. I wonder sometimes what they remember. What stories they tell. Perhaps there are angels in their stories that I know nothing of.

Sunlight on My Face

I have played Hide and Seek most of my life. It has been long enough. There comes a point when every hider gets tired of hiding, climbs out of his cubby hole, says: *Here I am. Let's start over.*

These words are now my voice. This writing, my hand waving.

A funeral is, of necessity, a public thing. It needs mourners to attend. Look in the open coffin and grieve. Listen to the story. Lay it to rest.

Africa held me buried these long years, but a voice calls me out of the tomb and there is sunlight on my face. It is an astonishing thing to be alive.

The long funeral is over.

KAREN AN-HWEI LEE

Dream of Ink Brush Calligraphy

FROM *Poetry*

In prayer:
quiet opening,
my artery is a thin
shadow on paper—
margin of long grass,
ruderal hair, sister to this
not yet part of our bodies
your lyric corpus of seed
in rough drafts of pine ash,
chaogao or grass calligraphy
in rough drafts of pine ash—
your lyric corpus of seed
not yet part of our bodies:
ruderal hair, sister to this
margin of long grass,
shadow on paper,
my artery is a thin
quiet opening
in prayer.

BK LOREN

What It Is That Feeds Us

FROM *Orion*

COYOTES ARE CONSUMMATE ILLUSIONISTS. TAKE A WESTERN landscape, a few piñon pine gnarled like arthritic knuckles, chamisa blooming like handfuls of sunlight, mesas miraged in the distance, and there, on that wide horizon, they will materialize. Where there was nothing, now there is something, long-legged, loping. They give you their tough-guy glance and, panting, they move on. You barely believe you've seen them before they sink back into the earth. You think of the word *vanish*, and understand the sound of it now, the hard *v* at the beginning, the hush by the time it ends, how quickly something comes to nothing.

The Hubble telescope pointed its powerful lens at a bigger expanse of nothingness than any poet's wasteland could ever define, and more than ten thousand galaxies appeared, 78 billion light-years away, the distant past of them emerging before our eyes in a place that was once empty.

Place is never empty.

When I was a kid, my brother told me the Rocky Mountains surrounding our home were wolves, their jagged shoulder blades hunched up, heads lowered. Their coats changed with the seasons: snow white in winter, granite gray in summer. But to me the mountains looked like a sleeping dragon. The crags to the north: the spiny tail. The lumpy hogbacks to the south: the dragon's snout. I have always needed stories. Mountains were my first stories. They've been telling my life over and over ever since.

Now I am a writer, and I understand characters as bodies of land; they rise up from place like coyotes, like mountains, like me. I see the red dirt of Colorado and it looks like the marrow of my bones: gritty, rust-colored mud.

Without place, all stories become weightless, their characters dangling from dog-eared pages, hoping for a word to give them marrow, bone, body. Even the way we speak is formed by wind whistling across certain landscapes, the words of New Yorkers streetwise enough to turn corners too early, dropping *r*'s as they run to grab a cab; and the voice of a rural girl saying *haa-ay*, making it two syllables, as if she had all the time in the world.

Without place, every sentence is from nowhere.

For years after I'd grown, after my parents died, I lived in my childhood home. Over my lifetime, the small field behind the house had become a Hubble galaxy. On first glance: some land. Years later: the migrations of birds I knew better than any calendar could predict, down to the day—Swainson's hawks in mid-March, barn swallows in May. The turn of the day ticked in my ears like the rhythms of wings flying home. Night saturated me: howls of coyotes in the fields, wind skittering across ponds, predawn meadowlarks singing. The sound of the nearby train rumbled through my sleeping, a comfort, not an intrusion.

When I am embraced in place, I don't need to buy anything to organize my life. Each step appears in the sway of the day. I don't need anything to fill me. I sense what is possible, my day brimming with discovery where there was once familiarity, the land a palimpsest that layers with time.

The pretense that place does not matter turns us all into straw dogs subjected to the whims of marketing. If we are unattached, we need. We need so many things. If we point the lens into the core of us and no galaxy appears, then what? We dangle, storyless, bland words rolling across the windy landscapes of our tongues. We stay awake all hours of the night, peering out windows, until, at last, we let go of longing and accept the constellations that connect us all. We rest our eyes on a horizon that tells a story from the bones out, embraces us from the skin in, lets us rise from the dust of where we've been and where we are, like coyotes, hunting, hungry, finally knowing exactly what it is that feeds us.

PAUL MYERS

Apparitions & Visitations

FROM *Portland*

ONE DAY I WAS AT A CONFERENCE OF HEALTH CARE PROFESSIONALS when the speaker asked if anyone present had ever been visited by a dead relative. No one moved. Then a few hands inched upward, and everyone began to squirm. But the hands in the air kept multiplying until the vast majority of people in the room held a hand in the air.

What a relief I thought. I am not alone.

Jesus raised people from the dead, and He came back from the dead Himself, chatting amiably with friends and followers who had perhaps seen Him die. Saint Paul brought a boy back from the dead; the story is told that Paul was up late talking, and the boy fell asleep sitting in a window, and fell to his death; Paul interrupted his talk, went downstairs, brought the boy back to life, and went back upstairs to finish his story.

Three men were walking a trail in Yellowstone National Park, fly rods in hand. Suddenly one stopped and said *There's my dad coming down the trail.* The other men stopped also. No one spoke. A hawk sailed over. The wind combed through the pines. The man's father had been dead for many years. He had often taken his sons fishing in Yellowstone as the boys were growing up. Some things should be accepted for what they are. *Under the rocks are the words*, as Norman Maclean wrote, in his fishing memoir.

Saint Bernadette Soubirous was fetching firewood along a river when she saw the Madonna hovering in the air. She spoke to Bernadette in French and Latin. For more than a hundred years since that moment, people from all over the world have walked along that river, watching, listening, praying. I have done so.

One time when my cousin was in college he fell asleep in a house by a lake and when he awoke there was a woman with grey hair pulled into a bun and a dark flower-print dress sitting on the stool next to the couch looking at him. She smiled and leaned down and touched his head gently. He sat up suddenly, wide awake. There was no one there.

Five times in recent years a voice has whispered *Paul* in my ear, and when I turn there is no one there. I am not the only one this has happened to, even in my own house.

I know a young man whose cousin was killed. A few weeks later he was asleep when he felt a disc pressing his stomach and chest and shoulder, pressing down with enough force to wake him. He sat up in bed and saw a disc of light hovering in the air. He says he knew instantly it was his cousin's spirit. He reached over and turned on the light and the disc of light vanished.

There was a woman who came to America from Italy. She was a most kind, generous, and vivacious soul. Her house was always filled with visitors enjoying food and debate. She dearly loved birds and kept one as a pet. She was a devout woman and lived a long life. When she was buried the birds in the trees around her plot grew so loud you could hardly hear. Her granddaughter told me later that a small wild bird had flown into the house before the funeral and perched a while in the kitchen. When the granddaughter opened the front door the bird shot straight out of the house and was not seen again.

In the house where I grew up sometimes there would be a strong rapping on the front door and when my dad went to open it no one was there. Maybe this was a prank every time, but maybe not. Maybe it was a former resident or relative, now deceased. Maybe.

There was a man named George who had been in a war and never quite came home. He was an edgy man, especially harsh to his uncle Johnny. One day Johnny suddenly died from rheumatic fever. George was racked with guilt. On the day of the funeral, as the family trooped back into the kitchen after Johnny's funeral, the phone rang. George answered it. There was a long silence as he listened to the speaker at the other end of the line. George hung up the phone and fell into a kitchen chair, slack-jawed. That was Johnny, he said. He told me he forgave me and everything was fine between us and that I shouldn't feel so guilty. To the day he died George swore that it was Johnny on the phone that day.

A father died and his daughter climbed up to the lectern in church to eulogize him. She said in his last days she asked him if he was afraid to die. He said no, he was sure he would be reunited with family and friends who had died before him, but that he *had* been frightened by a dream he'd had about the afterlife. He had dreamed that after his death he was walking along a dirt road, passing people occasionally, and he was terrified that one of the strangers he passed on the road was Jesus, and he didn't recognize Him. He wanted all of us to hear his dream, said the daughter, so that you would all keep this in mind: *whatever you did for the least of my brothers, you did for me.*

A girl is asleep in her college dorm room. She feels a pressure on her stomach and chest and shoulder, pressing down with enough force to wake her. She sat up and saw her grandfather at the foot of the bed. He had died a month before. *I love you, he said. Don't worry about a thing. Everything is going to be just fine.* She felt a great peace and confidence and reassurance and fell back to sleep. Thornton Wilder's last words in *The Bridge of San Luis Rey:* "But soon we shall die . . . and we ourselves shall be loved for a while and forgotten. But the love will have been enough; all those impulses to love return to the love that made them. Even memory is not necessary for love. There is a land of the living and a land of the dead and the bridge is love, the only survival, the only meaning."

A nun once told me about her vibrant and lovely sister. The sister was flayed by cancer far too young. Sitting with her sister the nun in the hospital room, moments before her death, the sister said, intently, *I am going to be just fine. Everything will be alright.* Months later, the nun had a dream in which she was walking along the beach and her sister walked up to her and said again, *I am going to be just fine. Everything will be alright.* And the nun awoke and knew all was well.

The Gospel of Mark: When he saw that they were straining at the oars against an adverse wind, he came towards them early in the morning, walking on the sea . . . when they saw him walking on the sea, they thought it was a ghost and cried out; for they all saw him and were terrified. But immediately he spoke to them and said, Take heart, it is I; do not be afraid. Then he got into the boat with them and the wind ceased. And they were utterly astounded, for they did not understand . . .

. . .

For all of my years of training as a scientist and clinician, I have had experiences that I cannot explain away in sensible fashion, and I have come to the conclusion that sensible explanations only block the gift you may receive. I saw my brother-in-law's spirit leave a river canyon the day he drowned. I heard my dead grandfather call my name as I was wading along a trout stream. I felt a tremendous call to forgive my enemies the instant I finished drinking from the chalice that Blessed Basil Moreau used to celebrate Mass. I have spoken with the dead in my dreams. I knew the moment my beloved cousin died in a wreck far away. I have learned to wonder and ache and dream at this end of Thornton Wilder's bridge, as I see and hear from people at the other end. I believe with all my heart and soul that there is more on heaven and earth than I could ever dream of, and that this is God, from whom all blessings flow.

SEYYED HOSSEIN NASR

Harmony of Heaven, Earth and Man—Harmony of Civilizations

FROM *Sophia*

> *The following is the text of the keynote speech given at*
> *the Beijing Forum in October 2000. It is dedicated to*
> *Huston Smith.*

ANYONE SERIOUSLY CONCERNED WITH THE HUMAN CONDITION
today cannot but observe the presence of unprecedented crises and
disorder on so many planes of our existence from the spiritual, phil-
osophical and psychological to the social, economic and political to
the environmental that now threatens the very web of life here on
earth. Instead of seeking that harmony between Heaven, Earth and
Man, to use the terminology of classical Chinese tradition, which
has its correspondence in the other major traditions of humanity
from the Hindu and Buddhist to the Christian and Islamic, so
many today seek to live in disregard of this inner harmony and
there are even those who go so far as to deny that such a thing is
even possible or has any meaning. Ours is a world dominated by
self-interest of individuals, ethnic entities, economic groupings and
nations. We speak often of humanity but usually only in an abstract
sense and when we do seek to be unselfish, it is usually in making

our interests subservient to those of the group, organization or nation to which we belong and not to humanity as a whole, there being some exceptions that are still, however, very much a minority voice.

One can of course claim that it has always been and will therefore continue to be so, but such an assertion overlooks the radically changed situation in which we now live, one that requires our extending our view of "us" to embrace ultimately the whole of humanity. Before modern means of communication and production disrupted traditional patterns of life, brought different segments of humanity close to each other in an unprecedented manner, and caused the actions of people in one part of the world to affect vitally other parts, before the radioactive clouds of Chernobyl killed people in Lapland in Sweden and the carbon emission of one country caused devastating floods in lands far away, for men and women of one segment of humanity, *their* world was *the* world. A thousand years ago for a person living in China, China was for all practical purposes the world as such and Chinese society humanity itself; the same was also true *mutatis mutandis* for a Muslim, a Christian or a Hindu. There were seers and sages who did have a global vision of humanity, but for the vast majority such a vision seemed only theoretical and did not concern their practical lives in a concrete fashion. Nor did it need to do so except in rare cases. Even religions address the particular humanity for which they have been destined as humanity as such. For members of each civilization, their civilization was civilization pure and simple and those outside of it were often treated as uncivilized, barbarians, unbelievers, etc.

Into this natural order of things came modern Western civilization which not only sought to monopolize for itself the condition of being civilized and did so in a new totalitarian manner, but also attempted to destroy other civilizations in a fundamental way by negating the very legitimacy of any worldview other than its own. As its power spread all over the world, being civilized came to mean, for those who had become subservient to it no matter where they were living on the globe, being Europeanized (or Westernized) and modernized. This process itself made it unfashionable and redundant to speak in modern circles of civilizations in the plural. During the colonial period even opposition to this Western domination by Asians, Africans and others came usually not in the name of other civilizations and their traditions but in the form of the modern European idea of nationalism, the case of the movement of Mahatma Gandhi in India and some of the anti-colonial movements in the Islamic world being exceptions to the rule. It is therefore quite significant that during the past two decades, due partly to the otherwise flawed thesis of Samuel Huntington, discourse on civilizations in the plural has again become prevalent.

It is indeed significant that we now speak of civilizations, the importance of their harmonious existence and the dangers inherent in their possible confrontations. To speak in these terms is to realize already the truth that, despite its spread world-wide, Western civilization has *not* been able to destroy until now, nor is it likely to do so in the future, the other major civilizations of the world and the worldviews or "presiding Ideas" that have created various civilizations. In fact as a result of major crises within Western civilization itself, many in the West have become deeply attracted to the philosophies, religions, arts, social teachings, and even sciences and technologies of the other civilizations which were considered as being irrelevant by so many until recently. Much has been written in the West itself, on the basis of unprecedented access to the sources of the wisdom of other civilizations and driven often by the search for truths largely lost as a consequence of the triumph of modernism in the West, about the remarkable similarity in the teachings of various wisdom traditions including that of the traditional West, the wisdom to which many of us refer as the *sophia perennis* or *philosophia perennis*.

Furthermore, on the basis of these teachings many have come to understand the deeper reasons for the crises of modernism, chief among them being what can be called the rebellion against Heaven and consequently the loss of harmony with the Earth. They have come to realize how the spread of the modern worldview has resulted in unprecedented conflicts on so many levels, in the rise of individualism resulting in the weakening of the social order, in the spread of psychological imbalance among so many members of modern society, in the unprecedented environmental crisis with terrifying consequences for the future of all of humanity if the crisis is allowed to continue, in the weakening of the moral order individually and collectively, in the unprecedented disparity between the rich and the poor, in the existence of abject material poverty amidst economic prosperity for some, in the injustice of a so-called global political order which in reality is a disorder based on the domination by force of the weak by the strong and in many other problems whose solutions are vital to humanity as a whole. It does not take a prophet to foresee that the solution to so many of our predicaments lies in the creation of harmony between and within our civilizations.

Harmony between civilizations is, however, not possible without harmony between Heaven, Earth, and Man, between *T'ien*, *Ti*, and *Jen*, within the being of each of us to the extent possible in the chaotic world in which we live. We must re-establish moral order within ourselves and on that basis in the world about us remembering what is written in the *Analects* of Confucius, "He who rules by moral force (*tê*) is like the pole-star, which remains in its place while all the lesser stars do homage to it." (Book II, Arthur Waley translation) Except that now the arena of our moral actions must be humanity and in fact creation as a whole. Our vision of such a global order must, moreover, be based not on the espousal of relativism and a secularist humanism anchored in the ever shifting sands of terrestrial human nature and on the destruction of our own traditions in the name of the bland least common denominator between our cultures, but on the true nature of man that is foundational to all of our traditions and as confirmed in the perennial philosophy lying at the heart of our wisdom traditions, to what we can also justly call the "unanimous tradition." The task of those who possess this global and at the same time universal vision is to seek harmony, based on mutual respect, between different civilizations on the basis of the re-establishment at first within ourselves and then within the being of those we are able to lead to this vision of harmony with both Heaven and Earth. Without the establishment of this inner harmony, our discourses about the harmony between civilizations cannot but remain mere talk, the creation of a lot of sound and fury signifying nothing, to reformulate the famous line of Shakespeare.

Man is a thinking being and how he thinks usually determines how he acts. Let us then mention a few concrete ideas that can play a crucial role in how we can act in trying to achieve that harmony between civilizations that we all seek.

The present-day *de facto* interconnectedness between different individuals, societies and civilizations requires us to go beyond all parochialism. We must re-examine what we consider to be our ethnic, national, cultural and even civilizational interests in light of the inevitable role that the interests of the "other" can and does have for our own ultimate interests. We must realize that every other civilization also considers itself as the "Middle Kingdom," to use the classical Chinese concept, and that "center" where Heaven and Earth meet exists in one form or another for the "other" as it does for us. We must respect the integrity of other civilizations and the precious truths and realities they bear within themselves no matter how different they might be on the outward plane from what we consider to be "ours." In this context one should recall the wise words of the ancient sage of China, Confucius. In his *Analects* he says, "The man of perfect virtue (*jen*), wishing to be established himself, seeks also to establish others; wishing to be enlarged himself, he seeks to enlarge others." (Book VI; James Legge translation) In light of and on the basis of this mutual respect, all of those who seek harmony between civilizations must oppose the establishment of a global order based on purely material factors and bent on destroying the precious diversity of human civilizations and cultures. Harmony after all presumes the existence of diversity whose destruction results not in harmony but in a deadening uniformity that can only impoverish humanity and be most destructive for the rich spiritual heritage that we have received from our traditions.

We must seek to revive the idea of what the eminent Chinese Confucian scholar and philosopher Tu Weiming has called anthropocosmic man. This idea is profoundly Chinese but it is not only Chinese. Rather, it has its correspondence in other cultures. According to this thesis taught by all of our wisdom traditions, man is not an island unto himself, a subject who creates his own objective reality. Rather, his true nature binds him to an objective world that has its ontological reality independent of his subjectivism and his being includes an organic link to both the society in which he lives, an idea so much emphasized in classical Chinese thought, and also to humanity as a whole. It also includes the profoundest relations with the world of nature and in fact the whole of cosmic reality, with both Heaven and Earth of classical Chinese cosmology.

The revival of awareness within us of the reality of the anthropocosmic man as our true nature should have direct consequences for how we act on every level in our lives. It means the recreation of balance between ourselves and the natural world that surrounds us. It means the regaining of that state of "naturalness" of which classical Far Eastern schools such as Ch'an or Zen in Japanese have spoken so eloquently. It means a new understanding of the boundaries with which we define ourselves as individuals, societies, nations and even civilizations and of how we see ourselves in relation to all those we consider as "others." On the basis of the inner harmony attained through the realization of this "naturalness," which is the antipode of giving free reign to what we call our natural instincts, we can then seek harmony with the society in which we live and create an economic and political order based not simply on selfishness, greed, aggression and domination, but on harmony in relation to the "other" based on integrity and the preservation of wholeness.

Let us not forget that harmony is based on the existence of plurality. One cannot create musical harmony if one can play only a single note. Uniformity that destroys all pluralism does not result in a life of harmony but leads to the monotony of death. The harmony between civilizations and also with the world of nature of which we speak so often these days and whose realization has now become not a far-fetched ideal but a matter of life and death for humanity, implies forming a new attitude towards pluralism whether it be concerned with the ethnic, the religious, the cultural, the social or the civilizational and ultimately with even non-human forms of life.

Moreover, this pluralism must be understood not as what those philosophers who defend modernism consider as a so-called "universalism" that is based on sheer relativism and denial of all truth claims. This is but a pseudo-universalism that cannot but lead to intellectual suicide. The pluralism of which I speak is itself based on the truth and means clinging to the truths of our own tradition while respecting the "other" without denying that there is such a thing as error. If there is no truth, there is no error and if there is no goodness, there is no evil.

As far as civilizations are concerned, authentic pluralism means cultivating respect for other civilizations and honoring the way of life, thought, culture and actions of others even if they are different from our own. It requires the cultivation of the attitude of cooperation rather than aggression and domination. Surely there cannot be harmony between those who are aggressors and who seek to dominate by force and those who are the subjects of aggression and domination.

In speaking of harmony between civilizations it is necessary to mention also the significance of harmony within civilizations. Rarely in history have there been civilizational wars and confrontations. Most discord has come between nations, tribes, and ethnic groups within a single civilization and even between the alliance of elements belonging to two different civilizations against other alliances of groups also belonging to the two civilizations in question. Our histories are replete with such occurrences as for example when the Ottomans and the Safavids, both belonging to Islamic civilization, made alliances with different European powers such as the French, British and the Austro-Hungarians all belonging to Western civilization with the aim of gaining the upper hand in the confrontation with each other. Some in fact have criticized the whole thesis of the "clash of civilizations" on the basis of this historical and also present-day reality. But they are wrong as far as this particular criticism is concerned for civilizations remain powerful realities even if there does not exist harmony among various nations and the diverse groupings within them. If we do not exert ourselves to create that harmony, conditions are such that the world could in fact move towards confrontations of colossal dimensions among civilizations themselves. Already those who speak of "the West and the rest" are propagating civilizational confrontation. We must, therefore, seek both inter- and intra-civilizational harmony here and now.

To achieve this harmony both among ourselves and with the "others" we must cultivate a holistic view of life, a vision that is deeply embedded in our wisdom traditions no matter to which civilization we belong. We must strengthen our organic bond with not only our own social group, not only with minorities living among us, whether they be of an ethnic, racial, linguistic or religious nature, not only with the rest of our own civilization with whom we share profound commonalities, but also with people belonging to other civilizations, with the whole of humanity. We must be ever mindful that the Heaven with which man must be in harmony is symbolized by the sky that covers us all and the Earth with which man must seek to live harmoniously is one upon which we all walk. A situation has been created in these times in which awareness of this holistic vision is no longer only an ideal of a few seers and visionaries, as it has always been, but an imperative reality without whose realization we shall face impending disaster collectively. Nowhere is this more evident than in the global environmental crisis where we see so clearly that discord rather than harmony with the world of nature affects not only those who have created, live and act on the basis of this discord, but humanity as a whole.

Being the first Muslim to be given the honor of delivering a key-note speech at this prestigious Forum, I find it necessary to say in conclusion a few words about the possibility of harmony between Islamic and Chinese civilizations which have had such a long historical relation with each other and which possess geographical contiguity. Already during the Sassanid period the Persian Empire, which later became a major center of Islamic civilization, had profound relations with the Chinese. The Silk Road was even then not only a route on which goods from silk and jade to carpets were transported back and forth, but also a means of communication of ideas and cultural elements, of arts and sciences and even of religions. Let us not forget that Buddhism first came to China from the eastern provinces of the Persian Empire. And this exchange in so many domains became more accentuated with the establishment of Islamic civilization.

The city of Kashghar that is now in China was a thriving center of Islamic civilization in its Persianate form. Over the centuries Chinese painting began to influence the Persian miniature. Chinese astronomers were to be found in Tabriz and Persian ones in Beijing. Works on Chinese medicine were translated and paraphrased in Persian. Stories from China appeared in Persian literature including some of its masterpieces such as the works of Nizāmī. Islamic science had some influence on the development of Chinese science. A technology as central as the production of paper (the Persian word for which, *kāghaz*, comes from Chinese) reached the Islamic world from China and it was from the Islamic world that it reached Europe. And then there is the whole question of the presence of Muslims in China and the transformation brought about in classical Islamic learning in China in the 17th century through the translation of a number of seminal Persian texts by Jāmī and others into the language of classical neo-Confucianism.

The full account of the historical contact on numerous levels from technology to astronomy to philosophy between Islam and China has yet to be written. It is one about which much needs to be said for many reasons not least of which is that it is one of the most fascinating inter-civilizational contacts in world history. Moreover, this long history can play a fundamental role today in the creation of harmony between these two civilizations on the basis of more than expediency. Huntington considers the alliance between Islamic and Chinese civilizations to be of the greatest danger to the West. But is this really true? Such an alliance might be against certain interests of the West in Asia and Africa, but surely if we understand the value of harmony of civilizations in the sense noted above, surely such an accord does not need to be at the expense of the destruction of harmonious existence of either civilization with the West itself. In fact the creation of harmony between any two civilizations cannot but be of benefit to the whole of humanity as long as it is not created simply for the sake of political or economic interest and in order to strengthen the hands of those in accord to confront and combat another civilization seen as the common enemy.

In light of the reality of the dire situation existing in the world today resulting from consideration of only selfish interests and the domination of the weak by the strong, the vision of intra- and inter-civilizational harmony appears to many as simply an illusion and at best a dream. But in fact it is our only hope for the avoidance of global disaster. To live a life of harmony with both Heaven and Earth, to realize the organic nexus that binds us to all of creation, to seek harmony and peace among ourselves, among our civilizations and with the natural world, these are our only means of survival as a species, our only means of salvation as real human beings. They are not simply niceties to be spoken of and then forgotten—they must be put into action in our everyday lives as individuals, societies and civilizations.

As the famous Chinese proverb states, "The journey of a thousand miles begins with a single step." As far as the journey to create harmony between civilizations and prosperity in both its spiritual and economic sense are concerned, that single step must of necessity be the creation of harmony within ourselves, harmony with both Heaven and Earth. Only after having taken that first step can we take the other steps necessary to create harmony both within our own civilization and with other civilizations. Upon the success of our endeavor in this task depends the future of the life of humanity in this world. Let us take this first step and then strive to complete with hope and determination the difficult journey of a thousand miles that lies ahead, bringing the caravan of our civilizations safely home to the terminal point of our journey wherein is to be found the abode of peace and harmony.

DAVID NOVAK

Why Are the Jews Chosen?

FROM *First Things*

ONE WAY ANTI-JEWISH SENTIMENT HAS BEEN INTERPRETED IS
simply as a *quid pro quo*. Gentile animosity, in this view, does to the
Jews what the Jews have done, or at least would like to do, to
Gentiles—because we Jews present ourselves as the *chosen* people.
In the seventeenth century, Baruch Spinoza suggested that the Jews
made the Gentiles hate them by claiming to be God's people and
setting themselves apart by their practice of circumcision—the
bodily sign of God's covenantal election. In 1938, immediately after
the Nazi pogroms of *Kristallnacht*, George Bernard Shaw wondered
why the Jews were complaining so loudly; after all, wasn't this what
the chosen people did to the Canaanites in the process of conquer-
ing the promised land?

In this view of Jewish chosenness—given its clearest expression,
after the Holocaust, in George Steiner's 1999 novel *The Portage to
San Cristóbal of A.H.*—envy of the Jews' claim made the Nazis do
two things. The first was to accuse the Jews not only of having in-
vented their chosenness but also of having invented the God who
chose them. As Steiner's Hitler asks, "Was there ever a crueler in-
vention, a contrivance more calculated to harrow human existence,
than that of an omnipotent, all-seeing, yet invisible, impalatable, in-
conceivable God?" And the second was to argue that, because there

can be only one chosen people, it must be either the Jews or (in this case) the Germans. One must extinguish the other from the face of the earth. There is no possible middle ground, no possible compromise.

There are Jews today who seem to hold this view, even if they do not like to ascribe it, as Steiner does, to Hitler. They have concluded that if the affirmation of chosenness by God is the cause of near extinction, Jews must root that affirmation out entirely. And for some Jews, this denial of election means denial of God—a denial that fits, unfortunately, with the atheistic agenda of some of the more radical Jewish secularists, who think they can build a thoroughly secular Judaism. The denial lives at a primal, emotional level: "Since God's choice of us Jews has led to death and destruction, we now *unchoose* Him!" This is the dead-god atheism of Nietzsche rather than the there-never-was-a-god atheism of Feuerbach.

I remember this myth being thrown in my face little more than ten years after the Holocaust, when, as a Jewish teenager, I was confronted in our Chicago high school by another Jewish student—Sam, who screamed at me for wanting "to be chosen by *that* god," after most of his family in Europe was murdered in Auschwitz. Compared to Sam's anger, the occasional taunts from Gentile classmates were mild. And ever since that afternoon in 1956, I have tried to think of what I should, or could, have said in response.

Along the way, I also have found that Sam is legion.

We might begin with the obvious point that biological identity is natural while national identity is constructed. Even when God chose Israel, he did not create the people of Israel as he created its human members, as natural beings. Instead, God formed the people of Israel from individual human beings already living in the natural world, calling them into a new historical identity.

These identities are necessarily related, but they are not the same. No one lives without some sort of political-cultural identity, and all political-cultural groups are made up of individual human members—but persons are not a people, and a people is not a person.

Most Jews, like most rational persons, know that their personal identity and their ethnic identity are not one and the same. Some Jews, in fact, seem to have concluded that their political-cultural survival might work against their individual biological survival. If there is a much greater chance that I and my children will be killed because we are identifiable as Jews than if we become (or pass as) Gentiles, then isn't assimilation the most reasonable means? Some evidence for this exists in the extremely low birth rate among more secularized Jews, their high intermarriage rate, and the fact that they are much more likely to convert to other religions than are religious Jews. They've chosen to be unchosen, and many of them have been quite successful in their practical denial of election, at least by this-worldly criteria.

To reach the idea that physical survival trumps ethnic survival, however, we have to assume that ethnic survival must be for the sake of personal survival. Jewish tradition teaches the opposite: The survival of the Jewish people takes precedence over the survival of individual Jews. A Jew is required to marry, bring children into the world, and rear them with a Jewish identity, even if this means that their chances of individual survival will be lessened. Under the most extreme conditions, the cultural-religious survival of the Jewish people altogether trumps the physical survival of any individual Jew.

Privileging ethnic survival makes sense only when one understands that the survival of the Jewish people is not self-justifying: As a genuine task for Jews, survival requires a transcendent purpose and reason for existence, and a claim that without ethnic survival, Jews will sink into individual or collective nihilism. Even though, according to Jewish theology, Jews cannot, *de jure*, cease being Jews, they can, *de facto*, hide that theological fact from human eyes. Moreover, a Jew can terminate his Jewish familial lineage by siring Gentile children with a Gentile woman. According to Jewish law, a Jewish woman can give birth to Jewish children sired by a Gentile father; the chances are great, however, that such children will not identify with the Jewish people in any tangible way, and their descendants will be even less likely to do so.

Jewish ethnic and religious survival thus depends on the active choice of Jews to advocate Judaism in authentically Jewish ways—which means Jews must actively choose to be chosen. They confirm the theological fact that God has chosen Israel for an everlasting covenant, the constitution of which is the Torah. And this requires that the Torah be taught, and its commandments kept, as much as is humanly possible.

All of this is a way of expressing what I should have told Sam all those years ago: There is a necessary connection between the choice of the Jewish people to survive and the central doctrine of God's election of Israel in the giving of the Torah.

The centrality and ultimacy of the Torah is expressed in one of the most famous stories in the Talmud: the story of the martyrdom of Rabbi Akiva ben Joseph. This event occurred around 135 C.E., when the imperial Roman authorities in Palestine had outlawed the rabbis' public teaching of Torah. The Romans, no doubt, regarded the Jews' public religious gatherings as potentially revolutionary, and in the case of Rabbi Akiva, an outspoken supporter of revolutionary leader Simeon bar Kokhba, they were right.

When Rabbi Akiva defied the ban, he set himself up for an inevitable, painful execution. When another Jew asked him why he was engaging in what seemed, to someone of little faith, to be a suicidal course of action, he answered with this parable: A fox was walking alongside a river and saw fish, who were forming groups in the stream. He asked, "What are you fleeing?" And they answered, "From the nets humans cast over us." He said to them: "Wouldn't you like to come up here to dry land so that I and you can dwell together like my ancestors dwelt with your ancestors?" They said to him: "You're the one reputed to be the smartest of the animals! You're not smart, but a fool! If in our vital habitat [*bi-mqom hayyutenu*] we are afraid, in a place where we will certainly die, how much more so?"

For Rabbi Akiva, the Torah is the vital public habitat of the Jews. As scripture says, "It is your life [*hayyekha*]." Without Jewish engagement in the public teaching and learning of Torah, the Jewish people as a distinct community cannot survive. Neither can individual Jews survive as Jews in private without the public dimension of their covenantal religion.

This leaves open, of course, the question of whether the Torah exists for the sake of the survival of the Jews, or the Jews survive for the sake of the Torah. Because the Jewish people are chosen by God and commanded by him to "choose life," and because this life means more than mere physical existence, a Jewish life can be lived cogently only when its purpose transcends its own contingent presence in the world. God chose us to live both in body and in soul, but the body functions for the sake of the soul more than the soul functions for the body.

The perfect Torah "restores the soul," as the Psalms say, which means the soul does not restore itself without being in a strong covenantal relationship with God—a relationship constituted by the Torah and nothing else. Without the public teaching and practice of Torah, not only have the Jews lost their reason for existing but the whole world has lost its reason for existence. To emphasize creation's dependence on the Torah, the Talmud cites Jeremiah 33:25: "Were My covenant not by day and by night, I would not have made the very structures of heaven and earth."

Only humans can be the free subjects of commandments. And only humans can freely relate back to God—the perpetual giver of the Torah—as the active recipients of the Torah, in the context of God's covenant. As in God's covenant with all creation at the time of Noah, both covenanted partners are irrevocably pledged to remain faithful forever. There are no exit clauses in this asymmetrical mutual partnership in which God is the senior partner and the elected community is the junior partner.

The covenanted community should have been universal humankind, uniquely created in the image of God. But since the debacle of the Tower of Babel, there has been no universal human community—only the separate and distinct peoples in this world. Indeed, a real universal human community is only a messianic desideratum, not a human project. That is why—as it seems from the juxtaposition in Genesis of the Tower of Babel event and the life and career of Abraham—God chose Abraham and those born from him (and those who have attached themselves to his house) to be the covenanted community that God needs for the Torah to do its work in the world.

God seems to see, in a way that is hidden from human eyes, potential in the children of Abraham for the Torah to be kept in their midst until the end of days. That potential will be fully actualized in the future; it is not reward for past meritorious human achievement. Jews by themselves cannot actualize their covenantal potential.

Acceptance by Jews of our chosen status—when we do accept it—is much more an acceptance of God's electing claim on us than a demand that the world recognize our this-worldly superiority, whether moral, political, or even religious. Whatever George Steiner's fictional Hitler and others more real might think, we are a chosen people, not a master race. We were chosen to be the trustees of God's Torah, and this is why we must survive as a people, even if it entails walking a dangerous path in this world. Just as a commandment is best fulfilled when a Jew understands *why* God gave each commandment the way he did, so the Jews' chosenness is best lived for—and died for—when we understand the uniquely divine purpose for which God chose us.

Here and now, this prepares us to understand how we can survive the shadow of the Holocaust, surviving it without forgetting it. We must survive, even living as fully as possible in this world, because God needs Israel for the sake of his holy Torah, so that God's presence does not vanish from the earth because there is no place for it here. We do not know *why* we have suffered; we know only *for what and for whom* we have survived our suffering.

Those who have truly made God's Torah their purpose in this world will survive not only the Holocaust but also the memory of all the lesser holocausts; they will remember them without ever being done in by them. They will live again to see the time when God's Torah will "be written on their hearts" (Jer. 33:31–33), and they will keep its commandments freely. They will not commit the suicide of the Jewish soul by succumbing to the despair that follows when the Holocaust becomes our central point of reference rather than something the Torah teaches that God Himself will conquer, when he "will destroy death forever, and will wipe away tears from every face" (Isaiah 25:8).

The Holocaust, taken by itself, is a black hole. To look at it directly is to be swallowed up by it. The Holocaust can be glanced at only sideways, from the safe haven of being God's chosen people, here and now. Only everlasting life will finally explain death. Death can never explain life; it can only try to destroy it. "I shall not die but live to declare the works of the Lord" (Psalms 118:17), doing the work that God has placed before Jews to do in this world. It is work that anticipates the joyous life of the world yet to come. Yet even that anticipation never lets us forget the agony of this world, even as it helps us survive it.

EVAN OSNOS

The Next Incarnation

FROM *The New Yorker*

THE DALAI LAMA'S BIRTHDAY PARTY, AN EVENT HE HAS NEVER much cared for, was set to begin at 9 A.M. on July 6th, in the Indian Himalayan town of Dharamsala, where he lives. He skips the party most years, but he had promised to attend his seventy-fifth, so five thousand people turned up at the temple that morning, in a humid downpour, to await his arrival.

The exiled spiritual and political leader of Tibet—His Holiness to Buddhists, and HHDL to his Twitter followers—settled in Dharamsala half a century ago, after rejecting China's claims to his homeland and trekking over the mountains to India. He was followed by thousands of refugees, many of whom expected a short stay; when they were urged to plant trees in their settlements, they waved off the idea. "People said, 'We're going to be going back in a few years,'" Thubten Samphel, a writer and spokesman for the government in exile, recalled. "Trees will take fifty years to grow, so what's the point?"

Today, Dharamsala is the capital for more than a hundred and fifty thousand Tibetans in exile worldwide. Set high on a ridge, in the shadow of snowbound peaks, the town is a mix of refugee community and hippie retreat, with dreadlocked Israeli backpackers jostling among freshly shorn monks. For the more than five million

Tibetans living inside Chinese borders, the Dalai Lama remains a venerated figure, and he is surprisingly present in their daily conversation. Families in Tibet routinely contact his office with the request that he name their newborns.

A few minutes after nine, a band with drums and bagpipes marched into the temple courtyard, playing the Tibetan national anthem, which is illegal in Tibet. After the band came a throng of monks in maroon-and-saffron robes, and at its center was the Dalai Lama, ambling up the path from his office with a side-to-side gait, stooped forward "like a middle linebacker," as his friend the late Abe Rosenthal, of the *Times*, once put it. At the stage, he pivoted to face the audience with a look of wide-eyed astonishment, an expression that he applies to many things. He sat down beneath a banner inscribed in his honor: "The sun in the sky, the jewel of the world, the light of our hearts, may you live a long life."

The festivities that followed seemed to owe less to temple rituals than to those of a Midwestern ice-cream social. The Dalai Lama took in some school-dance-troupe performances, greeted members of the local Lions Club, and handed out public-service prizes. Then came some of the supremely odd moments that one has come to expect in the company of the Dalai Lama: A smiling Indian man approached the stage and unrolled a gift, a large portrait of the birthday boy, which the artist had painted in his own blood. Later, the Dalai Lama accepted a present from an eight-year-old Indian girl who is regarded as a prophet. She once predicted that he would fall ill, and he subsequently contracted a gallbladder infection. (Recently, she prophesied that Tibet would be an independent country by 2016.)

In the past decade or so, the Dalai Lama has also required hospital visits for a pinched nerve and dysentery, facts that are carefully recorded not only in Dharamsala but also in Beijing and Washington, D.C., where his future figures into some complicated political prognoses. When I asked him how it feels to have his aches and pains become a matter of geopolitical record, he smiled and said, "Some Chinese—I think, ten years ago—created a rumor: 'Dalai Lama is suffering from cancer, only a few months left!'" He said that he had been having regular checkups. "According to physicians, my body is very good. But it seems the Chinese know more about my condition!" He erupted in laughter.

The Dalai Lama's death, which he calls a "change of clothing," is not a taboo subject; as a Buddhist, he says, "I visualize death every day," and the political stakes are too large to ignore. As a practical matter, he believes that the traditional practice of identifying a young Tibetan boy as his reincarnation may no longer make sense, not only because he lives in exile but also because times have changed. He has taken to musing aloud that he might be reincarnated as a woman, or that Tibetans might vote on whether the institution of the Dalai Lama should continue at all. Or, he says, he might select his own reincarnation while he is still alive—a theological twist known as *madhey tulku*—which would give him the chance to train a successor and avoid the gap in leadership that has always been a time of instability for Tibetans. Only one thing is certain, he says: his successor will be found outside Tibet.

China disagrees. The government has passed a series of laws stipulating that it has ultimate authority over the "management of living Buddha reincarnation," an act of remarkable intellectual flexibility for the officially atheist Communist Party. After the 1989 death of the Panchen Lama, the second most prominent lama in Tibet, the Dalai Lama identified Gehdun Choekyi Nyima, a Tibetan boy who was six years old at the time, as the reincarnation, but Chinese authorities were incensed by the Dalai Lama's involvement from abroad, and the boy and his family were placed in seclusion. They have not been seen since. The government says the Panchen Lama does not want to be disturbed. In Dharamsala, his face appears on flyers with the tagline "The World's Youngest Political Prisoner."

The Chinese government eventually named its own choice of a child as Panchen Lama: Gyaltsen Norbu, who now holds several official posts. Unless something changes, a comparable standoff is almost certain after the Dalai Lama dies, a scenario that is likely to fuel unrest in Tibet and, potentially, affect the behavior of the Chinese government, making it one of the few foreign-policy questions that hinge on matters of reincarnation. A senior Obama Administration official told me that the White House is expecting "something like the Avignon popes," the feud that upended Europe in the fourteenth century with a competition among multiple Catholic authorities.

The Fourteenth Dalai Lama—Jetsun Jamphel Ngawang Losang Yeshe Tenzin Gyatso, known to many Tibetans as "the Presence"—has a biography so ripe for mythmaking that Hollywood has sought to capture it on film several times—once directed by Martin Scorsese and once starring Brad Pitt. Despite his oft-stated intention to abandon political life ("Retirement is also my human right"), the Dalai Lama has served longer than Queen Elizabeth, Fidel Castro, and other durable leaders, having taken the throne at the age of five, notwithstanding the fact that, for most of that time, he has not had much to rule.

Officially, the Dalai Lama is the senior religious leader of Tibetan Buddhism, though most of his admirers know him from other pursuits. He has lent his name to at least a hundred books, on subjects ranging from ethics to the interaction between science and religion, and, more recently, "Business, Buddhism, and Happiness in an Interconnected World." (Some of these he wrote; many are edited collections of his speeches.) He is the unlikeliest avatar of the global age: a reincarnate lama who didn't set foot in the West until he was nearly forty and, to this day, holds no passport. (He travels on the yellow document of a refugee.) He has evolved from an oddity to a sage and a reluctant icon of endurance. When he alighted in Vancouver in 2004, tickets for his stadium speech sold out within twenty minutes, a spectacle that seemed to his biographer Pico Iyer as if "a president was visiting, in the company of Mick Jagger."

Along the way, the Dalai Lama has prevented Tibetans from being relegated, with the Chinese Uighurs and the Nordic Sami people, to the fringes of history. In the words of Robert Thurman, the Columbia professor and former monk, Tibetans became "the baby seals of the human-rights movement."

That has poisoned his relationship with the one country he needs most: China. Its government considers him a "criminal" and a "false religious leader," intent on "splitting the motherland." The Communist Party chief in Tibet has called China's struggle against the Dalai Lama "a fight to the death." Just as his friend Pope John Paul II was once an icon of opposition to the Soviet empire, the Dalai Lama has become the face of resistance to Chinese rule.

The conflict has taken an especially bitter turn in recent years. On March 10, 2008, several hundred monks in Lhasa conducted a march to demand the release of Tibetans detained for celebrating the U.S. government's awarding of the Congressional Gold Medal to the Dalai Lama. Dozens of the monks were arrested and, on March 14th, a demonstration to protest their detention became violent: gangs of Tibetans attacked Chinese police and turned on other symbols of China's presence, throwing stones at Chinese civilians and burning and looting about a thousand Chinese-owned shops. The violence resulted in the worst riots in Tibet since the eighties; eleven civilians and a Tibetan were burned to death after hiding in buildings set on fire by rioters, and a policeman and six civilians died from beatings or other causes, according to the government. Security forces eventually moved in with armored vehicles to take over the city, and the authorities began a roundup of suspects, leading to hundreds of arrests. Tibetan exile groups alleged that eighty Tibetans were killed in the crackdown in Lhasa and elsewhere, a claim that China denies. The Chinese government eventually blamed the riots on what it called the "Dalai clique," though the Dalai Lama called for calm and vowed to resign his political duties if the violence did not end.

The uprising was a turning point for both sides. For the Chinese, it shattered a fragile confidence in Tibetan loyalty. For the Dalai Lama, it forced him to confront a gap between Tibetans' rage and his own aversion to violence. Though he is sharply critical of Chinese policy in Tibet—especially the restrictions on religion and language—he disavows even nonviolent marches and hunger strikes, in the belief that they lead to confrontation. The violence left him shaken; in a remark that startled his supporters worldwide, he said, in October of that year, "As far as I'm concerned, I have given up."

His aides later softened the comment, but the Dalai Lama's patience was fraying, as was that of many of his followers. They revere him as a religious authority, but many exiles have concluded that his political strategy is hopeless. "It's time for His Holiness to recognize the reality that China has no need to talk to us. They are playing for time," Lhasang Tsering, an outspoken Tibetan exile who fought as a guerrilla against China in the early seventies, told me. "Soon, Tibet will be filled with Chinese. We will be wiped out." To invoke patience and virtue in the face of "genocidal and colonial rule," Tsering says, is akin to "national suicide, and that, to me, is the ultimate violence."

The Dalai Lama's predicament is especially striking because it reflects deep changes in the global balance of power. In 1989, his thirtieth year abroad, he won the Nobel Peace Prize and had recently been invited to address the Human Rights Caucus of the U.S. Congress as well as the European Parliament. China, meanwhile, was isolated and reeling from the bloodshed in Tiananmen Square, and straining to jump-start an economy that was smaller than Spain's. Craving international support, Beijing authorities invited the Dalai Lama to make his first trip there in decades, to attend the funeral of a high-ranking lama. But his advisers worried that accepting the trip could weaken his bargaining position and he declined, a decision that senior aides now regret and some scholars say is symptomatic of the Dalai Lama's unwillingness to make the compromises needed to reach a resolution with Beijing. In the words of Melvyn Goldstein, a Tibet scholar at Case Western Reserve University, the Dalai Lama's ostensible successes at building support in the West "look more and more like Pyrrhic victories." Of the decision to appoint a Panchen Lama, Goldstein writes, "From China's perspective, once again, at a critical time, the Dalai Lama had thumbed his nose at Beijing."

By the Dalai Lama's fiftieth anniversary in exile, China had entered the World Trade Organization, invested heavily to raise the standard of living in Tibet, and emerged as an economic behemoth. In recent months, Chinese authorities have arrested Tibetan artists and intellectuals in a wave of suppression that activists describe as the most widespread in years. But the Dalai Lama and his advocates struggle to be heard. "It's almost impossible now," the actor Richard Gere, who chairs the board of the International Campaign for Tibet, told me recently.

Gere, since coming into contact with the Dalai Lama three decades ago, has helped turn Tibet into a favored cause in Hollywood. The Tibetan movement once lobbied to keep China out of international organizations. Today, Gere describes more modest goals: "We're working with every government and saying, 'You have to bring up Tibet. In every discussion, that's the minimum.' And they all say they do it." He added, "Whether it's just checked—'O.K., we spoke the word "Tibet,"'—or how deep are they getting into it? That's a state secret."

In recent years, China has declared Tibet a "core interest" of national importance, and has been remarkably successful in lobbying foreign governments to refrain from meeting with the Dalai Lama: since 2007, the leaders of Australia, the Netherlands, and New Zealand, as well as the Pope, have declined to see him. Between 2005 and 2008, he met with twenty-one national leaders; in 2009, that count dropped to two, according to Robert Barnett, a Tibet scholar at Columbia. In 1998, Apple annoyed the Chinese government by featuring a photograph of the Dalai Lama in a series of ads that included Muhammad Ali, Gandhi, and Picasso. These days, the online store for Chinese iPhone users does not offer such applications as "Dalai Lama Quotes" and "Nobel Laureates." ("We continue to comply with local laws," an Apple spokesperson said.)

One of the starkest measures of the Dalai Lama's precarious position, however, has come from an unexpected source. When Barack Obama entered the White House, Tibet activists expected a swift embrace. As a senator, Obama had met the Dalai Lama, who is a rare crossover star in Washington, with advocates from both the Bay Area and the Bible Belt. (In October, 2007, he stood between George Bush and House Speaker Nancy Pelosi in the Rotunda of the Capitol to receive the Congressional Gold Medal, the government's highest civilian honor.) But, as he prepared for his first visit to the new Administration, the Washington *Post* broke the news that he and Obama would delay their White House meeting until after the President's official trip to China, that November. It was the first time since 1991 that the Dalai Lama would come to the U.S. capital without seeing the President. Tibet supporters were taken aback. "We all had the first initial reaction: How could you possibly do that?" Gere said.

At the time, the White House was seeking China's support on North Korea, Iran, climate change, and other issues. According to a senior Administration official, Chinese diplomats had privately and adamantly sought a delay in the Dalai Lama's visit, arguing that a visit in the run-up to the Beijing summit would, in the official's words, "prejudice the trip." White House officials believed that if they delayed a meeting China would respond by resuming a series of talks with Tibetans and revitalizing the broader relationship with the U.S. "From our point of view, the timing was less important than the substance," the official told me, adding, "If we could get a resumption of dialogue with the Dalai Lama and get U.S.-China relations on a stable footing—which would enable us to have the Tibet issue less confrontational—we thought that was worth doing." When the delay became public, critics faulted the White House for acceding to Chinese pressure in the name of broader objectives. In an interview with the *Times*, Václav Havel, the former Czech dissident and President, said of Obama, "With these minor compromises start the big and dangerous ones, the real problems."

Lodi Gyari, the Dalai Lama's special envoy and lead contact with the U.S. government, says the criticism of Obama was unwarranted: "The decision not to do the meeting beforehand was absolutely mutual." Nevertheless, he added, in the months since, some foreign governments have used it as an excuse to avoid irritating China. "They said, 'Look, if the big United States is shying away, then, please, give us a break,'" he told me. China did resume talks with the Dalai Lama's representatives, but the talks were not fruitful; other hoped-for concessions from Beijing have yet to materialize.

The experience left the Administration bruised, though it stands by the decision. "If we facilitate dialogue, at some stage the Tibetans and the Chinese might find a way to actually make the dialogue fruitful," the official said, adding that the domestic political cost was unavoidable. "From a foreign-policy point of view, it made sense. We knew we were going to take a hit. We took a hit, and we did it."

The Dalai Lama eventually visited Obama in February of this year; the Administration said that the seventy-minute meeting in the Map Room was longer than any previous Presidential meeting with the Dalai Lama. The Chinese complained that it was "seriously damaging" ties between China and the U.S., and summoned the American ambassador to lodge a formal complaint.

The Dalai Lama wakes most mornings at three-thirty, at his two-story stone-and-concrete bungalow. First, he meditates, followed by full-body prostrations—part ritual and part exercise. Before breakfast, at five-thirty, he walks outside or on a treadmill. He tunes in to the BBC, and occasionally Voice of America's Tibetan-language broadcast, before returning to meditation and readings in philosophy. After a day of work and meetings, he performs a final hour or two of meditation before bed, at 8:30 P.M.

High Tibetan lamas traditionally carry themselves as remote, commanding figures. The Dalai Lama, by contrast, usually runs late, because he has a Clintonian appetite for handshakes. "We were in this hotel in downtown L.A., and they're trying to get him from point A to point B," Ronny Novick, who has frequently filmed the Dalai Lama, told me. "And, all of a sudden, boom! He breaks off and goes into the gift shop, where they're selling chewing gum and 'I Love L.A.' Teddy bears, just to say hello to the shopgirls."

For someone so involved in diplomacy, the Dalai Lama is willfully unconcerned with status. He tugs the beards of sombre religious clerics and holds hands with heads of state. He cuts short meetings with dignitaries whom he finds overly self-impressed. (When he settles deep into his chair, aides warn, he has lost interest.) Oprah once asked him if the whole world should meditate, and he replied cheerfully that it was a "stupid question." He then answered it in detail.

He tires of what he calls the "old courtesies," and one of the first changes he made after leaving Tibet was to declare, despite the protests of his retinue, that his visitors should henceforth be given a chair of equal height. Unlike many Buddhists, he eats meat, because, he says, his health suffered during a spell as a vegetarian. (Paul McCartney later wrote to him, urging him to reconsider. "It just doesn't seem right—the Dalai Lama, on the one hand, saying, 'Hey, guys, don't harm sentient beings. . . . Oh, and by the way, I'm having a steak,'" he told the *Guardian*.)

The Dalai Lama's romance with the West makes him vulnerable to detractors: learned Buddhists who cringe at the sound of Scripture being boiled down to bromides; liberals who point out that although the Dalai Lama calls for full legal rights for gay men and women, he cites Buddhist doctrine, which condemns anal and oral sex, and considers it unsanctioned for Buddhists; decided atheists like Christopher Hitchens, who called the Dalai Lama's following "a Hollywood cult that almost exceeds the power of Scientology."

To get those around him to relax, he has honed a sense of "radical informality." He giggles, makes jokes about digestion, cleans his glasses with a handkerchief, and, if the meeting follows lunch, marches off to the washroom with a toothbrush and an admonition about oral hygiene. Spalding Gray, the late writer and performer, once asked him in an interview how he deals with distractions like "women in bikini bathing suits." The Dalai Lama, who has been bound by a vow of celibacy since childhood, responded, "Sometimes in my dreams, there are women. And, in some cases, fighting or quarreling with someone. When such dreams happen, immediately I remember, 'I am monk.'"

He tends to make a deep impact on those he meets not only because of his spiritual stature but also because he is unusually interested in what they say. "It's quite disarming, because he'll say, 'Well, what do you think I should do?'" Robert Barnett told me, adding, "I've always wondered whether he would ask the same question if I were a nutcase, because as far as one can tell he listens patiently to them, too."

The Dalai Lama's effect on others has drawn the attention of scientists. The psychologist Paul Ekman, a professor emeritus at the University of California at San Francisco, and a pioneer in the study of emotion, had long regarded Buddhism as "another crazy cult that was attracting people in the Bay Area." Then, ten years ago, he met the Dalai Lama at a conference and experienced what he calls "a sensation I've never had before or since." The best way to describe it, he told me recently, was "when you get a CT scan and they inject you with a radioactive fluid that makes your whole body tingle." Ekman, who went on to co-author a book with the Dalai Lama, titled "Emotional Awareness," said, "It is a concept you can find described all the way back in history: there were people whom others wanted to be around because it just felt good to be in their presence. They were usually spiritual leaders of one kind or another, and that's what he is. From my vantage point, it's a mutation."

The Dalai Lama does one or two big U.S. tours every year, and in May he flew in for a two-week swing, starting in Bloomington, Indiana, which holds special significance for him, because his elder brother, the late Thubten Jigme Norbu, lived there for more than forty years, teaching Tibetan language and history at Indiana University. Bloomington sits on rolling hills that break up the un-Himalayan landscape of southern Indiana, and it prides itself on a college-town broadmindedness that has accorded local sainthood to Bobby Knight, the homegrown violinist Joshua Bell, and the late sex researcher Alfred Kinsey.

Although the Dalai Lama's early visits were greeted by protest from a local fundamentalist church, that resistance subsided, and Indiana fans now describe him as a kind of management consultant for the soul. "There's a whole group of us out there who consider ourselves Christian Buddhists," Lisa Morrison, a local organizer, told me. "I believe in Jesus Christ—that he lived is not a question, it is a fact—but I have also been touched so deeply by His Holiness."

The Dalai Lama was booked for two days in front of a sellout crowd of about three thousand people. His success is due in part to the West's long-standing fascination with Tibet as the "cure for an ever-ailing Western civilization, a tonic to restore its spirit," as the Buddhist-studies scholar Donald Lopez said in his book "Prisoners of Shangri-La." Many Americans were introduced to Tibet by the novelist James Hilton, who conjured up an earthly paradise in the Himalayas which he called Shangri-La, in his 1933 novel "Lost Horizon."

After Bloomington, the Dalai Lama was booked at the Indianapolis arena that is home to the Pacers of the N.B.A. Signs advertised upcoming visits by the gospel singer Bill Gaither and the W.W.E. SmackDown World Tour. One of the Dalai Lama's strengths as a speaker is his ability to tailor different products for different audiences. In Bloomington, he gave a formal Buddhist teaching on "The Heart Sutra," but for the stadium crowd in Indianapolis he sat forward on a plush burgundy armchair with a tiny headset microphone protruding from under his left ear and deployed a reliable laugh line: "Some people may have the feeling that the Dalai Lama has some kind of miracle power. After 2008 October, I went through surgery. Gallbladder." Beat. "So that scientifically proves Dalai Lama has no healing power."

During the next hour and a half, he conducted a high-speed tour of his vision of the good life, rooted in his conviction that, "physically, mentally, emotionally, we are the same." He staked out the widest possible circle of agreement—praising believers of all religions as well as believers of none. He was animated and jokey, folding his hands into paws to act out the role of a kitten whose survival depends on a mother's compassion. To drive home his point that a "happy life is entirely dependent on the rest of the community," he held his wrist in the air and said, "I love my watch, but if I kiss my watch the watch has no ability to return affection." It was vintage Dalai Lama: light on eloquence, and alive with energy and common sense. The crowd was absorbed.

Afterward, during a question-and-answer period, a woman in a yellow T-shirt and jeans asked about managing anger toward others, adding, "Like, maybe, in my instance, an ex-husband?" The Dalai Lama smiled, straightened his back, and answered by drawing a comparison between her divorce and the fate of Tibet. "We lost our own country, we lost our freedom. Everything. But then think about the situation: this is something beyond our control. No use for too much worry."

Later, I ran into the woman who had asked the question, a thirty-eight-year-old certified dog groomer named Erin Pattison. She was still beaming from the exchange, which, as she put it, confirmed that "what I'm doing is what I should be doing." After her divorce, she'd begun studying to become a veterinarian. "It's like what His Holiness said to me: The worst is nothing compared to losing your country. I'm blessed with what I have."

After the Dalai Lama wrapped up one afternoon in Indiana, I saw a flyer for a talk by the president of the Tibetan Youth Congress, an exile group. I followed signs to a classroom nearby, where fewer than twenty people were seated. Brochures were fanned out on a table. When it was clear that nobody else was coming, Tsewang Rigzin, the group's president, stepped up to the lectern and said, "We were expecting a few more people." He gave a short, forceful speech about Tibetans—"They're being tortured, they're being imprisoned, they're being executed, but they've never given up"—and, when it was over, I asked him what he made of the turnout. "If you look at all the teachings that His Holiness does, you have thousands of people," he said. "But in terms of the support for us politically? It's, well, less." He added, "What we need is concrete support, not just sympathy."

Being the Dalai Lama has never been a guarantee of good fortune. Since the lineage began, more than six hundred years ago, only half of the men who held the title have lived to see their thirties. At least four are believed to have been killed amid palace intrigue. In 1682, a government minister hid the death of the Dalai Lama for fifteen years, secretly ruling with the help of a look-alike.

The current Dalai Lama was born to a family of farmers in northeastern Tibet. His mother bore sixteen children, seven of whom survived. His father was a horseman with a short temper. When the son was two years old, a search party was roaming the countryside looking for a toddler who might be the latest incarnation of the Dalai Lama. The family was not rich, but it was well established: the boy's elder brother and great-uncle had been recognized as high-ranking lamas. As the Dalai Lama wrote in a 1990 memoir, "Freedom in Exile," the search party proceeded under the guidance of mystical signs: the corpse of the previous Dalai Lama had turned its embalmed head to face northeastern Tibet; a senior monk peered into the waters of a sacred lake and saw letters that suggested "Amdo," the region in the northeast, as well as an image of the toddler's family house. When the party reached the home, they monitored the boy for days and then tested him by laying out prayer beads, drums, and other objects and asking him to identify which ones had belonged to the previous Dalai Lama.

He chose correctly and was eventually whisked off to Lhasa, to be "hidden away like an owl," as he put it, in the thousand-room Potala Palace, a childhood of lonesome splendor. Apart from tutors, and occasional visits with his family, his closest contacts were the sweepers who maintained the grounds, and whenever he was called to preside over long, elaborate ceremonies he worried, most of all, about whether his bladder would hold out.

For fun, he dissected watches, a music box, and other devices, and he spent so much time gazing at the night sky through a telescope that he concluded, contrary to Tibetan beliefs, that the moon was not illuminated from within. Though he remains intensely interested in science, he has never entered the computer age. "His Holiness finds it difficult even knowing where to press the button," his longtime private secretary Tenzin Geyche Tethong once said. His blog and other online accounts are tended by others.

The Dalai Lama was fifteen in 1950, when the newly triumphant Communist Party raided a Tibetan outpost, promising liberation. The conflict hinged on whether Tibet was a part of China or an independent country. Both sides agreed that China's Mongol rulers had amassed great authority in Tibet by the thirteenth century. But Tibetans say the bond was based principally on a shared religion, and they argue that the Mongols did not represent the Chinese. Historians in China consider the Mongol era the beginning of seven hundred years of political sovereignty over Tibet. One fact, however, is undisputed: by the time Communist forces marched into Tibet in the twentieth century, the former empire was ill-prepared to defend itself. It had a poorly trained army, no paved roads, and no more than a few speakers of any Western language. Had the country modernized earlier instead of shunning reforms, the Dalai Lama writes ruefully, "I am quite certain that Tibet's situation today would be very different."

By the end of the decade, he faced a stark choice: stay in Tibet or escape into exile. China was pressing a "socialist transformation"; the Dalai Lama was receiving reports of atrocities. For advice, he turned to what he calls his "supernatural counsels," a private world of divination and soothsaying that has helped him make difficult decisions ever since.

He relies most heavily on the "state oracle," a deity called Nechung, who communicates through a human medium, usually a monk. According to the Dalai Lama's description in his memoir, the medium slips into a trance "with bulging eyes and swollen cheeks. . . . His breathing begins to shorten and he starts to hiss violently." The Dalai Lama poses questions, and the oracle responds with enigmatic advice. On complex affairs of state, he writes, "I seek his opinion in the same way as I seek the opinion of my Cabinet." For further help, the Dalai Lama relies on a form of *mo* divination, in which choices are written on pieces of paper and placed in balls of dough. He then swirls the balls in a cup until the right answer tumbles out.

This confidence in the supernatural is common among Tibetans, though not universally celebrated. Jamyang Norbu, a prominent writer and critic of the Dalai Lama, bemoans the practice of "burying our collective head in the sands of superstition and inertia." When I asked the Dalai Lama how he balances his trust in science with his faith in the supernatural, he said that he views the oracles as "consultants."

"After I consult human beings and these oracles, if there's something clear, something which I can now decide, then I decide," he told me. He said he had made "all major decisions" from the age of sixteen with the help of the oracles, and he had become convinced that they are correct.

These days, the Nechung medium is Thupten Ngodup, an amiable fiftyish monk who likes to garden in his spare time. When I visited him one morning in Dharamsala, he explained that he'd been an ordinary monk, overseeing the sculptures and incense at a monastery, until one day, in 1987, when the deity suddenly chose him as the medium—a physical sensation that he compared to an electric shock. "My position is very difficult," he said. He had joined the monastery at the age of nine, never expecting much drama. "When the oracle chooses me, I'm just a normal monk." His job now requires him to be on call whenever the Dalai Lama needs a consultation. "Anytime His Holiness needs, he calls."

When it came to the crucial decision, in 1959, whether to stay or go, the oracle, in a trance, advised the Dalai Lama to escape, reached for a pen and paper, and drew a map of the route through the mountains. One night in March, the Dalai Lama donned a disguise—"unfamiliar trousers and a long black coat"—and slipped out the door of the palace with a group of guards who pretended to be on patrol. After two weeks of trekking and hiding in the Himalayas, the escape party reached the Indian border.

In exile, the Dalai Lama looked for allies, but no nations recognized Tibet's claim to independence. Some of the Dalai Lama's brothers pursued another strategy: the C.I.A. was eager to cause problems for the new Chinese government, and by 1958 it was air-dropping weapons and tutoring Tibetans in guerrilla warfare. Some of them trained in Colorado, where they learned radio and parachute skills, and, for inspiration, watched "The Bridge on the River Kwai." By the early sixties, the insurgents were attacking Chinese convoys, but U.S. priorities changed abruptly. President Nixon began to initiate diplomatic ties with Chairman Mao, and the C.I.A. dropped the operation. One of the Dalai Lama's brothers settled in Bloomington; another moved to Hong Kong; a third went to New Jersey, where, at one point, he worked as a school custodian known as Sam.

In the sixties, reports from inside Tibet told of ill-fated farming experiments and brutal ideological campaigns. The Dalai Lama focussed on absorbing refugees, while deepening his religious studies, especially Buddhist conceptions of compassion, interdependence, and "emptiness," according to which any person or phenomenon is by itself devoid, or "empty," of intrinsic identity. He studied the religious and political lives of Mahatma Gandhi and Baba Amte, and they left a lasting impression on him. At the time, Robert Thurman, of Columbia, was studying to become a Tibetan Buddhist monk and visited India. (He had ended a marriage to an heiress after deciding that he didn't want to spend his life, as he told the *Times*, "drinking Champagne and staring at Rouaults.") When he met the Dalai Lama, in the early sixties, he "wasn't blown over by him as a guru," Thurman told me. But when Thurman saw him again, in 1971, "he had come alive philosophically."

The Dalai Lama was travelling and lecturing, and he had discovered that esoteric teachings had a limited Western audience; he developed talks that focussed on a more accessible concept of "basic human values." One day in the late seventies, he asked for a meeting with Elie Wiesel, the author and Holocaust survivor. According to Wiesel, the Dalai Lama said, "I'm familiar with your work, what you wrote about the Jewish people losing a homeland two thousand years ago, and how you're still here. Mine has just lost its homeland, and I know it's going to be a very long road into exile. How did you survive?"

Wiesel replied, "When we left Jerusalem, we didn't take all our jewels with us. All we took was a little book. It was the book that kept us alive. Second, because of our exile we developed a sense of solidarity. When Jews left one place for the next, there were always Jews to welcome and take care of them. And, third, good memory. Survival takes a good memory."

Then Wiesel took the Dalai Lama to Washington, where he met Tom Lantos, the only Holocaust survivor in Congress and a vocal human-rights advocate. Lantos introduced him to other lawmakers (and, years later, to Nancy Pelosi, who became a stalwart supporter).

At the time that he was exploring Washington, the Chinese

leaders were experimenting with a more relaxed policy in Tibet, and they opened talks with the Dalai Lama's representatives. Privately, some Tibetan officials argued for a bargaining strategy of demanding independence from China, even if they never expected to get it, as a means of obtaining at least some concessions. But the Dalai Lama rejected that idea, saying the approach was morally flawed. "They're saying something, but their real hope is for something different. It's wrong," he told me.

The talks failed, and, in the years since, many Tibetan leaders have looked back regretfully. "I think those of us serving His Holiness maybe could have been a little bit more bold," Gyari, the Dalai Lama's envoy in Washington, told me recently. He added, "Many decades later, with more gray hair, I sometimes pinch myself to say, 'Maybe . . .'" He trailed off.

But, in truth, China never expected much of the talks. "The dialogue between Dalai and the central government is not a dialogue between two political entities," Lian Xiangmin, a researcher at the government-supported China Tibetology Research Center, in Beijing, told me. "What is it? It came about because Dalai—as a Chinese citizen—has the right to inform the government of his pursuits. This is the way we look at it."

In 1984, when negotiations stalled, China made a momentous change: if the Dalai Lama could not be enticed back to China, then Beijing would buy stability in Tibet through economic development. It approved forty-two major construction projects in Tibet and encouraged other ethnicities to seek work there. Thanks to what Chinese economists called a "blood transfusion" from the East, Tibet now has highways, bridges, and factories on a par with other parts of China. But the influx of non-Tibetans has become a leading cause of unrest. In March, 1989, Tibetans in Lhasa held the largest anti-Chinese demonstrations there in decades, in honor of the anniversary of the 1959 unrest that coincided with the Dalai Lama's flight into exile. The task of restoring order fell to Hu Jintao, a promising young cadre who was the Party boss in Tibet. He asked Beijing to declare martial law and cracked down on rioters. (He was rewarded for keeping the peace. Today, he is China's President and Party chief.)

The Dalai Lama became increasingly convinced that the quest for independence was doomed, not only because of his belief in pacifism but also because of simple demographics. "A holistic view brings realistic action," he told me. China is a "huge country. . . . So, therefore, the best way to deal with China is not confrontation but through reason." In 1988, he publicly abandoned the goal of independence in favor of what he calls the Middle Way, which seeks greater autonomy within Chinese borders. For the first time, he was at odds with many Tibetans, including some of his closest advisers. "He often used to say, 'We have no hatred towards the Chinese,'" Tethong recalled. "So one day I gathered my courage and I said, 'Your Holiness, instead of saying 'We have no hatred,' say 'I have no hatred.'"

From afar, the Chinese government's comments about the Dalai Lama can sound like a relic of the Cultural Revolution. On the very day that one arm of the government is helping to craft a strategy for global economic recovery, another arm is likely to be denouncing the Dalai Lama as "a devil with a human face." But in order to understand the rationale and emotion that drive China's intense—and surprisingly polarized—views of the Dalai Lama, you have to get close enough to see what lies behind the vitriol.

In Beijing, I live a couple of hundred yards from the Palace of Peace and Harmony, better known as the Lama Temple. The largest Tibetan monastery in the capital, it is a quiet maze of shrines and cypress trees that is popular with Chinese and foreign tourists. The temple's history is entwined with that of the Dalai Lama, which makes for an awkward balance between celebrating the past and ignoring the present. I once bought a Chinese book from the gift shop on the history of the place. In a hundred and twenty-four pages, the current Dalai Lama—the most famous in history—is mentioned in two sentences.

Officially, China has fifty-six ethnic groups; Han Chinese are by far the most numerous, representing more than ninety per cent of the population, and, historically, the vast majority of Han are proud of their role in Tibet, which they see as a long, costly process of extending civilization to a backward region. The Han in the lowlands had little in common with the pastoral people in the mountains—no shared language or diet—and Chinese historians explained that a Tang-dynasty princess taught Tibetans about agriculture, silk, paper, modern medicine, and industry, and stopped them from painting their faces red. (Tibetan historians see things differently.) In the twentieth century, when China secured Tibet, Inner Mongolia, and Xinjiang within its borders, the move was hailed by the Chinese people as the end of a century of foreign invasion and humiliation. The Dalai Lama, from that perspective, stood in the path of history, and when he went into exile Chinese newsreels recorded images of farmers denouncing their former landlords and destroying records of hereditary debts.

Anyone over fifty years old in China today has grown up with those scenes dramatized in influential films like "Serf," a 1963 drama about a freed Tibetan servant and his grateful encounter with the People's Liberation Army. Han Chinese who are only a generation or two removed from poverty are inclined to view China's investment as a sacrifice. A Chinese graduate student at Yale told me, "My father is an educated man. He has worked all over Tibet for years and, to this day, he can't really respect Tibetans. He doesn't see any intellectual output from them."

One of the most consistent and ardent beliefs among the Chinese I know is that Tibet is an inalienable part of their country. For many, Tibet is China's glamorous Wild West, a chic destination associated with spirituality and rugged individualism. "When I'm in Tibet," a young Chinese rock musician told me recently, "I can be free." That appeal has spurred interest in the religion, and a small but growing number of Han Chinese consider themselves followers of Tibetan Buddhism. The Dalai Lama believes this could eventually alter Chinese policy. "If thirty years from now Tibet is six million Tibetans and ten million Chinese Buddhists, then maybe something will be O.K.," he told Pico Iyer. The Dalai Lama is increasingly intent on cultivating Chinese fans. In July, he answered questions on Twitter from Chinese users for the second time in two months, telling them that he hopes to "build up a big family that enables Chinese and Tibetans to coexist in a friendly fashion."

I know a number of Chinese adherents of Tibetan Buddhism, including two well-off friends in their late thirties, whom I'll call Feng and Liu. Feng has glasses and a medium build and works in private equity; Liu is an elegant stay-at-home mom who speaks with a serious, philosophical bent. She told me that she found Buddhism at a moment of anxiety around her thirtieth birthday. "I was in bad shape," she recalled with a chuckle. In college, Feng had gravitated toward psychology and religion, and later settled on Tibetan Buddhism, but with apprehension. "When I was learning from my Tibetan teachers, I used to ask them, 'Are you Chinese or Tibetan? Are you going to use my money to buy weapons?' I could sense that some of these masters really hated Han Chinese."

Over time, his nervousness subsided, and he became interested in the Dalai Lama. "He's written about sixty books, and I've probably read thirty of them," Feng told me. The Dalai Lama is one of the masters I admire the most." We were at an outdoor café in Beijing, and another friend at the table, who happens to be a Party member, gave a theatrical gasp, and said, "He is brave for saying that."

Feng rolled his eyes and continued, "I think the Dalai Lama is not actually a Tibetan separatist. If he were, Tibet would have been out of control by now." Even so, Feng urged me not to mistake his opinion for that of the majority. "I have a friend who is a lawyer at a private-equity firm, and he firmly believes that the Dalai Lama is a wolf in monk's clothing."

Indeed, the sheer force of China's official denunciation of the Dalai Lama makes any imminent change in public opinion hard to picture. A Tibetan monk in Qinghai Province estimated that eighty per cent of the visitors to his monastery are now Han Chinese, but he's not convinced that this will alter Chinese policy. "It's like pouring water over a stone," he told me recently. "It looks like it's wet, but nothing seeps in."

Recent Chinese leaders project a tougher line on Tibet and the Dalai Lama than any leaders have since Mao. That's partly because officials have come to blame the collapse of the Soviet Union, to some degree, on a policy of granting too much ethnic autonomy to the reaches of the empire. When protesters in Kazakhstan took to the streets in 1986 to declare that "Kazakhstan belongs to Kazakhs," Mikhail Gorbachev, after sending in the military, tried to appease the rioters by installing a Kazakh apparatchik and changing unpopular language laws. Other ethnic groups eventually rose up as well. That chain of events "reminded that P.R.C. leaders of the political risk in managing ethnic relations, and made them very cautious," according to Ma Rong, an influential sociologist at Peking University.

"The former Soviet Union took a great risk by handling its nationality/ethnicity issues the way it did," Ma wrote in an academic journal in 2007. The Soviets wrongly assumed that Communism would bind their ethnicities together, but the "nation was at risk of disintegrating if the ideological linkage among the ethnic groups collapsed." Today in China, where Communism is only a wisp of an ideology, the fifty-six officially recognized ethnic groups live side by side. In 2008, President Hu Jintao said, "Stability in Tibet concerns the stability of the country." When human-rights activists accuse Beijing of repressing Tibetan intellectuals, Chinese authorities counter that they face a grave threat to national security and stability, an argument that is persuasive to a population that recalls the chaos of the Cultural Revolution.

Chinese leaders see the Dalai Lama as an especially potent threat. Although he repeatedly renounces efforts to seek Tibetan independence, they say that he harbors a covert intention to split Tibet from the rest of China, as evidenced by his willingness to allow others in the exile community to call for independence. At times, China's leaders have been swayed so completely by their own newsreels that it has left them vulnerable. In 1979, when a delegation from Dharamsala was allowed to visit Tibet, Party officials urged Tibetans not to throw stones or spit at the Dalai Lama's representatives, out of hatred of the old society. But when the contingent arrived it was mobbed by thousands of adoring Tibetans, prostrating themselves and clamoring to touch the Dalai Lama's brother. (A stunned Party chief complained that all the efforts of the previous decades had evidently been no more effective than throwing money into the Lhasa River.)

And, yet, offering an alternative perspective on Tibet is risky. In 1998, after months of research in Tibet, the Chinese writer Wang Lixiong noted that the region "is more prosperous now than ever before in its history. However, this has not gained the People's Republic of China the allegiance of the Tibetans, more and more of whom have become attached to the Dalai Lama." In another piece, Wang warned, "The present stability is superficial." For his writings on Tibet and elsewhere, he was eventually placed under house arrest.

When the 2008 protests erupted in Tibet, the world focussed largely on the drama in the capital, but at least a hundred and fifty incidents of unrest were rippling across other areas as well, including remote parts of neighboring provinces like Qinghai, where the Dalai Lama was born. One afternoon in July, I hailed a gypsy cab for a trip to his birthplace, a small town known in Tibetan as Taktser, an hour by car from the provincial capital of Qinghai. The driver was a genial thirty-four-year-old Tibetan whom I'll call Jigme. Though he was brought up in the area, he had never heard of Taktser. But he figured he could find anything eventually, and we set off at a fare of thirty dollars.

Jigme wore green cargo shorts and a black T-shirt with a mug of Guinness silk-screened on the front. He was an enthusiastic travel companion. His father was a traditional Tibetan opera musician who had received two years of schooling before going to work. When his father was growing up, he would walk seven days from his home town to Xining, the provincial capital. Jigme now makes the same trip three or four times a day in his Volkswagen Santana. A Hollywood buff, he was eager to talk about his favorites: "King Kong," "Lord of the Rings," Mr. Bean. Most of all, he said, "I like American cowboys. The way they ride around on horses, with hats, it reminds me a lot of Tibetans."

Jigme spoke good Mandarin. The central government has worked hard to promote the use of standard Mandarin in ethnic regions like this, and a banner beside the train station in Xining reminded people to "Standardize the Language and Script." Jigme was married to an accountant, and they had a three-year-old daughter. I asked if they planned to enroll her in a school that taught in Chinese or in Tibetan. "My daughter will go to a Chinese school," Jigme said. "That's the best idea if she wants to get a job anywhere outside the Tibetan parts of the world."

We passed frequent reminders that China is determined to pull this region closer to the rest of the country. We saw a crew of hundreds of workers erecting pylons that will carry a new highway, and another team sinking a tunnel into a mountain. Jigme turned off the main road, and the buildings thinned out. The car climbed through a valley flanked by cliffs of brilliant red stone.

In his comments and appearance, Jigme seemed to be constantly negotiating what it means to be both Tibetan and Chinese. When I asked how the Han Chinese and the Tibetans were getting along, he said, "In some ways, the Communist Party has been good to us. It has fed us and made sure we have a roof over our heads. And, where it does things right, we should acknowledge that." After a pause, he added, "But Tibetans want their own country. That's a fact. I graduated from a Chinese school. I can't read Tibetan."

We threaded through tiny villages, with mud-brick homes and sheep moving in single file by the roadside, until we reached Taktser (known in Chinese as Hongyacun)—two hundred and fifty or so households clustered on a red-rock hill that villagers say resembles a crouching lion. Only after we were in town did Jigme ask why I wanted to visit in the first place. Neighbors pointed us to the nicest home in the village, a courtyard house with double-height red wooden doors and Tibetan scarves fluttering from the latches. I'd read that it had been partly destroyed during the Cultural Revolution, but was later rebuilt, and is now maintained by a relative of the Dalai Lama's. The authorities keep him close; according to the state news agency, he receives a salary from the government and serves on a local political advisory body.

An old woman with silver teeth and a pair of braids opened the wooden doors. The courtyard was lined with cobblestones and flanked by flower beds; prayer flags fluttered overhead. When she saw me, she said, "Sorry, they've told us foreigners aren't allowed inside. If we let them, there will be problems for us." As I turned to leave, Jigme asked her if he could pray inside the threshold. The old woman ushered him in, and I saw him fall to his knees and press his forehead to the cobblestones.

That night, I stayed in the town known in Tibetan as Rebkong, and in Chinese as Tongren. During the uprising in 2008, local monks protested in front of government offices. An eyewitness quoted in a report by Human Rights Watch described a scene of "soldiers and police beating the crowd with electric batons." A man in his sixties reportedly began shouting, "May His Holiness the Dalai Lama live for ten thousand years!" and "Tibet is independent!" According to the witness, "Five or six soldiers threw him to the ground and beat him so severely that he seemed close to death."

After the unrest, the government expanded the military presence in the area. There is a sprawling military base of blocky white buildings on the edge of town. That was accompanied, as usual, by investments intended to demonstrate the advantages of peaceful development. Next to the base was a newly constructed five-story apartment complex in pastel colors; from a window hung a red banner inscribed with the phrase "Strengthen Ethnic Unity."

When I met the Dalai Lama in Dharamsala in July, we sat in a spacious reception room decorated with paintings of the Buddha, in a complex of offices beside his house. His aides had told him that I was coming from China, and, before I could pose a question, he asked me for an update on ethnic regions such as Xinjiang and Inner Mongolia. He seemed unnerved by the notion that Tibet might someday be as Sinicized as Inner Mongolia, where there are more Han Chinese residents than Mongolians.

"According to some Mongolian friends," he said, "now in Inner Mongolia the Mongol population is around three or four million, whereas Han immigrant population is nearly twenty million." He perched on a brown sofa chair, with a mug of plain hot water before him. He was still thinking about Inner Mongolia and asked, "So when you visit the appearance is of many Chinese?" Before I could answer, he said, "Lhasa is also now becoming like that: Chinatown."

I asked about his prediction that more Chinese followers of Tibetan Buddhism might alter China's policies, and I said that, from my experience, Chinese citizens appear to separate political and religious attachments to Tibet. He shook his head and told the story of a Frenchman who became a Tibetan Buddhist monk but wanted nothing to do with political issues. "I asked him whether you are praying for the survival of Tibetan Buddhism, and Buddhism in general. He said yes, every day he prays for that. Then I mentioned that the Tibetan struggle is mainly for the preservation of Tibetan Buddhism. So if you pray, then actually you are involved!" He erupted in a belly laugh.

In Dharamsala, I bumped into Tsewang Rigzin, whom I'd last seen in Indiana, where he was trying, in vain, to attract Americans to his cause. Rigzin, who has a buzz cut and serious, heavy-lidded eyes, used to live in Oregon, where he worked for a bank before he was elected president of the Tibetan Youth Congress. He moved to Dharamsala, but his wife and children remain in the United States. The Chinese press says that he runs a terrorist organization. In April, 2008, the Xinhua news agency quoted a government spokesman who alleged that Tibetan advocacy groups, including Rigzin's, planned to "organize suicide squads to launch violent attacks."

Sitting at the group's headquarters in Dharamsala, a one-story office with the threadbare quality of an old union hall, Rigzin said the accusation was absurd. "I get Chinese people here all the time, and they laugh when we talk about the Chinese calling the T.Y.C. a terrorist group," he told me. "I tell them, 'If we are a terrorist organization, you wouldn't be here.' You would probably need to pass through a bunch of security guards with AK-47s and what have you. We are a democratic and a transparent organization. Everybody is welcome here."

Rigzin said the group has never condoned violence, and yet he is content to be ambiguous about the future. "As long as His Holiness is around, the struggle will be nonviolent," he said. "But we have to be realistic that there will be a day when he will no longer be with us. And then we don't know. We'll have to wait and see."

That sense of anticipation, I discovered, is brewing in China as well. As a Tibetan intellectual in China put it to me, "The questions of Tibet and the Dalai Lama are separate issues. The Tibetan people have been here for thousands of years, and the Dalai Lama is just one man among many. The Tibetans and the Han will still have to live together. After he's gone, the stability will be harder to maintain."

He expressed deep admiration for the Dalai Lama, so I was surprised by what he said next: "The way that young people here see it, the Dalai Lama is received by foreign leaders. To do so, he has given up Tibet's independence, but what have the Tibetan people gotten in return? He had the right to protect independence, but who gave him the right to abandon it? There is a group of us who feel this way." He was growing excited. "People all over the world are the same," he said. "If they've lost everything, they don't fear death." Of the Chinese, he added, "They think they have succeeded. They are mistaken."

One way that the Dalai Lama hopes to prevent a violent future is by teaching younger figures to uphold his vision until a reincarnation comes of age—or a secular exile leadership can gain support. Among the people who might play a role is the Karmapa, a high-ranking Tibetan lama who was born in Tibet and was on track to become a "patriotic" religious leader, as Jiang Zemin, then China's President, said of him as a child. Instead, the Karmapa fled to Dharamsala at the age of fourteen, and now, at twenty-four, has matured into a calm, commanding figure who is sometimes seated at the Dalai Lama's side at public events. Compared with the Dalai Lama, the young Karmapa is a more earthly presence, quick to mention his fondness for the Internet, hip-hop, and video games. When I asked him if the growing numbers of Chinese followers of Tibetan Buddhism reassured him as it does the Dalai Lama, he sounded wary. "They have soft feelings, but I don't know if that means they support genuine autonomy," he said. "They are interested in the culture."

Another way that the Dalai Lama is trying to sustain the Tibet movement in the future is by promoting a secular Tibetan leadership. ("A religious leader having to assume political leadership—that period is over," he has said.) Through the years, he has called repeatedly for greater democracy among Tibetans in exile, but his people hold fast to his leadership. In previous elections, only half of eligible voters turned out. For the first time, campaign posters were plastered around Dharamsala, in advance of an election for Prime Minister in October. But Buddhist voters were still becoming acclimated to the sight of so much self-promotion. "Some feel it is rather 'un-Tibetan,'" Thubten Samphel told me.

In July, a few days before the Dalai Lama's birthday, a Chinese court handed down a verdict in the latest case against a Tibetan intellectual: the Chinese authorities sentenced Rinchen Samdrup, a well-known Tibetan environmentalist, to five years in prison on charges of inciting subversion. He was accused of posting an article on his organization's Web site which referred to the Dalai Lama favorably.

In Beijing, the spokesman for the Foreign Ministry, Qin Gang, when asked for comment on the Dalai Lama's birthday, replied that he did not bother to keep track of the date. Instead, he preferred to recall two other landmarks in history: the moment, in 1951, that the Chinese Army brought "peaceful liberation" to Tibet; and the day, in 1959, that the Chinese put down a rebellion and launched a political overhaul—a date that the government recently enshrined as Serf Emancipation Day.

As the Dalai Lama ages, the Chinese government grows more resolute in its determination to shun him. Nobody I spoke to—in

Beijing, Dharamsala, or Washington—thinks this will change anytime soon. In part, that's because China has narrowed its own options: by educating its citizens to perceive any concession where Tibet is concerned as an existential threat, China has left itself little room to bargain. So, for the moment, the two sides remain locked in a war of patience: the Dalai Lama waiting to win over enough ordinary Chinese followers to alter Chinese policy, and the Chinese government waiting to win over enough ordinary Tibetans to keep Lhasa stable.

Chinese leaders are betting that, if they wait for the Dalai Lama to die, whoever comes after him will be less galvanizing to lawmakers in Washington and dog groomers in Indiana—and they are probably right. But they might be overlooking the disruptive potential of Tibetans, which would not be the first time that Chinese decision-makers have been blinded by their own hopeful reading of Tibet. Wang Lixiong, the Chinese writer who has correctly predicted Tibetan unrest before, wrote not long ago, "While the Dalai Lama is still alive . . . Tibetans harbor hope. But once the Dalai Lama dies . . . grief will give rise to frenzy." And, yet, Lodi Gyari says that his Chinese counterparts across the table are more unyielding than ever. "They always say that the clock is ticking for you," he told me. "I say, 'Yes, it is certainly ticking for me. But it is also ticking for you.'"

When I visited the Dalai Lama at his compound, he had been wrapping up a meeting with a group of Chinese visitors, and he bid them goodbye with a few words in Mandarin. As we talked, China was on his mind. "So long as there is a separate Tibetan identity they feel fear," he said of the Beijing leadership. "The Chinese government must learn the experience of India: South Indians, East Indians, West Indians, North Indians—different languages, different scripts. Each is proud yet remains within one republic. No danger of separation if you realize a common interest."

Though he may have been idealizing India's fractious ethnic politics, his point was clear, and his faith in the power of a "common interest" reminded me of the Chinese sociologist Ma Rong's warning that the Soviet Union collapsed because it never united its diverse population around anything but a hollow economic philosophy. In this sense, the Dalai Lama and the Chinese leadership have unwittingly settled on a shared belief in the need to pull the country together. But on the best way to achieve this they differ fundamentally, and, probably, irreconcilably.

On the evening of the Dalai Lama's birthday, Indian television broadcast a talk-show-style interview with him, and the host, inevitably, inquired about his health. "If I don't commit suicide," he answered merrily, "then otherwise my body is very healthy. Another ten to twenty years . . . no problem. Maybe thirty years!" If his prophesy holds, he will be a hundred and five.

MARILYNNE ROBINSON

Thinking Again

FROM *Commonweal*

IT WILL BE A GREAT DAY IN THE HISTORY OF SCIENCE IF WE SOME-time discover a damp shadow elsewhere in the universe where a fungus has sprouted. The mere fossil trace of life in its simplest form would be the crowning achievement of generations of brilliant and diligent labor.

And here we are, a gaudy efflorescence of consciousness, staggeringly improbable in light of everything we know about the reality that contains us.

There are physicists and philosophers who would correct me. They would say that if there are an infinite number of universes, as in theory there could be, then creatures like us would be very likely to emerge at some time in one of them. But to say this is only to state the fact of our improbability in other terms.

Then there is the odd privilege of existence as a coherent self, the ability to speak the word "I" and mean by it a richly individual history of experience, perception, and thought. For the religious, the sense of the soul may have as a final redoubt, not as argument but as experience, that haunting I who wakes us in the night wondering where time has gone, the I we waken to, sharply aware that we have been unfaithful to ourselves, that a life lived otherwise would have acknowledged a yearning more our own than any of the daylit motives whose behests we answer to so diligently. Our religious traditions give us as the name of God two deeply mysterious words, one deeply mysterious utterance: I AM. Putting to one side the question of their meaning as the name and character by which the God of Moses would be known, these are words any human being can say about herself, and does say, though always with a modifier of some kind. I am hungry, I am comfortable, I am a singer, I am a cook. The abrupt descent into particularity in every statement of this kind, Being itself made an auxiliary to some momentary accident of being, may only startle in the dark of night, when the intuition comes that there is no proportion between the great given of existence and the narrow vessel of circumstance into which it is inevitably forced. "I am Ozymandias, king of kings. Look on my works, ye mighty, and despair."

There is much speculation about the nature of the mind, its relation to the brain, even doubt that the word "mind" is meaningful. In his book *Consilience*, the biologist E. O. Wilson claims, "The brain and its satellite glands have now been probed to the point where no particular site remains that can reasonably be supposed to harbor a nonphysical mind." But if such a site could be found in the brain, then the mind would be physical in the same sense that anything else with a locus in the brain is physical. To define the mind as nonphysical in the first place clearly prejudices his conclusion. The experimental psychologist Steven Pinker, writing about the soul in *How the Mind Works*, asks, "How does the spook interact with solid matter? How does an ethereal nothing respond to flashes, pokes and beeps and get arms and legs to move? Another problem is the overwhelming evidence that the mind is the activity of the brain. The supposedly immaterial soul, we now know, can be bisected with a knife, altered by chemicals," and so on. By identifying the soul with the mind, the mind with the brain, and noting the brain's vulnerability as a physical object, he feels he has debunked a conception of the soul that only those who find the word meaningless would ever have entertained.

This declension, from the ethereality of the mind/soul as spirit to the reality of the mind/brain as a lump of meat, is dependent, conceptually and for its effects, on precisely the antique dualism these writers who claim to speak for science believe they reject and refute. If complex life is the marvel we all say it is, quite possibly unique to this planet, then meat is, so to speak, that marvel in its incarnate form. It was dualism that pitted the spirit against the flesh, investing spirit with all that is lofty at the expense of flesh, which is by contrast understood as coarse and base. It only perpetuates dualist thinking to treat the physical as if it were in any way sufficiently described in disparaging terms. If the mind is the activity of the brain, this means only that the brain is capable of such lofty and astonishing things that their expression has been given the names mind, and soul, and spirit. Complex life may well be the wonder of the universe, and if it is, its status is not diminished by the fact that we can indeed bisect it, that we kill it routinely.

In any case, Wilson's conception of mind clearly has also taken on the properties of the soul, at least as that entity is understood by those eager to insist that there is no ghost in the machine. As Bertrand Russell pointed out decades before Gilbert Ryle coined this potent phrase, the old, confident distinction between materiality and nonmateriality is not a thing modern science can endorse. Physicists say a change in a split photon occurs simultaneously in its severed half, at any theoretical distance. As if there were no time or space, this information of change passes instantly from one to the other. Is an event that defies any understanding we have of causality a physical event? Yes. Can the seeming timelessness and spacelessness that mediate this change also be called physical? Presumably, since they have unambiguous physical consequences. Then perhaps we cannot claim to know the nature of the physical, and perhaps we ought not to be so confident in opposing it to a real or imagined nonphysical. These terms, as conventionally used, are not identical with the terms "real" and "unreal," though the belief that they are is the oldest tenet of positivism. The old notion of dualism should be put aside, now that we know a little about the uncanny properties of the finer textures of the physical. If, as some have suggested, quantum phenomena govern the brain, evidence for the fact is not likely to be found in scrutiny of lobes or glands or by means of any primitive understanding of the brain's materiality.

Let us say the mind is what the brain does. This is a definition that makes the mind, whatever else, a participant in the whole history and experience of the body. Steven Pinker offers the same definition, but modifies it differently. He says, "The mind is what the brain does; specifically, the brain processes information, and thinking is a kind of computation"—excluding the felt experience of thinking, with all its diverse burdens and colorations. Elsewhere he says, with the certitude typical of his genre, "Family feelings are designed to help our genes replicate themselves, but we cannot see or smell genes. . . . Our emotions about kin use a kind of inverse genetics to guess which of the organisms we interact with are likely to share our genes (for example, if someone appears to have the same parents as you do, treat the person as if their genetic well-being overlaps with yours)." Here we have the self we experience at a qualitative remove from what the brain really does. Presumably we are seduced into collaborating in the perpetuation of some part of our genetic inheritance by those moments of love and embrace. But why are these seductions necessary? Why are they lovely to us? Why would nature bother to distract us with them? Why do we stand apart from nature in such a way that the interests that really move us should be concealed from us? Might there not be fewer of these interfamilial crimes, honor killings, child abandonments, if nature had made us straightforwardly aware that urgencies more or less our own were being served in our propagating and nurturing? There is more than a hint of dualism in the notion that some better self—the term seems fair—has to be distracted by ingratiating pleasures to accommodate the practical business of biology.

This automaton language of Pinker's sounds a bit like Descartes. But Descartes theorized that the pineal gland, central and singular in the symmetries of the brain, moved one way or another to permit or obstruct the actions of the body, which he knew were governed by the brain. In his theory, the impressions of the senses, integrated in this gland, were appraised by the soul, which in Descartes is a term that seems pointedly synonymous with the mind. That is to say, his interest is in cognition and reason, not sin or salvation, and this in a physical and intellectual landscape inflamed by theological controversy in which those concepts figured prominently. Still, it is the soul that appraises what the mind integrates. In this way Descartes acknowledges the complexity of thinking, judging, and in his way incorporates the feeling of consciousness and the complexity of it more adequately than most theorists do now.

What Descartes actually intended by the words "soul" and "mind" seems to me an open question for Descartes himself. Clearly they are no mere ghost or illusion. What their meanings are for us as inheritors of the thought of the modern period is a more manageable question. I am excluding the kind of thinking on this point that tends toward the model of the wager. According to this model, we place our faith in an understanding of the one thing needful, and, ultimately, suffer or triumph depending on the correctness of our choice. By these lights the soul exists primarily to be saved or lost. It is hardly more our intimate companion in mortal time than is the mind or brain by the reckoning of the positivists, behaviorists, neo-Darwinists, and Freudians. The soul, in this understanding of it, is easily characterized by the nonreligious as a fearful and self-interested idea, as the product of acculturation or a fetish of the primitive brain rather than as a name for an aspect of deep experience. Therefore it is readily dismissed as a phantom of the mind, and the mind is all the more readily dismissed for its harboring of such fears and delusions.

Steven Pinker says, "The faculty with which we ponder the world has no ability to peer inside itself or our other faculties to see what makes them tick. That makes us the victims of an illusion: that our own psychology comes from some divine force or mysterious essence or almighty principle." But the mind, or the brain, a part of the body just as E. O. Wilson says it is, is deeply sensitive to itself. Guilt, nostalgia, the pleasure of anticipation, even the shock of a realization, all arise out of an event that occurs entirely in the mind or brain, and they are as potent as other sensations. Consistency would require a belief in the nonphysical character of the mind to exclude them from the general category of experience. If it is objected that all these things are ultimately dependent on images and sensations first gleaned from the world by the senses, this might be granted, on the condition that the sensory experience retained in the mind is understood to have the character the mind has given it. And it might be granted if sensory experience is understood to function as language does, both enabling thought and conforming it in large part to its own context, its own limitations. Anyone's sensory experience of the world is circumstantial and cultural, qualified by context and perspective, a fact which again suggests that the mind's awareness of itself is of a kind with its awareness of physical reality. The mind, like the body, is very much placed in the world. Those who claim to dismiss the mind/body dichotomy actually perpetuate it when they exclude the mind's self-awareness from among the data of human nature.

By "self-awareness" I do not mean merely consciousness of one's identity, or of the complex flow of thought, perception, memory, and desire, important as these are. I mean primarily the self that stands apart from itself, that questions, reconsiders, appraises. I have read that microorganisms can equip themselves with genes useful to their survival—that is, genes conferring resistance to antibiotics—by choosing them out of the ambient flux of organic material. If a supposedly simple entity can by any means negotiate its own enhancement, then an extremely complex entity largely composed of these lesser entities—that is, a human being—should be assumed to have analogous capabilities. For the purposes of the mind, these might be called conscience or aspiration. We receive their specific forms culturally and historically, as the microorganism does also when it absorbs the consequences of other germs' encounters with the human pharmacopoeia.

If the brain at the level of complex and nuanced interaction with itself does indeed become mind, then the reductionist approach insisted upon by writers on the subject is not capable of yielding evidence of mind's existence, let alone an account of its functioning. One who has inquired into the properties of hydrogen and oxygen might reasonably conclude that water is a highly combustible gas—if there were not his own experience to discourage this conclusion. As proof of the existence of mind we have only history and civilization, art, science, and philosophy. And at the same time, of course, that extraordinary individuation. If it is true that the mind can know and seek to know itself in ways analogous to its experience of the world, then there are more, richer data to be gleaned from every age and every culture, and from every moment of introspection, of deep awareness of the self.

The strangeness of reality consistently exceeds the expectations of science, and the assumptions of science, however tried and rational, are inclined to encourage false expectations. As a notable example, no one expected to find that the expansion of the universe is accelerating, and that the rate of its acceleration is accelerating. It is a tribute to the brilliance of science that we can know such things. And it is also an illustration of the fact that science does not foreclose possibility, including discoveries that overturn very fundamental assumptions, and that it is not a final statement about reality but a highly fruitful mode of inquiry into it.

The fact of the accelerating expansion of the universe is a conclusion arrived at in the first place by observation. Theory and hypothesis have followed. What was thought to be known about the effect of gravity, that it would slow cosmic expansion, could not be reconciled with new data, and a major and novel factor, in effect an antigravitational force, emerged as a hypothesis in a changed conception of the universe. The best wisdom and the most venerable of natural laws do not have standing to preclude our acknowledging solid data, though the grounds for refusing to take account of them could perfectly well be called "scientific." The exclusion of what the brain does from an account of what the brain is is "scientific" in just the same sense. By this kind of reasoning, the laws of nature supposedly tell us what we must exclude from what we might otherwise consider entirely relevant, one example being our own inwardness. This distinction between science and parascience is important in considering the mind over against the materialist position that would understand it in reductionist terms, that is, in terms that limit the kinds of interpretation that are appropriately brought to bear on it. The neo-Darwinists argue that the brain evolved to maximize the chance of genetic survival, to negotiate access to food and sex, presumably before the species evolved to the point where the prolonged helplessness of infants made genetic survival dependent in some degree on cooperation. Therefore, they tell us, we may not assume that any motive can depart from an essential qualitative likeness to these original motives. The "evolutionary epic" explains the brain exhaustively.

But "the material" itself is an artifact of the scale at which we perceive. We know that we abide with quarks and constellations, in a reality unknowable by us in a degree we will never be able to calculate, but reality all the same, the stuff and the matrix of our supposedly quotidian existence. We know that within, throughout, the solid substantiality of our experience indeterminacy reigns. Making use of the conceptual vocabulary of science to exclude a possibility which in a present state of knowledge—or a former one—that vocabulary would seem to exclude, has been the mission of positivist thinking since Auguste Comte declared scientific knowledge effectively complete. If doing so is a reflex of the polemical impulse to assert the authority of science, understandable when the project was relatively new, it is by now an atavism that persists as a consequence of the same polemical impulse.

The ancient antagonist that has shaped positivism and parascientific thought and continues to inspire its missionary zeal is religion. For cultural and historical reasons, the religions against which it has opposed itself are Christianity and Judaism, both of which must be called anthropologies, whatever else. "What is man that thou art mindful of him?" The very question is an assertion that mindfulness is an attribute of God, as well as man, a statement of the sense of deep meaning inhering in mindfulness. If I were not myself a religious person, but wished to make an account of religion, I believe I would tend toward the Feuerbachian view that religion is a human projection of humanity's conceptions of beauty, goodness, power, and other valued things, a humanizing of experience by understanding it as structured around and mirroring back these values. Then it would resemble art, with which it is strongly associated. But this would dignify religion and characterize the mind as outwardly and imaginatively engaged with the world, as, in parascientific thought after Comte, it never is.

Steven Pinker says, "Religion is a desperate measure that people resort to when the stakes are high and they have exhausted the usual techniques for the causation of success." Then a little farther on he lists the "imponderables" that lie behind the human tendency toward religion and also philosophy. These imponderables are consciousness in the sense of sentience or subjective experience, the self, free will, conceptual meaning, knowledge, and morality. He says, "Maybe philosophical problems are hard not because they are divine or irreducible or meaningless or workaday science, but because the mind of Homo sapiens lacks the cognitive equipment to solve them. We are organisms, not angels, and our brains are organs, not pipelines to the truth."

How odd that these "imponderables" should be just the kind of thing humankind has pondered endlessly. Neo-Darwinism allows for hypertrophy, the phenomenon by which evolution overshoots its mark and produces some consequence not strictly useful to the ends of genetic replication, the human brain as case in point. How strange it would be, then, that this accident, this excess, should feel a tropism toward what Pinker himself calls "the truth."

Science has arrived at a cluster of hypotheses about the first instant of creation. They attempt description, in the manner of science. In course of time, on various grounds, one description might prove to be more satisfactory than others. A consensus might be arrived at about the nature of a very fecund particle whose eruption became everything we know, and a great deal more beside. We might learn at some point whether time was created together with this universe or exists independently of it. The questions to which science in its most sophisticated forms has come would have been the imponderables of philosophy a few generations ago, of theology a few centuries ago, of religion a few millennia ago. Why this ancient instinct for the greatest questions? It is striking that Pinker identifies religion with the high-order questions humankind has posed to itself from antiquity. Then he dismisses these things as insoluble, as if that were a legitimate reason to dismiss any question. We may never know why gravity is so much weaker than, in theory, it should be, or know if we are only one among any number of actual and potential universes. But every real question is fruitful, as the history of human thought so clearly demonstrates.

And "fruitful" is by no means a synonym for "soluble." What is man? One answer on offer is: An organism whose haunting questions perhaps ought not to be meaningful to the organ that generates them, lacking as it is in any means of "solving" them. Another answer might be: It is still too soon to tell. We might be the creature who brings life on this planet to an end, and we might be the creature who awakens to the privileges that inhere in our nature—selfhood, consciousness, even our biologically anomalous craving for "the truth"—and enjoys and enhances them. Mysteriously, neither possibility precludes the other. Our nature will describe itself as we respond to new circumstances in a world that changes continuously. So long as the human mind exists to impose itself on reality, as it has already done so profoundly, what it is and what we are must remain an open question.

In order to arrive at a parascientific view of humankind we are obliged to put to one side whatever is not to be accounted for in the apparently simple terms of genetic self-interest. I say "apparently simple" because in every instance these theorists build in devices to account for the inadequacies of their theories. The Ptolemaic model of the universe worked well enough, given certain cogs and wheels, epicycles and deferents. Wilson and Pinker speak of the old error, that notion of a ghost in the machine, the image of the felt difference between mind and body. But who and what is that other self they posit, the hypertrophic self who has considered the heavens since Babylon and considers them still, by elegant and ingenious means whose refinements express a formidable pressure of desire to see and know far beyond the limits of any conception of utility, certainly any neo-Darwinist conception of it? Who is that other self needing to be persuaded that there are more than genetic reasons for rescuing a son or daughter from drowning? The archaic conundrum, how a nonphysical spirit can move a physical body, only emerges in a more pointed form in these unaccountable presences whom evolution has supposedly contrived to make us mistake for ourselves. These epigones exist because without them the theories would fail the test of comparison with human experience. Merely shift the balance toward manifest behavior, assuming that the genes do indeed look after themselves in ways and degrees we most likely cannot yet describe, but in any case that their functioning is consistent with manifest behavior. Then human nature, in its wholeness and complexity, is restored—as an unsolved problem, but as a phenomenon endlessly offering a very burdened testimony.

Each of us lives intensely within herself or himself, continuously assimilating past and present experience to a narrative and vision that are unique in every case yet profoundly communicable, whence the arts. And we all live in a great reef of collective experience, past and present, that we receive and preserve and modify. William James says data should be thought of not as givens but as gifts, this by way of maintaining an appropriate humility in the face of what we think we know. The gifts we bring to the problem of making an account of the mind are overwhelmingly rich, severally and together. This is not an excuse for excluding them from consideration. History and civilization are an authoritative record the mind has left, is leaving, and will leave, and objectivity deserving the name would take this record as a starting point.

The universe passed through its unimaginable first moment, first year, first billion years, wresting itself from whatever state of nonexistence, inflating, contorting, resolving into space and matter, bursting into light. Matter condenses, stars live out their generations. Then, very late, there is added to the universe of being a shaped stick or stone, a jug, a cuneiform tablet. They appear on a tiny, teetering, lopsided planet, and they demand wholly new vocabularies of description for reality at every scale. What but the energies of the universe could be expressed in the Great Wall of China, the *St. Matthew Passion*? For our purposes, there is nothing else. Yet language that would have been fully adequate to describe the ages before the appearance of the first artifact would have had to be enlarged by concepts like agency and intention, words like "creation," that would query the great universe itself. Might not the human brain, that most complex object known to exist in the universe, have undergone a qualitative change as well? If my metaphor only suggests the possibility that our species is more than an optimized ape, that something terrible and glorious befell us—if this is merely another fable, it might at least encourage an imagination of humankind large enough to acknowledge some small fragment of the mystery we are.

RICHARD RODRIGUEZ

Saint Cesar of Delano

FROM *The Wilson Quarterly*

THE FUNERAL FOR CESAR CHAVEZ TOOK PLACE IN AN OPEN FIELD near Delano, a small agricultural town at the southern end of California's Central Valley. I remember an amiable Mexican disorder, a crowd listening and not listening to speeches and prayers delivered from a raised platform beneath a canvas tent. I do not remember a crowd numbering 30,000 or 50,000, as some estimates have it—but then I do not remember. Perhaps a cool, perhaps a warm spring sun. Men in white shirts carried forward a pine box. The ease of their movement suggested the lightness of their burden.

When Cesar Chavez died in his sleep in 1993, not yet a very old man at 66, he died—as he had so often portrayed himself in life—as a loser. The United Farm Workers (UFW) union he had co-founded was in decline; the union had 5,000 members, equivalent to the population of one very small Central Valley town. The labor in California's agricultural fields was largely taken up by Mexican migrant workers—the very workers Chavez had been unable to reconcile to his American union, whom he had branded "scabs" and wanted reported to immigration authorities.

I went to the funeral because I was writing a piece on Chavez for *The Los Angeles Times*. It now occurs to me that I was present at a number of events involving Cesar Chavez. I was a teenager at the edge of the crowd in 1966, when Chavez led UFW marchers to the steps of the capitol in Sacramento to generate support for a strike against grape growers. A few years later, I went to hear him speak at Stanford University. I can recall everything about the occasion except why I was there. I remember a golden light of late afternoon; I remember the Reverend Robert McAfee Brown introducing Cesar Chavez. Something about Chavez embarrassed me. It was as though someone from my family had turned up at Stanford to lecture undergraduates on the hardness of a Mexican's life. I stood at the back of the room. I did not join in the standing ovation. I would not give him anything. And yet, of course, there was something compelling about his homeliness.

In her thoroughly researched and thoroughly unsentimental book *The Union of Their Dreams: Power, Hope, and Struggle in Cesar Chavez's Farm Worker Movement*, journalist Miriam Pawel chronicles the lives of a collection of people—farm workers, idealistic college students, young East Coast lawyers, a Presbyterian minister, and others—who gave years of their lives at subsistence pay to work for the UFW. By the end of her book, every person Pawel profiles has left the union—has been fired or has quit in disgust or frustration. Nevertheless, it is not beside the point to notice that Cesar Chavez inspired such a disparate, devoted company.

We easily forget that the era we call "the Sixties" was not only a time of vast civic disaffection; it was also a time of religious idealism. At the forefront of what amounted to the religious revival of America in those years were the black Protestant ministers of the civil rights movement, ministers who insisted upon a moral dimension to the rituals of everyday American life—eating at a lunch counter, riding a bus, going to school.

Cesar Chavez similarly cast his campaign for better wages and living conditions for farm workers as a religious movement. He became for many Americans, especially Mexican Americans (my parents among them), a figure of spiritual authority. I remember a small brown man with an Indian aspect leading labor protests that were also medieval religious processions of women, children, nuns, college students, burnt old men—under the banner of Our Lady of Guadalupe.

By the time he had become the most famous Mexican American anyone could name—his face on the cover of *Time*—the majority of Mexican Americans lived in cities, far from the tragic fields of California's Central Valley that John Steinbeck had made famous a generation before. Mexican Americans were more likely to work in construction or in service-sector jobs than in the fields.

Cesar Chavez was born in Yuma, Arizona, in 1927. During the hardscrabble years of his youth, he dropped out of school to work in the fields of Arizona and California. As a young man he accumulated an autodidact's library. He read books on economics, philosophy, history. (Years later, Chavez was apt to quote Winston Churchill at UFW staff meetings.) He studied the black civil rights movement, particularly the writings of Martin Luther King Jr. He studied most intently the lives and precepts of St. Francis of Assisi and Mohandas Gandhi.

It is heartening to learn about private acts of goodness in notorious lives. It is discouraging to learn of the moral failures of famously good people. The former console. But to learn that the Reverend Martin Luther King Jr. was a womanizer is to be confronted with the knowledge that flesh is a complicated medium for grace. To learn that there were flaws in the character of Cesar Chavez is again to test the meaning of a good life. During his lifetime, Chavez was considered by many to be a saint. Pawel is writing outside the hagiography, but while reading her book, I found myself wondering about the nature of sanctity. Saints? Holiness? I apologize for introducing radiant nouns.

· · ·

The first portrait in *The Union of Their Dreams* is of Eliseo Medina. At the advent of the UFW, Eliseo was a shy teenager, educated only through the eighth grade. Though he was not confident in English, Medina loved to read *El Malcriado*, the feisty bilingual weekly published by the UFW. He remembered that his life changed the Thursday night he went to hear Chavez in the social hall of Our Lady of Guadalupe Church in Delano. He was "disappointed by the leader's unimpressive appearance." But by the end of the evening, he had determined to join the union.

No Chavez speech I have read or heard approaches the rhetorical brilliance of the Protestant ministers of the black civil rights movement. Chavez was, however, brilliantly theatrical. He seemed to understand, the way Charlie Chaplin understood, how to make an embarrassment of himself—his mulishness, his silence, his witness. His presence at the edge of a field was a blight of beatitude.

Chavez studied the power of abstinence. He internalized his resistance to injustice by refusing to eat. What else can a poor man do? Though Chavez had little success encouraging UFW volunteers to follow his example of fasting, he was able to convince millions of Americans (as many as 20 million, by some estimates) not to buy grapes or lettuce.

Farmers in the Central Valley were bewildered to find themselves roped into a religious parable. Indeed, Valley growers, many of them Catholics, were distressed when their children came home from parochial schools and reported that Chavez was used as a moral exemplum in religion class.

At a time in the history of American entrepreneurialism when Avis saw the advantage of advertising itself as "Number Two" and Volkswagen sold itself as the "bug," Chavez made the smallness of his union, its haphazardness, a kind of boast. In 1968, during his most publicized fast to support the strike of grape pickers, Chavez issued this statement (he was too weak to read aloud): "Those who oppose our cause are rich and powerful and they have many allies in high places. We are poor. Our allies are few."

Chavez ended his 1968 fast in a tableau that was rich with symbol and irony. Physically diminished (in photographs his body seems unable to sustain an erect, seated position), he was handed bread (sacramental ministration after his trial in the desert) by Chris Hartmire, the Presbyterian minister who gave so much of his life to serving Chavez and his union. The Protestant activist was feeding the Catholic ascetic. Alongside Chavez sat Robert F. Kennedy, then a U.S. senator from New York. The poor and the meek also have allies in high places.

Here began a conflict between deprivation and success that would bedevil Chavez through three decades. In a way, this was a struggle between the Mexican Cesar Chavez and the American Cesar Chavez. For it was Mexico that taught Chavez to value a life of suffering. It was America that taught him to fight the causes of suffering.

The speech Chavez had written during his hunger strike of 1968, wherein he compared the UFW to David fighting Goliath, announced the Mexican theme: "I am convinced that the truest act of courage, the strongest act of manliness is to sacrifice ourselves for others in a totally non-violent struggle for justice. To be a man is to suffer for others. God help us to be men." (Nearly three decades later, in the program for Chavez's funeral, the wording of his psalm was revised—"humanity" substituted for "manliness": *To be human is to suffer for others. God help me to be human.*)

Nothing else Chavez would write during his life had such haunting power for me as this public prayer for a life of suffering; no utterance would sound so Mexican. Other cultures in the world assume the reality of suffering as something to be overcome. Mexico assumes the inevitability of suffering. That knowledge informs the folk music of Mexico, the bitter humor of its proverbs, the architecture of its stoicism. *To be a man is to suffer for others.* The code of machismo (which in American English translates too crudely to sexual bravado) in Mexico derives from a medieval chivalry whereby a man uses his strength to protect those less powerful. *God help us to be men.*

Mexicans believe that in 1531 the Virgin Mary appeared in brown skin, in royal Aztec raiment, to a converted Indian peasant named Juan Diego. The Virgin asked that a church be erected on the site of her four apparitions so that Mexican Indians could come to her and tell her of their suffering. Our Lady of Guadalupe was a part of every UFW demonstration.

Though he grew up during the American Depression, Chavez breathed American optimism and American activism. In the early 1950s, while still a farm worker, he met Fred Ross of the Community Service Organization, a group inspired by the principles of the radical organizer Saul Alinsky. Chavez later became an official in the CSO, and eventually its president. He persuaded notoriously apathetic Mexican Americans to register to vote by encouraging them to believe they could change their lives in America.

If you would understand the tension between Mexico and the United States that is playing out along our mutual border, you must understand the psychic tension between Mexican stoicism—if that is a rich enough word for it—and American optimism. On the one side, Mexican peasants are tantalized by the American possibility of change. On the other side, the tyranny of American optimism has driven Americans to neurosis and depression—when the dream is elusive or less meaningful than the myth promised. This constitutes the great irony of the Mexican-American border: American sadness has transformed the drug lords of Mexico into billionaires, even as the peasants of Mexico scramble through the darkness to find the American dream.

By the late 1960s, as the first UFW contracts were being signed,

Chavez began to brood. Had he spent his poor life only to create a middle class? Lionel Steinberg, the first grape grower to sign with the UFW, was drawn by Chavez's charisma but chagrined at the union's disordered operations. "Is it a social movement or a trade union?" Steinberg wondered. He urged Chavez to use experienced negotiators from the AFL-CIO.

Chavez paid himself a subsistence annual wage of $5,000. "You can't change anything if you want to hold onto a good job, a good way of life, and avoid suffering." The world-famous labor leader would regularly complain to his poorly paid staff about the phone bills they ran up and about what he saw as the misuse of a fleet of second-hand UFW cars. He held the union hostage to the purity of his intent. Eliseo Medina, who had become one of the union's most effective organizers, could barely support his young family and, without even the prospect of establishing a savings account asked Chavez about setting up a trust fund for his infant son. Chavez promised to get back to him but never did. Shortly after, discouraged by the mismanagement of the union, Medina resigned.

In 1975, Chavez helped to pass legislation prohibiting the use of the short-handled hoe—its two-foot-long haft forced farm workers to stoop all day. That achievement would outlast the decline of his union. By the early 1970s, California vegetable growers had begun signing sweetheart contracts with the rival Teamsters Union. The UFW became mired in scraps with unfriendly politicians in Sacramento. Chavez's attention wandered. He imagined a "Poor Peoples Union" that would reach out to senior citizens and people on welfare. He contacted church officials within the Vatican about the possibility of establishing a religious society devoted to service to the poor. He grew interested in the Hutterite communities of North America and the Israeli kibbutzim as possible models.

Chavez visited Synanon, the drug rehabilitation commune headed by Charles Dederich, shortly before some of its members were implicated in a series of sexual scandals and criminal assaults. Chavez borrowed from Synanon a version of a disciplinary practice called "the Game," whereby UFW staff members were obliged to stand in the middle of a circle of peers and submit to fierce criticism. Someone sympathetic to Chavez might argue that the Game was an inversion of an ancient monastic discipline meant to teach humility. Someone less sympathetic might conclude that Chavez was turning into a petty tyrant. I think both estimations are true.

From his reading, Chavez would have known that St. Francis of Assisi desired to imitate the life of Jesus. The followers of Francis desired to imitate the life of Francis. Within 10 years of undertaking his mendicant life, Francis had more than 1,000 followers. Francis realized he could not administer a growing religious order by personal example. He relinquished the administration of the Franciscans to men who had some talent for organization. Cesar Chavez never gave up his position as head of the UFW.

In 1977 Chavez traveled to Manila as a guest of President Ferdinand Marcos. He ended up praising the old dictator. There were darker problems within the UFW. It was rumored that some within the inner circle were responsible for a car crash that left Cleofas Guzman, an apostate union member, with permanent brain damage.

Chavez spent his last years protesting the use of pesticides in the fields. In April of 1993, he died.

In death, Cesar Chavez became a Mexican saint and an American hero. The year after his death, Chavez was awarded the National Medal of Freedom by President Bill Clinton. In 2002, the U.S. Postal Service unveiled a 37-cent stamp bearing the image of Cesar Chavez. Politicians throughout the West and the Southwest attached Chavez's name to parks and schools and streets and civic buildings of every sort.

In 1997 American painter Robert Lentz, a Franciscan brother, painted an icon of "Cesar Chavez of California." Chavez is depicted with a golden halo. He holds in his hand a scrolled broadsheet of the U.S. Constitution. He wears a pink sweatshirt bearing the UFW insignia.

That same year, executives at the advertising agency TBWA/Chiat/Day came up with a campaign for Apple computers that featured images of some famous dead—John Lennon, Albert Einstein, Frank Sinatra—alongside a grammar-crunching motto: THINK DIFFERENT.

I remember sitting in bad traffic on the San Diego Freeway and looking up to see a photograph of Cesar Chavez on a billboard. His eyes were downcast. He balanced a rake and a shovel over his right shoulder. In the upper-left-hand corner was the corporate logo of a bitten apple.

RON ROSENBAUM

Rescuing Evil

FROM *First Things*

AT THE CLOSE OF THE FINAL 2010 TEMPLETON-CAMBRIDGE JOUR-nalism Fellowship seminar series in Cambridge this June, after writer Rob Stein's informative discussion of "Conscience," as everyone be-gan packing up, one of the moderators, Sir Brian Heap, turned to me and asked (presumably because I'd once written a book entitled *Explaining Hitler*): "Did Hitler have a conscience, Ron?" Having spent a decade examining that very issue, which was at the heart of my book, I was able to reply, crisply and cogently: "Um, well, I'm not sure . . . I mean, it all depends." Yes, it all depends. It all depends on how you define conscience, and how you define conscience depends on how you define evil, the cancer for which conscience is the soul's MRI.

Evil has gotten a bad name lately. It always was a name for some sort of badness, yes; but lately the word sounds antiquated, the prod-uct of a less-sophisticated age. Evil belongs to an old, superstitious world of black and white, and we all know now that everything is gray, right? It belongs to a world of blame in which the Enlighten-ment tells us that "to understand all is to forgive all"—no blame, just explanation. There are some who argue it's an unnecessary word: Having no ontological reality, no necessary use, it's merely a semantic trap, a dead end.

After a century that saw the slaughter of more than a hundred million souls, we seem to be insisting on one more casualty: the word evil. Perhaps because by eliminating its accusatory presence and substituting genetic, organic, or psychogenic determinism, we escape the accusatory finger it points at the nature of human nature. Things go wrong with our genes, or our amygdalas, or our parenting, but these are aberrations, glitches. The thing itself, the human soul, is basically good; the hundred million dead, the product of unfortunate but explicable defects, not the nature of the beast.

But there are losses to the glossing-over process that has made the concept of conscious evil so unfashionable. If we could rescue free-will evil from the various determinisms that have been substituted for it, we could also set free will—the freely made choice to do good or evil—free again. Doing so would reestablish the possibilities of freely chosen courage and nobility, of altruism and self-sacrifice, rather than reducing them to some evolutionary biology survival stratagem. We diminish and marginalize the idea of evil because we don't want to face the accusatory consequences that the free choice of evil—a choice contrary to conscience—entails.

Serial killers and mass murderers are frequently spoken of, in the mumbo jumbo of popularizing science, as people "without conscience." But if they lack conscience, they lack transgressiveness; they cannot consciously violate an entity they lack. Consider Derrick Bird, a cabdriver in England's West Cumbria, who, on a June morning in 2010, with no evident warning signs, turned into a spree killer who murdered twelve people and then shot himself. The murders took place at a time when I was in Cambridge for the Templeton-Cambridge Journalism Fellowship and so was able to observe the cultural schism over the notion of evil and free will as it played out in the intensive coverage (virtually absent in the United States) of the murders and their aftermath.

Bird—or "PSYCHO-CABBIE" as the tabloid *News of the World*'s front-page headline dubbed him—became an emblematic case study of how science and religion have shaped the split in society and culture over the nature of evil. Just take that headline moniker, PSYCHO-CABBIE. On the one hand, it melodramatizes the killings. On the other hand, it serves to defuse their malevolence: The murders were performed by a "psycho," not a "normal" person, and psychologists tell us that psychos suffer from a disease, not from evil. They have poor "impulse control," and so it's not something we have to fear from normal people like ourselves.

On yet another hand, on its inside pages the *News of the World* featured an exclusive photo of PSYCHO-CABBIE's dreary kitchen, a shot taken from outside his kitchen window that spotlighted a bottle of HP sauce on his sad, loner's kitchen table. The headline on that read "THE DEVIL'S KITCHEN."

Tabloids believe in evil. And yet, if someone is possessed by evil spirits, does that mean he's a victim, too? Was the headline saying that the devil was cooking up evil in that kitchen, using his special brew of satanic HP sauce on the previously nondevilish PSYCHO-CABBIE?

It's complicated. But at least evil is still a problem to the moralists of the tabloid press. To the bienpensant columnists of the serious press, it's virtually a vulgarism. On the day after the PSYCHO-CABBIE's killing spree, *The Independent* ran a story on the killings by an "investigative psychologist" with the headline, "A simmering anger fuelled by low self-esteem and paranoia."

Ah, that old (and shopworn) villain, low self-esteem. The allegedly more sophisticated media, with their investigative psychologists of various stripes, think we're on the way to giving evil a local habitation and a name in the brain. Neuroscience will clear up the problem of evil that has troubled philosophers and theologians since before St. Augustine: Pinpoint the site of evil on this or that temporal lobe or cortical matrix and predict and perhaps interdict evil behavior.

Geneticists have recently proclaimed, with all the confidence of Columbus discovering the Indies, that they have located evil in the "evil twin" copy of the "warrior gene." Brain-scan analysts say it's located in "an imbalance between the orbital cortex and the amygdala," as neuroscientist James Fallon recently informed listeners to National Public Radio. The morning before PSYCHO-CABBIE started on his murderous rounds, the ever-dependable *Independent* credulously informed us, at breakfast, of a different finding, in a story headlined "How a deprived childhood leaves its mark on the brain." Written by "Social Affairs Correspondent" Sarah Cassidy, the story promoted the brain scan-based theory being peddled by a charity called The Kids Company, which, we were told, spent £1.6 million on a study to establish that "over-exposure to fright hormones damages children's brain development and leaves them prone to violent outbursts and unable to calm themselves" when they grow up and perform evil acts.

The story was accompanied by two scary-looking brain-scan slices, in each of which a sinister-looking, crescent-shaped swath was helpfully highlighted by *The Independent* in blood red to demonstrate the effects of "cortical atrophy," seen in the difference between a "healthy three-year-old" and one who "suffered severe sensory deprivation with minimal exposure to language, touch, and social interaction." It turns out that Rousseau's child of nature, the epitome of unsocialized innocence, untainted by "social interaction," is likely to harbor evil—or "cortical shrinkage"—rather than natural nobility within.

The red areas bore an unmistakable, if perhaps inadvertent, resemblance to Satan's horns, growing inside the brain, but the story was another instance of the organizing of evil, the implicit determinism: Anyone with cortical shrinkage showing up on the brain scan, like anyone with the wrong orbital-to-amygdala ratio, was destined to commit evil acts—and to be absolved of them by science because they were only the product of neuronal defects.

The Kids Company study also showed "enlarged ventricles in the center of the brain." Now we're talking. Hasn't evil as an "absence of being" been a theme of post-Thomistic discussions of the subject? Hole in the brain = absence of being, no? Curiously, on the page opposite the damaged-brain scans was a story about human remains found in the river Aire in West Yorkshire that turned out not to belong to two murdered prostitutes; evidently there had been speculation that a serial killer—a cortical-atrophied, poorly ratioed orbital / amygdala type—was at work emulating the famous "Yorkshire Ripper." The juxtaposition of stories suggested an account of evil: Cerebral atrophy means murdered prostitutes. A description of evil that, in effect, exculpated the evildoer by blaming his crimes on a bad brain scan.

Indeed, brain scans are the new phrenology of forensics, with the key bumps actually inside the head, on the soft parts of the brain, rather than outside, on the knobby protrusions of the skull. To my great satisfaction, the story in *The Independent* ended by quoting one of my favorite skeptics of pseudoscience, Raymond Tallis, a doctor and philosopher more well known in the U.K. than here, who suggested we not get too excited: "I do not think brain scans will add anything to what we already know," he said. "The trouble is that that leads to a general sort of claim that 'My brain made me do it.' This neuromitigation of blame has to be treated with suspicion."

Neuromitigation! Exactly the word we need to describe this organizing of evil. But evil is a problem not just for science. To promoters of a new religiosity—such as Terry Eagleton, who writes so well for someone whose thinking is so muddled, strangled in his own sophistry like Laocoön by the snakes—evil really isn't a problem, barely exists at all. Of course, Eagleton's sophistic denial of evil's relevance, in a book called *Evil*, demonstrates even more strongly what a problem it is. As Alan Wolfe noted in the *New Republic*, Eagleton thinks evil is "boring, supremely pointless, lifeless, philistine, kitsch-ridden, and superficial. Indeed, lacking any substance, it 'is not something we should lose too much sleep over.' People can be wicked, cruel, and indifferent. But the concept of evil, with which theologians and philosophers have wrestled for centuries, can be safely tucked away. When it comes to evil, we must be social and economic realists. 'Most violence and injustice [Eagleton argues] are the result of material forces, not of the vicious dispositions of individuals.'" The neo-Marxist Christian view of evil.

There have been few takers lately for Jung's view that evil has an ontological reality—that it has real being, something to watch out for. Although I have met two very different people whose sanity and stability I respect who have said they have encountered the presence of palpably ontological evil. One was a New York City cop, from the Dominican Republic originally, who, because of his background, was assigned to investigate allegations of Santeria killings and a subterranean ring of exorcists who were actually extortionists.

In effect, he was often called upon in his job to try to distinguish who was truly possessed by evil spirits and who was being conned into believing it or was suffering delusions of possession. I watched him perform an exorcism in his off-duty role as spiritual counselor in an old, candlelit Lower East Side church. It was chilling. And somehow convincing. He told me something much like what I also heard from Fraser Watts, a thoughtful, mild-mannered Anglican priest in Cambridge, also a trained psychologist, who described his experience of "deliverances," as the Anglicans call exorcisms of those possessed by evil spirits. He conceded that most of the cases he saw were likely psychogenic, but he believed that in a few instances he felt he had been in the presence of genuine evil spirits.

Of course, even evil spirits are a problem for evil, since belief in them displaces responsibility from the individual possessed to the possessor. Still, it's more than intriguing that similar language would be used by a hard-bitten New York cop and a soft-spoken Anglican priest in Cambridge.

Evil remains a problem, not just for its victims, though they should not be forgotten in all this theorizing, but for those who try to conceptualize it. This first came to trouble me during an exchange with the late historian Hugh Trevor-Roper, who has grown in estimation as one of the most scrupulous and discerning historians of his time. At the end of the Second World War, as a member of MI-6, Britain's secret intelligence service, he was tasked with going into Hitler's bunker to reconstruct the details of Hitler's death, in part to halt rumors of the Nazi leader's escape and survival. In the process, Trevor-Roper learned an immense amount of previously unavailable information. This included the discovery of Hitler's "final testament," in which, shortly before he killed himself, he commanded the German people never to cease and desist from their war to exterminate the "eternal poisoners of humanity, the Jews"—a job he'd left unfinished.

From the evidence he gathered, Trevor-Roper produced perhaps the first, certainly one of the finest, early biographies of Hitler. He agreed to be interviewed by me in the Oxford-Cambridge Club, to which I had brought a tape recorder, which I nested in the shelter of what looked like a five-century-old chess set and at which he looked disapprovingly. "A solecism," he said tartly, indicating the recorder. I decided to brazen it out, and I'm glad I did because I might not have retained the stark reply he gave to my question, "Did Hitler know he was doing wrong when he was committing his crimes?"

"Absolutely not," he shot back without hesitation. "He was convinced of his own rectitude." Yes, rectitude. All that Trevor-Roper discovered confirmed him in his belief that Hitler was a true believer—a man who did not consider himself evil but a heroic doctor, a veritable Pasteur, a great benefactor to humanity purifying the human race of infection.

This is an old—but still unresolved—philosophical question: Can someone be evil if he thinks he's doing good, no matter how deranged his thought process? It has troubled everyone from Plato to Augustine and their heirs, but it remains a genuine problem—because most people we think of as doing great evil think of themselves as doing the right thing. Indeed, who does evil while thinking he actually is doing evil? Only a few characters in literature—Shakespeare's Richard III, notably—and those cartoon villains twirling mustaches.

This is a hard notion to assimilate. In fact, the following week at Oxford, I placed it before Alan Bullock, Trevor-Roper's rival as an early historian of Hitler and the author of *Hitler: A Study in Tyranny*. He exclaimed, with North Country bluntness: "If we can't call Hitler evil, then who can we?" One way to sort all this out is to note that it is possible for evil to inhere in ideas as well as in men. There are evil ideas that men can become true believers in—thinking they are doing good in carrying them out. It is the intellectual version of possession by evil spirits.

In any case, back to PSYCHO-CABBIE, who raises a whole host of new questions about evil and its depiction in our culture. Beginning at 5:30 on that morning in June, the man whose name was not PSYCHO-CABBIE but the oddly cheerful name of Derrick Bird, began a killing spree that racked up twelve murders, not including his own suicide, in what was almost invariably referred to as the "sleepy seaside town of Whitehaven."

Was he feeling "simmering anger fuelled by low self-esteem" that morning? Other psychiatrists and savants lined up to weigh in. In a full-page diagnosis in a later edition of *The Independent* entitled "There is no one either good or bad, but circumstances make them so," Julian Baggiani junked "self-esteem," "paranoia," and other such old-fashioned jargon for "situationism," which he announced was "the dominant school of thought in psychology and philosophy now."

Ah, situationism, which, we were told, "claims that the best predictor of how people behave is the circumstances they find themselves in, not their predispositions." In other words, "everyone was doing it, you can't blame me." As the leading theorist of situationism, Philip Zimbardo, has put it, "We have underestimated the power of social situations because we overestimate the power of individual dispositions."

It's sad that conventional wisdom has thrown in its lot with "situationism." One dramatic refutation of it can be found in Christopher Browning's study *Ordinary Men*, which examined the choices made by the members of one of Hitler's killing squads in the period before mass murder had been industrialized in death camps such as Auschwitz.

Browning studied letters and diaries from members of a reserve police battalion which slaughtered whole towns full of Jews and buried them in mass graves. Browning learned that participation in the slaughter was not mandatory; troops had the choice to opt out, and some did. Despite the fearfulness of making such a choice, they refused, of their own free will, to participate in the evil. Which removed the "situationist" exculpation from those who did.

But there's no indication, contra Julian Baggiani, that situationism has the slightest relevance to PSYCHO-CABBIE's choices. He made them himself. Derrick Bird left the Devil's Kitchen at approximately 5:30 A.M. Shortly thereafter he arrived at the much larger, more luxe home of his twin brother David and shotgunned him to death.

Here we enter into one perplexing question raised by PSYCHO-CABBIE's spree—the degrees of evil. "The primal eldest curse" is on the murder of a brother, *Hamlet* tells us. And a twin? It more than recapitulates the First Murder. And indeed there were other Biblical elements to the PSYCHO-CABBIE's first murder. There was a struggle over a birthright and who was favored by the father's blessing. Apparently the younger but better-off of the twins (David) had received a £25,000 chunk of the father's estate—and then, when the father died, he didn't feed it back into the evidently depleted estate to be shared with his brother.

PSYCHO-CABBIE seemed to be wrought up over this, and over the way his solicitor had been handling it, and over the concomitant problem of Derrick's keeping £60,000 pounds of his cabbie earnings under the floorboards of the Devil's Living Room. He believed his brother and solicitor were "stitching him up" for the Inland Revenue so the brother wouldn't have to come up with the £25,000 pounds.

So one could see Derrick "simmering with rage and paranoia" and perhaps even the dread low self-esteem, too. But we are all simmering to some extent. And yet: Murdering his twin in cold blood and then driving over to his solicitor's house and shotgunning him in bed, too? Are these bad choices psychogenically determined, organically inevitable? Crimes just waiting to happen if we'd had a proper brain scan to warn us? Or are they evil? Can we utterly eliminate the fact that he had a choice, that he made a choice, and that it was an evil choice? Or do we just look at his brain scan posthumously for the real trigger? And what do we make of the nine further killings that morning, and of the dozen or so attempts that left several critically wounded?

From the murdered solicitor's office Derrick drove to his customary post in the cabbies' rank in Whitehaven, where he shot to death one of his fellow cabbies. There was talk that he did it because of a rumor that this poor fellow had gone out with Derrick's ex-wife. In each of those cases one could say there was a rationale, a reason—not a good one, not an excuse, not an exculpation, but a reason, however inadequate. Does the existence of a reason, however selfish and prideful, make these killings less or more evil? Less, one could say, because they weren't killing for killing's sake. They were killing for ancient human grudges against twins and lawyers, perhaps. More, one could also say, because they were killings for selfish, greedy, felonious reasons. Felonious in the sense that they were about money and rivalry and ego and emotional wounds of being second twin in a father's love.

In capital-punishment law in most American states, premeditated murder in the first degree is not enough to put one in jeopardy of the death penalty. It must be murder in the service of, or accompanied by, another felony—kidnapping, robbing a liquor store, and or the like—to put it over the top, because the murder is then done for some kind of gain beyond mere murder.

I wonder if here the law has it backward, that killing for the sake of killing is worse than killing with some further motive. At this point, after murdering three he knew, PSYCHO-CABBIE started killing complete strangers, killing for the sake of killing. He set out in his cab and started shooting just about everyone who crossed his path, shotgunning motorists, bicyclists, and pedestrians point-blank in the face and head.

In other words, virtually every time he saw anyone—a person with whom he did not have any kind of psychogenic, emotional, legal relationship—he chose evil, more and further evil, until he totaled a dozen dead victims and then shot himself. He was in a world of utter freedom offered by the fact that he could not become any more morally or legally culpable than he already was. He was free to be as evil as he wanted to be. He could have shot himself after the first three, but he chose to blast open the faces of a dozen or so more, nine of them fatally.

The reason I focus on the factor of choice in thinking about evil, rather than its ontological status, is that giving evil ontological status—positing that it is something external that may enter into or possess a previously nonevil being—makes that being less culpable.

Perhaps it could be argued that some people are culpable in "leaving the door open" for evil. Tempting evil. But what I want to emphasize is not that I know what evil is, but that abandoning the concept of evil, refusing even to see it as a problem that cannot be reduced to organic dysfunction, is to abandon free will. Because if we are not free to choose evil, we are not free to refuse it.

SHEROD SANTOS

Are You Now or Have You Ever Been

FROM *The Gettysburg Review*

When I emerged from the hospital annex,
the rain had stopped, and though numerous umbrellas
still floated past, the streets were starting to dry.
As the sun struggled to part the last remaining clouds,
a slight vibration in the courtyard caused
by an idling transport van traveled up through
the soles of my shoes and joined a slight vibration
in my hands. Perhaps the life of sensation
had already returned, the life that in my time away
I'd often stood back and reflected on.

. . .

Without shading my eyes, it was difficult
to make out where I was, though each step I took
the closer to home I felt. Relieved in any case
to be alone (but relieved of what—responsibility?),
I no longer cared, it no longer mattered,
which way I turned, right or left, forward or back,
in the end I'd arrive at my apartment door.

. . .

A taxi pulled up in front of me, and a woman
beside me stepped in. Across the street,
a man handing out leaflets did so standing
on the balls of his feet. What I'd thought
was the smell of dampened ash turned out
to be sweat from a window washer, his squeegee
canted like a guillotine, at the telecom office
next door. Even more significantly,
each of those images seemed to arrive
of its own accord (not "seemed," of course,
but "did"), and I was there, not to witness
but to "behold" it as it came. Was I,
I wondered, spilling over into the world,
or was the world spilling over into me?

. . .

As if awakened to the sound of someone
sobbing in the room next door, a voice raised,
a memory of pain but not the source of it:
a Portuguese Fado (Amália Rodrigues?)
through a third-floor open window above
The Babylon Mattress in Pilsen.

. . .

Each session I entered with what I was told
were "natural" feelings of dread, each session
I left with mixed emotions of solitude,
anxiety, pettiness, conceit, emotions
whose meanings "remained to be seen,"
or at least seen from a "broader perspective,"

for something somewhere inside of me
was always worth learning more about.
Nevertheless, there were days when I felt that,
easily enough, I might actually kill someone,
anyone, to escape whatever those meanings were.

. . .

My head heavy sometimes, sometimes light.
Sitting at my desk, coffee cup on the left,
stack of loose-leaf paper on the right,
I couldn't always tell if a minute or an hour
had passed between one line and the next.
In the afternoon, when asked how I was doing,
I answered, "I don't feel quite myself,"
though even as I said it, I remembered how
as a child I'd happily exchanged my identity
for whoever I pretended to be that day:
daredevil, cowboy, private detective, etc.

. . .

Having breakfast in a local coffee shop,
the brief but nonetheless cheerful thought
that whatever came next would come for the sake
of appearances, and only as a way of distracting
my attention. In on the secret, the waitress
who brought the coffee spoke in the low, island
patois of characters in a South Seas tale.

. . .

At the sound of the approaching subway train,
the sitters stood up at the same time, the standers
stepped forward at the same time, at the same time

the newspaper readers folded their papers,
the parents took their childrens' hands.
Once the train came to a stop, all of us
like-minded people stepped into our individual lives
where an inspired theatricality prevailed:

. . .

A man with a tracheal breathing tube,
his sunburned face covered with stubble
as though he'd just returned from a climb.
A teenage girl, her eyes closed, her hands
folded in her lap, the new tattoo on her ankle—
a Zoroastrian Ram?—still raw and slightly
inflamed. A marine with the laces of his desert-
issue boots untied (a coded protest against the war
slipped through the bars of my cell?). A woman
who moved her lips as she read but never
turned the page. A couple so happy, so at home
in their happiness, they might've been taken
right out of a Renoir boating-party scene.

. . .

The childlike reassurance I felt when,
as if turning back to a passage in a book
and reading it all over again, she answered
my questions the same way, with the same words,
the same turns of phrase and gestures
that she'd answered them with the week before.

. . .

More squatter than bird, dozens of sparrows
perched along a cross-street telephone line,

their wing-barred feathers tucked against the wind.
One or two newly arrived, one or two lifted
and settled back, most of them never stirred.
When I stopped to think about it—that is,
when I waited at the curb for the light to change—
it didn't seem all that hard to imagine
that a saint once liked to preach to birds,
or that birds once gathered to listen.
Certainly, it wasn't any more implausible
than a hundred other things
I'd scribble in my notebooks day to day.

.   .   .

In the morning, in the sun, in a public park
with a book, *Come Dance with Kitty Stobling*.
And a small boy beside me who asked if I'd like
to race him to the basketball courts and back.
When I told him I'm too old to race a boy like him,
his mother looked at me sharply, as though I'd knowingly
taken it upon myself to give her son a lesson in life.
"O tedious man with whom no gods commingle."

.   .   .

At an intersection where the farmer's market
had been set up in the morning, a line of cars
waited to turn at the crosswalk. There was no
light at the corner, and bustling about
with their plastic bags, the pedestrians rarely
paused to let the traffic through. The driver
of the car at the head of the line was forced,
therefore, to nose forward into the crowd,
and as he did a loosely dividing channel formed,

a streamlet of people passed behind
and another passed in front of the car,
an encroachment played out in a series
of intricate feints and starts by which, at length,
the car crossed over to the other side.
In this way, a camel might pass
through a needle's eye, a thought that eased,
or at least momentarily compensated for,
the fear that I'd been watching this
wholly independent of my will,
and with no more interest than I might've had
for any chance event that came my way.

.   .   .

At the station where I got on, an LED said
"Traffic normal through Cermak." And,
in fact, the lines at the turnstiles were normal,
the number of tourists in the concourse
was normal, the occasional stranger
approached with a look of such familiarity,
we passed with a friendly nod of the head.

.   .   .

I left my apartment in the afternoon, headed south
by a roundabout route to avoid the traffic,
crossed the river at State and continued downtown
to the public library. The Napoleon-red granite blocks
and high-arched windows, the great horned owl
above the entrance, all were visible from a distance.
I was walking fast, working my way through
the passersby, and it seemed I arrived
at each intersection just as the light turned green.

With everything going so well, I continued on
beyond the library, slowed my pace and, as though
searching for an address, carefully studied
the numbers on the buildings along the way.

. . .

And then one morning a shadow fell,
in happiness or tranquility, the breath-held
physical sensation of it, fleeting, yes, an aftermath
already in the saying, but nonetheless there,
a spot of warmth that, because it depended
so little on me, spread throughout my body.
An emotion so tenuous it could only be experienced
by canceling out whatever emotions I already felt.

. . .

After a while, I thought myself away.
Or perhaps some random word or phrase
overrode my thoughts, and an audible silence
filled my head. I could feel my heartbeat
through my shirt, the rise and fall
of my lungs, myself living on without me.
Myself not *for* but *as* the time being.

. . .

To take it for what it is, at face value.
To record it without making it into something.
To make it effortless, unconstrained, meaningless.
To escape the impression that what I see,
the images I respond to, are who I am,
and that everyone I notice is, at that moment,
who they appear to be. To keep to myself.

To do no harm. To know that tomorrow
I can try again. That was the dream,
that was the beginning, when I got
out of bed on a warm spring morning
in the middle of June. And for the next
few hours, that's what I attempted to do.

BETSY SHOLL

Pears, Unstolen

FROM *Image*

I was stopped on the sidewalk by pears
glowing on their tree like antique ornaments
with flaking paint, a green metallic shimmer,
hinting at yellow, mottled with a few flecks of red.

As light flickered over them, they seemed
to flutter like candles in the leaves.
But no—they were pears, and probably hard,
I told myself, probably inedible and holding

their juices tight, if they had juices at all.
Besides, something was pitting them like brass,
splotching, as if trying to spoil. Still, I wanted them.
I wanted that September light fingering each fruit,

so it seemed lit from without and within,
a fleshy tallow. I wanted the season's clock
stopped before the next strike, stopped
in this amber afternoon, my walk halfway,

the shiny leaves just starting to curl,
but still far from falling, and the pears

half hidden among them like birds singing
so sweetly you step closer, peer in,

careful, careful, wanting to touch that song,
but not spoil it. I stood there wanting
to hoard time, a thief trying to steal
a song I couldn't hear, a fool believing

there's something sweet that won't disappoint,
that pears in the hand could be anything
like pears dreamed in the mind, or a moment
stopped could be kept from rotting.

But what's so bad, a thief will ask: How is
plucking a piece of fruit worse than worms
tunneling in, or bees sating themselves
on that honeyed light, or mold blotching it?

Surely a saint has an answer to that,
something about how too much sweetness spoils,
or there's another sweetness that grows within.
For weeks I went back and forth, stopping

at the tree, watching first one pear let go
of its limb, then many begin to fall,
flickering briefly like coals in the grass
before they shrivel, letting their seeds slip out.

"That's the way it goes," mutters the thief.
"As scripture says they must," muses the saint,
while a few last pears glow on their brittle stems,
and the wind-strummed boughs bend toward earth.

GEORGE STEINER

Tritones

FROM *Salmagundi*

The Musician:

Why should I *speak* when I can *sing*?

Music is older than speech. Countless birds sing. The dark songs of whale drum through oceans. The winds make wires and hollow tubes sing. Cosmology intones a music of the spheres. We hear it in the *harmonia mundi* of Pythagoras and Kepler, in the "background noise" of today's astrophysical creation models. Were man to perish—a plausible conjecture—music would persist. So said Schopenhauer. Speech came late. Probably only after the most recent ice age. And splintered into innumerable, mutually incomprehensible, often ephemeral tongues. Music is universal. This is the sovereign fact. Very many cultures, ethnic communities or societies have no literature in any definable sense. No human gathering, be it a family, a hamlet or megalopolis lacks music. It is the only planetary idiom. Shared by, intelligible to all. It neither requires nor admits of translation. The same tune, the same 'hit' is sung, played, danced to in Kamchatka and Patagonia. Musical cadences, the "beat" reach the foetus in the womb; the very old, even the deranged hum, whistle, mouth music at their end.

No one can attach to anything but programme music any singular, limited sense. Music cannot be paraphrased. It can be enacted, imaged in dance. It cannot be transposed into any other medium. But though 'senseless', it is infinitely charged with meaning. This is its inexhaustible, paradoxical core. What is more meaningful to human reception and consciousness, to the nerve of our being than a piece of music, than a melody ("invention of melody, supreme mystery for the sciences of man" remarks Lévi-Strauss)? Music can help heal the bruised mind and inflame it. Yet what ideological, determinant, logical content has it? Hence the scandalous enigma whereby identical compositions can be harnessed to opposite political, social ends. Beethoven's setting of Schiller's Ode in his Ninth symphony provides a Nazi marching song, a communist hymn and the chorale of democratic freedom when the Berlin Wall crumbles. The selfsame *Heil*-choruses in Wagner's *Rienzi* inspire Herzl's vision of Zionism, of a homecoming to Jerusalem, and the young Hitler's hypnotic prevision of a third *Reich*. An identical tune, the same cadence submerges one man or woman in joy and another in heartbreak. There is, confided in Noel Coward, nothing on earth more potent than cheap music. Thus music alone lies beyond good and evil. It alone is transcendent, which is to say unbounded by any rational, analytic understanding or static equivalence.

Language is almost risibly helpless in the face of death. Verbal endeavours to prove, to define the existence of God amount to a dusty accumulation of verbiage and self-delusion. What is theology other than jargon? Only music can make in some sense existential, even sensible the possibility of experience beyond experience. Only music can intimate the possibility of some form of being beyond our empirical lives, of dimensions that are radically 'other.' Listen to the *andante sostenuto* of Schubert's Opus 163. The fact that we can neither explain rationally nor verbalize coherently this reaching into 'otherness' points precisely to the limitations of all discourse. In a Bach fugue or, to an almost suspect degree, in a Mahler *adagio*, the immediacy of the transcendent, the wealth of felt meanings in the *unsayable* are made manifest to us. Music both declares and supervenes (*Aufheben*) the tremendous banality that is death. Torn from its body, the head of Orpheus continues its song:

> Et (mirum !) medio dum labitur amne,
> Flebile nescio quid queritus lyra, flebile lingua
> Murmurat exanimis, respondent flebile ripae.

And the rocks listened.

(The Musician strikes a sorrowful but defiant chord on his guitar.)

The Mathematician:

No, my amiable friend. No. Music falls short of being a universal language. What of the deaf, of the tone-deaf? Oriental scales, pentatonic conventions are fully accessible solely to those who have grown up in the relevant cultures. The vast majority of men and women, the young especially in the third world find those high compositions you invoke to be a monotonous, inert bore. In turn, there are many to whom pop or rock are nothing but dehumanizing, deafening cacophony. By your own admission, music grows out of imitation. It mimes, it echoes natural and animal sounds. No. There is only one absolutely universal language, one all-embracing semantic code. It is that of mathematics.

The deaf-mute, those who share no syllable of each other's natural languages, can work together on a mathematical problem at the same blackboard. The silent idiom of geometric figures, of algebraic equations belongs to all women and men in equal measure. The rules which generate and govern its grammar know no frontiers, no political or ideological discriminations, no class barriers. There are indeed celebrated mathematicians, practitioners of virtuosity. In essence, however, all mathematics is anonymous. Proper names do attach to certain theorems—Pythagoras, Fermat, Poincaré—out of historical piety or courtesy. They are irrelevant. A mathematical formulation is lost or forgotten, but it can be re-discovered. This process robs it of nothing of its validity. As you yourself say, languages come and go. An estimated fifty become extinct every year. Texts become indecipherable or perish altogether. Only mathematics is *everlasting*. As that great mathematician G. H. Hardy famously put it: Aeschylus will be forgotten, indeed the bulk of his work has long disappeared, but a Euclidean theorem and its proof are eternal. A diophantine equation is as iron-clad or as unresolved (cf. Gödel's proof of incompleteness) as on the day it was first constructed or pursued. First and foremost, we are a primate that calculates. *Mirum!* as your friend Ovid exclaims. Animal species communicate by means of organized sound. Apes and rappers bellow. Only *homo sapiens* has engendered the axioms of geometry, the unfolding of calculus and algebraic functions. He or she alone can respond to the challenge of the Riemann hypothesis or perceive the dervish dance of irrational numbers and of zero. What is your strumming compared to that?

Justly, you claim that music is beyond good and evil. I would prefer to say that it is irrelevant to them. Which, in a significant way, makes it less than human, if not inhuman. Recall the ferocity of western music's foundational myths: the dismemberment of Orpheus, the flaying of Marsyas, the treacherous cannibalism of the Sirens. Blood-soaked but iconic tales. If it is immune to good and evil, music is no less extrinsic to truth and falsehood. Naively, music, notably operatic—Mozart's Queen of the Night, Verdi's Iago—can seek to express, to mime falsehood. But *per se* it cannot lie. By the same token, it cannot postulate, let alone verify or falsify the truth of any human proposition. It is precisely this capacity which mathematics possesses and enacts at every move. Mathematics can commit errors. It can temporarily deceive itself as to the soundness of an axiom or a demonstration. There is a sense in which the postulates of non-Euclidean geometries amend the compass of certain Euclidean definitions. They do not falsify them but show them to have been a special case. Relativity does not cancel the mathematics of Newton's celestial mechanics. Self-scrutiny, falsifiability are inherent in mathematical proceedings. But where the *demonstrandum* is sound, where it has resisted all deconstruction, its verity is both transparent and everlasting. Natural languages are inwoven with lies, half-truths, illusions, hypocrisies and fables. Their utterances are more often than not arbitrary, ephemeral and self-serving. What religious dogma, what metaphysical edifice, what moral, political or legal principle is susceptible of authentic *proof*? Not one. What are "self-evident truths" but rhetorical flourishes? What historical document, what decalogue or legal code stands intact? It is both the license and the infirmity of language to be ineluctably fused with fiction, with the fertilities and infantilism of the imaginary. When he is doing mathematics a human being inhabits the only realm of absolute truth open to him. The only terrain without bluff or deceit. It was as if he had been allowed to visit Eden. Where whatever Adam named was exactly that, where human speech had the benediction of tautology.

There is more. In manifold ways, alas out of reach of the unqualified, pure mathematics can, very often does exhibit radiant beauty. This is not a vague, indulgent metaphor. It is, on the contrary, a stringently precise attribute. Its crystalline facets are those of harmony, of formal equilibrium, of elegant closure. Most difficult to characterize but sensible to austere wit in certain proofs. To the counter-intuitive stroke springing from certain demonstrations in algebraic topology or number theory (that orange whose peels could circumscribe our universe). Frequently—the resolution of Fermat's 'last' theorem provides a ready example—there are differing approaches to a problem.

The successful one almost invariably turns out to be the most beautiful, where 'beauty' comprises both economy and rigour. Where Occam's razor cuts closest.

That such orders of beauty attach closely to uselessness seems tangible but difficult to show. Unforeseen pragmatic applications and consequences do arise out of pure mathematics. Via Relativity, tensorial calculus does relate, ultimately, to the physics of the atom bomb. But in essence, in its dynamic flowering, pure mathematics is proudly useless, non-utilitarian, autistic. It performs, in Kant's terminology, the one completely *disinterested* passion and pursuit of man. Why it arose in the first place—that Ionian and Greek miracle—whether it reflects external data in a Platonic sphere or is generated entirely from within man's playful, even irresponsible intellect, remain epistemological, psychological topics of unbounded fascination and debate. But the choreography of transfinite numbers, of elliptical functions, of the distribution of primes remains useless. It has the innocence of the absolute. It points toward some strenuous amusement (watch those 'Muses') in the deeps of the human soul. Keats's equation of truth and beauty can be demonstrated neither in music nor in spoken or written language. It is the summation, the informing equality in all mathematics. Hence Leibniz's persuasion—he was himself a towering mathematician—that when God sings to Himself, He sings algebra!

(**The Mathematician bends down and inscribes a non-linear equation in the sand.**)

The Poet:
Gentlemen, I have listened to you with attention and delight. Poets are listeners elect. I have taken in the deftness of your quotations, the charm of your similes, the devices of your rhetoric. And that of course is the point. Your instruments have been neither that guitar

nor this algebraic formula. They have been words, they have been sentences, they have consisted of lexical, grammatical and semantic units. In short, but also *in toto* they have been *language*. How could it be otherwise? You are human beings, what our ancient Greek teachers called *zoon phonanta*, which is to say "language animals." "The limits of your language are the limits of your world" (Wittgenstein). Human existence, in any completion, in any ripened mode is linguistic. We speak being, both to ourselves and in silence, and to others. We articulate reality so far as we can experience and grasp it. It is the evolution of intelligible speech, the gradual irradiation of the cortex by the fine-spun, compendious filaments, internets, synaptic interactions of neuronal speech-centres which have, perhaps not so very long ago, made us human.

Physiological dictates do declare themselves in our bodies in often imperative and complicated ways. I grant you that. Pain and ecstasy have their own communicative means. But there can be no *thought* prior to or without language. No pre-linguistic conceptualization. In the instant in which I attempt any such condition, my imagining has to adopt linguistic expression and the performative resources of syntax. We speak thought, *cogito*, silently or aloud: therefore we are. There is no terrain on the 'other side' of language. As you have pointed out, intimations of the transcendental remain just that: images, symbolic scenarios, metaphoric conjectures inevitably grounded in, circumscribed by the executive conventions of spoken or written discourse. This may indeed be a limitation, or, as I intuit, a safeguard against madness. But it is only via language that man can question, can test such limits or strive to enlarge them through incursions into the *almost* unsayable by poetry or metaphysics.

You advert to the fragility of languages, to their perennial extinction. True and sad enough. But new languages are continually being generated. As between age-groups, social classes, regions, professional needs. No *lingua franca* rules for ever. It succumbs to historical, political, commercial change. It fractures into new vulgates. By its very nature language is infinitely creative and innovative. Each dictionary, however compendious, is a transient snapshot of realities in perpetual motion. It is history on the day it is published. No normative or descriptive grammar is anything but an abstract shorthand, already obsolete when its rules and ideals are formulated. Human speech is as prodigal, as various, as fertile and mutinous as life itself. It *is* life itself. Silence is not its negation or opposite. It is as functional in language as it is in music.

To be sure, there are, as you have urged, other semiotic codes. Perhaps more formally exact than language, perhaps of more immediate sensuous appeal, as in pictures. But more likely than not, these are at key points language-based, meta-linguistic. Music has its phrasing, its signifying organization and punctuation. Even pure mathematics seems to entail deep structures which are kindred to logic, where logic derives ultimately from the rudiments and linearities of speech-acts. You cite Leibniz's beguiling trope about the algebraic song of the Almighty. May I remind you that there is on this loquacious planet hardly any mythology, any narrative of creation and genesis which does not postulate a verbal-grammatical origin. The Deity, the Demiurge, the Prime Mover *speaks* the world into being. God *said* and substance ensued. In the beginning was the Word. Not the tune nor the algebraic equation. The *Logos*. Source of all words thereafter, of the alphabet of reasons, of the signifying syllables which I address to you now.

We are so immersed in language—our dreams are talkative, our delirium chatters—that we take for granted its fantastic powers. Human time turns on the verb tenses in our grammars. Remembrance of things past inhabits, is preserved by language. Future tenses empower us, scandalously, to posit, to discuss phenomena long beyond our own deaths; the floral arrangements for billions of aeons hence. Optatives, subjunctives, counter-factual conditionals—"if Caesar commanded in Irak"—allow us to construe alternative worlds. It is this capacity of language to alter, to subvert the brute fact which defines hope and enabled us to endure, to circumvent the otherwise unbearable fixity of death. Hope is a matter of syntax. No other species, no pre-linguistic mentality can aspire to this evolutionary magic. Every future tense, every if-clause is a rebellion against the blind despotism of the organic. It is not only the voice out of the Burning Bush which proclaims "I shall be/what I shall be." It is man himself when he speaks the word 'tomorrow.'

It is this unique benefaction which has generated the arts, the sciences, the ideologies and philosophies produced by men and women, those architectures of imagination of which music and mathematics are only distinctive branches. We speak and write poems, we search out nature, we project audacious ideological blueprints in incessant investment in the future, in that *dure désir de durer* ancient as Pindar, modern as Eluard. Language allows us to create works, perceptions, hypotheses, symbolic forms which will outlast the cities in which they were devised, which will indeed outlast the particular tongues, social contexts, purposes in and for which they were initially voiced. Which, as Dante marmoreally has it, allow man his part of eternity: *come l'uom s'etterna*. Struck dumb, our species would be no more than a rapacious mammal, a malodorous predator howling to the apes.

Consider love. Mutual attraction, some mode of procreative intercourse is no doubt as universal as physiology itself. It is its minimal necessity. Mute sex is certainly feasible. The slavering moron can practice the libidinal. But the inexhaustible alphabet of eros, sexual

or not, the infinite prodigality and variousness of desire are en-
meshed with language. Inwardly or outwardly we articulate our
longings before we fulfill them. The discourse of lovers, differing in
every language, reaches into the very nerve-centres of sex. Where it is
mutually attained, orgasm is simultaneous translation. And in ways
which we do not as yet altogether understand, aesthetic and intel-
lectual passions, the obsessions which fuel serious art, scientific re-
search, ideological commitment, even economic derivatives have at
their deep buried roots, in their thrusting energies, modes of the
erotic. These, very precisely, modulate into the linguistic dynamics
of consciousness. It may be that Spinoza's virtually untranslatable
conatus comes nearest to this crucial generality.

No, my friends, I rejoice in music; I could scarcely imagine life
without it; the forbidding radiance of pure mathematics holds me
in awe. But my being is that of language. My humanity, imperfect,
half-baked as it is, exists because I speak. To you both.

(The poet takes out of his pocket a copy of Sophocles and begins re-
citing the choral ode on man from the Antigone.)

(The Musician doffs his imaginary cap, both in homage and irony.)

The Musician:
What eloquence! What oratory! You are indeed a master of words,
golden-tongued. What is a poor minstrel like myself meant to say?
Though I might remind you that the text you so poignantly de-
claimed was first *sung* not spoken.

(He bends over his guitar and begins to pick out the opening theme
of Mozart's Quintet in G-minor, K516. Those opening bars in which
the first viola takes the rôle of the bass towards the two violins. In

which the tonal light of the first violin then conjoins with the velvet dark of the viola.)

The wonders of sadness here are entirely beyond words. A ranking musicologist compares this passage "with the scene in the Garden of Gethsemane." But any such analogy is solemn chit-chat (*Gerede*). The effects need no specifically religious, no Christian invocation. They reach directly into the depths and quick of man's nature. They engage, as language does not, the sum of the human person. Nerves, viscera, the reticulations between body and consciousness of which we know so little. Language is no doubt instrumental in our public, cerebral, political, scientific business. But these are late acquisitions; conceivably symptoms of decay. Primordial responses, far more ancient, far more immediate are elicited by music. "G-minor, the key of melancholy." You will find that tag in every text-book. But what does it mean? How can a purely formal option in a technical, historically generated context, that of the *sonata tragica* produce within us a sense, an experience of desolation, pervasive, fundamental far beyond any verbal lament however inspired? What, in short, gives music, be it Mozart or heavy metal, authority over our innermost feelings, over the dance of our nerves and limbs incomparably more irresistible than that of any rhetoric? It is just this spontaneous, transforming authority, with its irrational, anarchic compulsions which all despots fear. Which provoked Plato's dreary attempts to domesticate, to militarize musical modes and Lenin's abstention from the *Apassionata*. And when you point to the verbal lineaments of eros, I need hardly counter that it is music which "is the food of love."

(He strums the harsh yet enigmatically life-enhancing final chords of the Quintet.)

The Poet:

I grant you the governance which music can exercise over all that is in-choate, unreasoned, immature in our make-up. And concede that such elements are the font of creative impulses. I am myself subject to rapture and sorrow "too deep for tears." Which music can unleash. The opening syncopation of Madame Piaf's *Non, je ne regrette rien* leaves me helpless, ideologically entranced, literally beside myself. (I know it to be sublime *kitsch*.) There is a cadenza in Berlioz which, each time I hear it, reduces me to tears. But this sensation of being beside oneself, of having lost some substantive degree of self-control is common, perhaps even more drastically, to the crazed automaton deafened by the 'wall of sound' at a rock-rave. It can be induced by the mass-chant of the football hooligan or the marching song of the totalitarian butchers. Its phenomenology is that of the narcotic, of individual or collective hypnosis. Witness the gyrations of the Dervish or the break-dancer. Mouths open, brains shut. Music is the most exalted of drugs. Our bodily and psychic responses to it can turn to addiction. Whereas language is our vulnerable, always subvertible but indispensable and finally unvanquished barrier against animality, against the eclipse of reason. It alone offers a contract with sanity. Hence a decisive correlative: it is via language that *homo sapiens* progresses, moves forward, enlists the dynamics and potential of history. Music does not progress. It does not activate the ascent of man.

The Mathematician:

Are you so sure? Intolerance, hatred, fanatical nonsense derive their power and dissemination directly from language. When western civilization lurched back into bestiality during the twentieth century, it did so under the lash of Hitler's unparalleled oratory, of communist and fascist "New-speak"; language can say, can ordain *anything.* It contains no barriers. This is a fact of crucial enormity. It presides not only over human progress but over inhuman regression. Only in mathematics is advancement both in-built and perpetual. The unfolding of mathematical questioning, the achievement of proof allow of no retrogression. Here is the only incontrovertible evidence of the growth, of the ripening of human reason.

The Poet:

A growth so esoteric that it is accessible only to a minute fraction of a fraction of the human race. How many of us have heard of, let alone understood such 'decisive' advances as the Langland conjecture for functional fields or the Selberg Integral? How many women or men can begin to apprehend why the local spacings of zeroes of L-functions over a number of fields may lead to the Holy Grail, as mathematicians call it, of a proof for the Riemann hypothesis? In what but an utterly hermetic, virtually solipsistic sense can these arcane games be representative of human progress which, *pace* temporary, contingent recursions of barbarism does depend, and depend intimately on language and its futurities?

The Mathematician:

A curious argument when put forward by a poet. Time and again, from Pindar to Mallarmé, from Góngora to *Finnegans Wake*, the leap forward of style and form has been intelligible only to the initiate. Already Hölderlin is forbidding; his greatest heir, Paul Celan, comes close to writing in a secret tongue "North of the future." Except at rudimentary levels, literacy, lexical and grammatical largesse have always been an élite principle and power relation. How numerous are those who seek out, who are endowed to seek out Kant on the synthetic a priori? "The truth has always been with the few" affirmed friend Goethe. Odi profanum vulgus. The fact that more or less all human animals chatter away using a minimal idiom masks but does not negate this finding.

The Musician:

Again, it is music which holds the balance. New instruments, such as the saxophone, may be invented, new key relations and chromatic effects may be explored. A tonality and aleatory structures can evolve. But *stricto sensu* there is no 'progress' in music. Webern does not supersede Monteverdi. Nor can there be regress when Stravinsky mimes Gesualdo. Because it internalizes and organizes time itself, music is timeless and, therefore innocent of error or corruption. And unlike mathematics, even the most 'difficult' music, whatever that term may signify, is at some level audible to all. Moreover, by some intriguing process, its difficulties, its off putting demands soon enter the mainstream. Symphonies, concerti first regarded as incomprehensible cacophony, now expend their charms from the juke box. Baroque counter-point has become a kind of tonal wall-paper in public and private spaces.

(Flourish on his guitar of a Boccherini phrase.)

(After a few moments of silence.)

The Poet:

I do not suppose that we shall convince one another. Would it not be more fruitful if we considered those elements which relate us, which we hold in common? Poetry, but also good prose, share with music criteria, ideals of rhythm, of cadence, of repeats and variation, of tone colour familiar to music. A poem seeks equilibrium, interaction between sense and sound. Sometimes it is the euphonic, the onomatopoieic which prevail; sometimes it is the semantic, those shadows of the prosaic which haunt even the purest of lyric verse. Ideally, there is collaborative tension between both. Assonance, consonance, rhyme itself are indissociably musical and linguistic. Verse displays its fortes and its pianissimos, its intervals and its codas. 'Measure' is a cardinal concept organic to both. In a deeper sense, poetic utterance, but also the discourse of theology and metaphysics aim at those spheres beyond everyday rationality, beyond routine logic and the utilitarian—a pursuit which you rightly ascribe to music. Both of us labour to enlarge the compass of human sensibility and perception in a unison of body and spirit.

The Musician:

Amen to that. When serious music sets a poem, when Bob Dylan sings to the wind, the most penetrating act of interpretation, of vital hermeneutics is operating. There are no finer readers of poetry, no more helpful critics than Schubert or Hugo Wolf when they set Goethe. What better elucidation have we of French lyric verse than Poulenc's chansons?

(He turns to the Mathematician.)

Our kinship with your mysteries is even closer. Harmonic progressions, proportions, symmetries, reversibilities such as inverse canons, resolutions or the unresolved as in dissonance are indispensable to us both. I have already alluded to the fusion of music and mathematics in ancient cosmogony, in the astronomy of Kepler. And although we cannot hear it, the vibration of strings which according to current sorcery determines the very fabric of our universe must emit its music, perhaps in C major! Thus there is far more than allegory to the millennial intuition that music is mathematics in motion, that algebra is also a choreography.

The Mathematician:

I rejoice in your suggestions. Where I do not observe a true affinity is in the parallel orders of mathematics and of natural language. They do remain mutually untranslatable. This untranslatability deepens as mathematics progresses. From Galileo and Descartes onwards. Mathematical analysis and demonstration can proceed in perfect silence. The mute, the deaf-mute might be a topologist of genius. There may, at psychic, pre-linguistic levels wholly out of our reach, be deep-lying structures of sequence, of combination, of rule-constrained development from which both mathematics and language originate, which made them possible. We do not know, and this dim supposition has no bearing on what we now experience as linguistic or mathematical. The gap is one of essence.

The Poet:

Even if this is so, we should celebrate the prodigious good fortune whereby 'a poor forked animal' such as we has engendered three majestic tongues. Whereby we can speak, sing and play music, argue mathematics, albeit in silence. We should look with proud wonder on phenomena, on creations in which these three codes conjoin, as they do in architecture (cf. Paul Valéry). Far too much of our social, political and even familial comportment has remained sadistic, deceitful or intellectually primitive. Our greed, our lust for massacre seem endless. The stench of money infects our lives. But when we produce a Shakespeare sonnet, when we compose a B-minor Mass, when we wrestle, over the centuries, with the Goldbach conjecture or the three-body problem, we transcend ourselves. Then, indeed, there is "no greater wonder than man."

(They join hands in the dance-garland of Matisse's great mural.)

The Day Continues Lovely

FROM *Tikkun*

With *Fear and Trembling* I studied my Kierkegaard, with
    Sickness unto Death
I contemplated with him my spiritual shortcomings, and it
    didn't occur to me then
but does now that in the Kierkegaard I've read he never takes
    time to actually pray.
Odd . . . This isn't to question his faith—who'd dare?—but
    his . . . well, agenda.
All those intricate paradoxes of belief he devotes his time to
    untying, re-tying.
Can it be that Kierkegaard simply *forgets* to pray, he's so busy
    untying, re-tying?
I understand that: I have times I forget to remember I can't
    pray. *Can't. Pray.*

This June morning just after sparkling daybreak and here I'm
    not praying.
My three grandsons asleep on their mats on the floor of my
    study,
shining, all three, more golden than gold, and I'm still not. *Not
    praying.*

Why aren't I? Even our dog Bwindi sprawled beside Turner, the
    youngest,
Turner's sleep-curled fist on her back: why haven't I prayed
    about them?
I can imagine someday something inside me saying: *Well, why
    don't you?*
Something inside me. As though suddenly would be *something
    inside me.*

There's a Buber story I'm probably misrepresenting that touches
    on this.
A Rabbi spends endless hours deciding whether to do good
    deeds or pray.
He thinks this first, then that: *This might be good; maybe that
    would be better,*
and suddenly a VOICE that can only be God's erupts: *STOP
    DAWDLING!*
And *God*, he thinks: he's been chastised by *God. STOP
    DAWDLING!*
And what happens then? In my anti-Bubering of the tale,
    everything's lost,
the fool's had his moment with God—even Moses had only
    how many?—

and he's squandered it because all he could do was stand
    stunned,
mouth hung metaphorically open, losing his chance to ask for
    guidance,
but he'd vacillated again and *What happens now?* he wonders in
    anguish.
*Maybe I should get out of this business, find a teaching job, write a
    book,*

on my desolation, my suffering, then he hears again, louder,
      STOP! STOP!
but this time it's his own voice, hopelessly loud, and he knows
      he'll forever be
in this waiting, this without-God, his glimpse of the
      Undeniable already waning.

And me? Leave aside Kierkegaard—who did, I've heard,
      pray—and Buber:
just *me*. Haven't I spent my life trying to make up my mind
      about *something?*
God, not God; soul, not soul. I'm like the Binary Kid: on, off;
      off, on.
But isn't that what we all are? Overgrown electrical circuits?
      Good, bad.
Hate, love. We go crazy trying to gap the space between on
      and off,
but there is none. Click. Click. Left: Right. Humans kill one
      another
because there's no room to maneuver inside those miniscule
      switches.

Meanwhile cosmos roars with so many voices we can't hear
      ourselves think.
Galaxy on. Galaxy off. Universe on, but another just behind
      this one,
one more out front waiting for us to finish. They're flowing
      across us,
sweet swamps of being—and we thrash in them, waving our
      futile antennae.

. . . Turner's awake now. He smiles, stands; Bwindi yawns and
    stands, too.

They come to see what I'm doing. Turner leans his head on my
    shoulder to peek.

What am I doing? Thinking of Kierkegaard. Thinking of
    beauty. Thinking of prayer.

Contributors' Notes

Stephen M. Barr is professor of physics at the University of Delaware and the author of *Modern Physics and Ancient Faith* and *A Student's Guide to Natural Science*.

John Berger is the author of many books, including, most recently, *From A to X: A Story in Letters*.

Robert Bly's many books include the bestselling *Iron John: A Book About Men*, *My Sentence Was a Thousand Years of Joy*, *The Night Abraham Called to the Stars*, and *The Light Around the Body* (National Book Award for Poetry, 1968).

Peter J. Boyer has been a staff writer for *The New Yorker* since 1992. His stories have appeared in *Best American Crime Writing*, *Best American Spiritual Writing*, *Best American Science Writing*, and *Best American Political Writing*. He won a George Foster Peabody Award and an Emmy as a correspondent for the PBS documentary series *Frontline*.

Katharine Coles's fifth collection of poems, *Flight*, is forthcoming from Red Hen Press. She is a professor in the English Department at the University of Utah, where she teaches creative writing and literature and codirects the Utah Symposium in Science and Literature. In 2010, she spent a month writing poems in Antarctica under the auspices of the National Science Foundation's Artists and Writers Program. In 2009 and 2010, she served as the inaugural director of the Harriet Monroe Poetry Institute at the Poetry Foundation. She is currently poet laureate of Utah.

Billy Collins's ninth collection of poems is *Horoscopes for the Dead*. He is a Distinguished Professor at Lehman College (CUNY) and a Distinguished Fellow at the Winter Park Institute of Rollins College.

Andrew Cooper is features editor at *Tricycle: The Buddhist Review*. He lives in Olympia, Washington, with his wife, Liz, and their daughter, Alana. Of the fruits of his long and varied study of Buddhism, he has written, "My failure to accomplish or attain any of what I had hoped I would when I set out on the Buddhist path is, I think, the thing that has most enriched my practice."

Kate Farrell's books include *Sleeping on the Wing: An Anthology of Modern Poetry with Essays on Reading and Writing* (written with Kenneth Koch) and *Art and Wonder: An Illustrated Anthology of Visionary Poetry*.

Eamon Grennan is the author of many books of poetry, including, most recently, *Out of Sight: New and Selected Poems*. He teaches in the graduate writing programs of Columbia University and New York University.

A. G. Harmon's fiction and essays have appeared in such publications as *Shenandoah, TriQuarterly, The Antioch Review, The Bellingham Review, Image*, and *Commonweal*. His novel, *A House All Stilled*, won the 2001 Peter Taylor Prize for the Novel. He teaches at The Catholic University of America in Washington, D.C.

Tony Hiss is the author of thirteen books, including the award-winning *The Experience of Place*. He is a visiting scholar at New York University's Robert F. Wagner School of Public Service and was a staff writer at *The New Yorker* for more than three decades.

Joe Hoover is in his tenth year as a Jesuit in formation. He is studying at Jesuit School of Theology in Berkeley, CA.

Pico Iyer is the author of several books about faith and crossing cultures across the modern globe, including *Video Night in Kathmandu; The Lady and the Monk; The Global Soul;* and *The Open Road,* describing thirty-four years of talks and travels with the Fourteenth Dalai Lama. His latest book, *The Man Within My Head,* out in early 2012, looks at Graham Greene and fatherhood to investigate how we might find kindness and conscience in our confused and confusing world.

Sam Jacobson is a lieutenant in the United States Marine Corps currently serving in Afghanistan.

Mark Jarman is the author, most recently, of *Bone Fires,* a collection of new and selected poems. He is Centennial Professor of English at Vanderbilt University.

Noa Jones is a writer of fiction and creative nonfiction. In addition to contributing to numerous newspapers and magazines, she has written and edited *Nature, Creativity, and Our Collective Future* and *A Story in Bhutan,* a coffee-table book about the making of Dzongsar Khyentse Rinpoche's film *Travellers and Magicians.* Her fiction has been nominated for a Pushcart Prize and she is currently living out of a suitcase, working on a novel in Bhutan.

Jill N. Kandel grew up in North Dakota and has lived in Zambia, Indonesia, England, and in her husband's native Netherlands. Her work has been published in journals such as *The Gettysburg Review, River Teeth, Brevity,* and *Image.* She recently finished writing a memoir, *The Sweet Thorn Tree: Six Years in an African Village.*

Karen An-Hwei Lee is the author of *Ardor* and *In Medias Res,* winner of the Kathryn A. Morton Prize and the Norma Farber First Book Award. Her chapbook, *God's One Hundred Promises,* received the Swan Scythe Press Prize. The recipient of a National Endowment for the Arts Grant, she lives and teaches in Southern California, where she is a novice harpist.

BK Loren's fiction and essays have been widely published in anthologies and periodicals including *Orion*, *Between Story and Song*, *Parabola*, *Spirituality and Health*, and *The Future of Nature*. She has received fellowships and awards from the Mary Roberts Rinehart National Nonfiction Fellowship, the Ucross Foundation, Colorado Art Ranch, New Millennium, and more. Her first book, *The Way of the River*, came out in 2001, and she has just completed her first novel.

Paul Myers is the University of Portland director of health, counseling, and disability services, and a practicing psychologist. He is a fellow of the American College Health Association and recipient of their Tunon Award in Human Dignity; he also founded the Spirituality, Religion and Student Health Coalition of the American College Health Association. His essays have appeared in *Portland*, *The Spokesman-Review Newspaper*, *College Health in Action*, and in the books *Volitional Action*, *Reading the Signs*, and *Research in Counseling*.

Seyyed Hossein Nasr is the University Professor of Islamic Studies at George Washington University and the author of many books, including *Man and Nature: The Spiritual Crisis of Modern Man*, *Religion and the Order of Nature*, *Knowledge and the Sacred*, and, most recently, *In Search of the Sacred*.

David Novak is the J. Richard and Dorothy Shiff Professor of Jewish Studies at the University of Toronto.

Evan Osnos is a staff writer for the *New Yorker*. He lives in Beijing and contributes the Letter from China blog to newyorker.com.

Marilynne Robinson is the author of many works of fiction and nonfiction, including *Home: A Novel* (2009 Orange Prize for Fiction), *Gilead: A Novel* (Pulitzer Prize for fiction, 2005), and *Absence of Mind: The Dispelling of Inwardness from the Modern Myth of the Self*. She teaches at the Iowa Writers' Workshop.

Richard Rodriguez is a contributing editor at *New America Media* in San Francisco and writes for various publications in the United States and Europe. He is the author of an autobiographical trilogy on class, ethnicity, and race: *Hunger of Memory*; *Days of Obligation: An Argument with My Mexican Father*; and *Brown: The Last Discovery of America*. He has been nominated for the Pulitzer Prize and the National Book Critics Award; he was honored in 1993 with the National Humanities Medal. Presently he is finishing a book on "the ecology of monotheism" (Viking) and an essay on why beauty matters (Yale).

Ron Rosenbaum is the author, most recently, of *How the End Begins: The Road to a Nuclear World War III*, *The Shakespeare Wars*, *Explaining Hitler*, and *The Secret Parts of Fortune*, a collection of his essays and journalism from *The New York Times*, *Harper's*, *The New York Observer*, and *The New Yorker*, among other periodicals. He cowrote the award-winning PBS documentary *Faith and Doubt at Ground Zero*. Currently a cultural columnist for *Slate.com*, he lives in New York.

Sherod Santos is the author of many books of poetry, most recently *The Intricated Soul: New and Selected Poems*. In 2005 he published *Greek Lyric Poetry: A New Translation*. He received an award for literary excellence from the American Academy of Arts and Letters in 1999.

Betsy Sholl is the author of seven books of poetry, including *Rough Cradle, Late Psalm, Don't Explain,* and *The Red Line*, which won the 1991 AWP Prize for Poetry. She teaches at the University of Southern Maine and in the Vermont College of Fine Arts MFA Program. From 2006 to 2011 she was poet laureate of Maine.

George Steiner is the author of many books, including *After Babel, The Death of Tragedy, Language and Silence, Antigones, Heidegger, Lessons of the Masters*, and most recently, *George Steiner at the New Yorker*.

C. K. Williams is the author, most recently, of a book of poems,

Wait, and a prose study, *On Whitman.* He is a member of the American Academy of Arts and Letters and teaches in the Creative Writing Program at Princeton University. He has won both the Pulitzer Prize and the National Book Award for his poetry.

Philip Yancey has written more than twenty books, including *The Jesus I Never Knew, What's So Amazing About Grace,* and his latest, *What Good Is God?* He also serves as editor at large for the magazines *Christianity Today* and *Books and Culture.*

Philip Zaleski is the editor of the Best Spiritual Writing series and the author of many books, including *The Recollected Heart, Gifts of the Spirit,* and *Prayer: A History* (with Carol Zaleski). He is a research associate in the Department of Religion at Smith College.

Other Notable Spiritual Writing of the Year

Susanne Antonetta, "Hosts," *Image*, Spring.

Andrew Boyd, "Death in Paris and London," *The Sun*, June.

Scott Cairns, "Lives Together," *The Christian Century*, April 6.

Lauren Collins, "Are You the Messiah," *The New Yorker*, November 29.

Thomas J. Cottle, "Our Thoughts and Our Prayers," *The Antioch Review*, Spring.

Brian Doyle, "Cub Scout," *First Things*, December.

Mary Eberstadt, "Christianity Lite," *First Things*, February.

Joseph Epstein, "T. S. Eliot and the Demise of the Literary Culture," *Commentary*, November.

Natalie Goldberg, "Blossoms Falling," *Shambhala Sun*, January.

Heather King, "One of Them," *Portland*, Winter.

Scot McKnight, "The Jesus We'll Never Know," *Christianity Today*, April.

Nancy Nordenson, "Spinning and Being Spun," *Comment*, September.

James Prosek, "Survivors," *Orion,* July/August.

Erik Reece, "In the Presence of Rock and Sky," *The Sun*, April.

Pete Rooks, "A War Story," *Portland,* Summer.

Nick Samaras, "The Alone of My Time," *Relief,* 2010.

Judith Shulevitz, "The Deconstructionist Sabbath," *Commentary,* April.

Richard W. Stevens, "Gandalf on Mars," *Salvo*, Winter.

Richard Wilbur, "Ecclesiastes II:1," *The New Yorker*, March 22.

Robert Wrigley, "Babel," *The Georgia Review*, Fall.